CUTTING BACK

My Apprenticeship in the Gardens of Kyoto

Leslie Buck

Timber Press
Portland, Oregon

FOR MY FIRST MOTHERS:

Anne Buck
Dorothy Whittaker
Betty McGrew

Published in 2017 by Timber Press, Inc.
The Haseltine Building
133 S.W. Second Avenue, Suite 450
Portland, Oregon 97204-3527
timberpress.com

This is a work of nonfiction. Events and quotations are
rendered true to memory, but to protect the privacy of
others some details have been changed.

Printed in the United States

Text design by Adrianna Sutton
Jacket design, lettering, and illustration by Kimberly Glyder

Library of Congress Cataloging-in-Publication Data

Names: Buck, Leslie, 1965– , author.
Title: Cutting back: my apprenticeship in the gardens of Kyoto / by
    Leslie Buck.
Description: Portland, Oregon: Timber Press, 2017.
Identifiers: LCCN 2016045504 (print) | LCCN 2017000520 (ebook)
    | ISBN 9781604697933 (hardcover) | ISBN 9781604698046
    (e-book)
Subjects: LCSH: Gardens, Japanese—Study and teaching—Japan—
    Kyoto. | Pruning—Study and teaching—Japan—Kyoto. | Buck,
    Leslie, 1965– | Apprentices—Japan—Kyoto.
Classification: LCC SB458 .B83 2017 (print) | LCC SB458 (ebook) |
    DDC 635.0952076—dc23
LC record available at https://lccn.loc.gov/2016045504

A catalog record for this book is also available from the British Library.

Contents

Preface

I am the person you spot up in the tree, dirt smeared across my face. "Is that a large bird up there?" you may wonder. My pruning shears busily clip away as I try to bring out the natural beauty in the tree in my playful, sometimes assertive, sometimes delicate way. The tree, shears, and I are dancing partners under the sun. We've been together for decades.

Passersby might step right over my pile, despite the rake I have lain across the sidewalk as a deterrent. Sometimes, without asking, they'll pick up a branch for their dog and walk on, hoping not to bother me. Or maybe I'll catch their eye as they walk right under a branch I'm sawing that is about to drop. People are curious about a female pruner high up in the tree, wielding sharp tools. Just as I covet the stylish outfits worn by the women who walk beneath my tree, I believe others want to be like a kid again, up in the tree with me.

This kind of interaction would never take place in Japan, where, starting late in the year 1999, I worked for three long seasons, watching the gardens explode with summer growth, morph overnight into radiant fall colors, and molt their leaves after the first bitter cold days of winter. Owing to their devotion and skills, traditional gardeners are treated like brain surgeons by the Japanese public. Clients and people walking by give them plenty of space, never talking to them unless summoned, so as not to break their concentration or pace. When addressing a gardener in Japan, people first apologize for interrupting, and then speak in reverent tones to the craftsman they know has trained like a star athlete, with much physical effort and years of sacrifice, in order to create over centuries some of the most beautiful gardens in the world.

But I don't mind if someone asks me a question while I'm up in a tree. I'm naturally friendly, having been born in the heart of the Midwest and raised from a young age in a sleepy California beach town. At the age of nearly thirty-five I went to Japan in pursuit of a gardening apprenticeship. I had to ask permission in person to join the company, to show I was serious, the way others have approached landscaping companies for centuries.

I didn't always feel daring. I'm an unusual adventurer: more worried than eager, unable to pick up new languages easily, and often getting lost. I'm willing to challenge myself, but my emotions, both anxiety and joy, always play a large role. Still I never let any flaws in my character keep me from going after a dream. My struggles were a gift. They taught me determination, and sometimes humor. In Kyoto I learned to work in silence, to run fast between projects, and to take breaks three times a day, with green tea and snacks. I grew to appreciate how hard I tried rather than how much I succeeded. I discovered a way to feel proud even when I came home dirty and exhausted.

In Kyoto I discovered that 90 percent of the private home gardens of Japan are native; the Kyoto private homes, monasteries, and imperial gardens I worked in were some of the most natural-looking gardens I'd ever seen. The miniaturized and overly sheared Japanese gardens I'd expected were surprisingly absent. Most of the gardens were designed and pruned to look so sincere that visitors might think they'd stepped into a piece of forest left behind in the city. One of my coworkers, who once fell asleep in a pine tree, said to me, "Leslie, tell your friends back home that Japanese gardens are as natural as possible."

I tend to work with serious focus. So I prefer answering inquires when sitting in a garden with a lovely table full of tea and cake nearby. A garden desires to be enjoyed. I love to teach others about my craft, and I enjoy pruning in the garden one day and writing in a café the next. Spending time in nature allows me to ruminate over my writing and ideas. The gardens inspire me and offer a paid workout. The feminine weeping red pine in one of my sixty-year-old gardens, or the two girls I always see walking by with their two well-fed boxers in San Francisco's Sea Cliff, give me an idea for my next chapter.

When I returned from my Japan apprenticeship, I built up my pruning business so I could buy a home and have access to health-care, two things every long-term hard worker should be able to afford. I joined volunteer pruning projects at nonprofit gardens with the Merritt College Pruning Club to teach others my craft. I continued to learn from classes, conferences, lectures, sketching, and almost thirty years of hands-on garden work.

The way to become a master craftsman in Japan is to practice one's craft and to teach. One garden craftsman told me that as a hobby he studied ikebana, the Japanese art of flower arranging. When I asked him how long he'd been doing this, he said, "Oh, not very long, only fifteen years. I'm just an amateur." It requires many years of hands-on experience to fully understand a craft. Japanese craftspeople take their work seriously. I begin my story at one of the first Kyoto gardens I worked in, where the garden craftsmen of Japan began to teach me not only about pride, but about how to find heart in the garden.

Watchful Turtle Is
Given a Pine Test

"This garden is not very old," my coworker softly whispered to me. "Only three hundred and fifty years." After driving for a while through the streets of Kyoto, we made a sharp left onto an almost hidden drive and entered the garden through a back gate. Our truck became enveloped by a lush woodland landscape. I found out later that, centuries before, the property had belonged to a wealthy Kyoto merchant. A formal restaurant now overlooks the wild, forested scene. Central to the landscape was a wide stream, an ancient canal once used to bring rice and goods on barges into Kyoto.

Two gently sloping embankments rose up from the stream, blanketed in ferns, azaleas, and nandinas in endless overlapping shades of green. Birds called from every direction. Insects buzzed and circled us like young playmates. Even the still turtles seemed to be tracking our movement with their eyes. A few stone lanterns dotted the landscape, but the flowing water held my attention. A building sat atop a hill, where diners watched the activity through large windows.

The youngest worker in our garden crew looked at me with a worried expression as he tentatively handed me a pair of *karikomi,*

Japanese hedge shears with long handles and narrow blades. I wondered if he thought I might throw the tool back. I tried to smile reassuringly as I thanked him softly in Japanese. I later learned that he'd been gardening for only seven months. I'd been studying horticulture and running a landscape pruning and design business for more than seven years. Nevertheless, he would eventually become my boss. Japanese craftsmen's hierarchy is determined by time in the company, not by experience. I had arrived just a few months after the shy teenager had joined our crew. This kind of hierarchy sometimes seems absurd to Westerners, but it produces efficient work teams with no competition between members because positions are set. With the possibility of having one's rank lowered by switching companies, hierarchy ensures that apprentices commit to the company that trains them.

I paid careful attention to the young gardener's energetic technique that day while we worked together on some overgrown azalea hedges. His *karikomi* sang out like a bird's melodic tune. Mine cried like a lost crow—sporadic, loud, and ineffective. *Karikomi* blades fit loosely like an old pair of scissors. To get a clean cut, I had to apply constant pressure to the handles so the blades would press together and cut properly. I worked clumsily and was frustratingly slow. I wondered if the tool had been designed this way on purpose, to strengthen the female gardener's arms, or perhaps her focus. My muscles began to ache. After a few hours of wondering if my arms might give out, I realized that if I relaxed, the blades pressed together more effectively. *I'm*—swish—*working with*—swish—*gardeners in Japan*—swish. *Or am I dreaming?* I felt both eager to show the men my enthusiasm and already worn out from excitement.

- - - -

At lunch, I walked over to examine a pine that an advanced worker had been styling. The styled black pine is one of the more mesmerizing trees in the natural Japanese garden landscape. Like all plants in a Japanese garden, the pine is styled to mimic its mature, wild form in nature. Usually the lower branches stretch wide and the top small like a mountain form, and each branch is staggered right and left, front and back searching for optimum light. Of course, there can always be exceptions to this generality, just like in nature. On this particular tree, the branches had been considerably thinned, and quite a few needles removed by hand. In fact, it looked to me as though he'd pruned the dickens out of it! I was used to pruning Japanese pines gently back home in California, where, outside their native environment, they grow with less vigor. Nevertheless, this pine looked more exquisitely styled than any I'd ever seen. Bright green needles contrasted with brown fissured bark on a timeworn trunk. Branches twisted and hung low at the ends so gracefully that it looked like only rain, sunshine, and snow had ever touched them, although I knew better. This tree had been carefully styled by craftsmen twice a year for hundreds of years.

I stroked my fingers along a few of the pine needles. They felt cool. I crushed a cluster with my fist and smelled the fresh sap. I pressed the palm of my hand against some upturned needles. *Yow!* The needle tips were sharp! These were all signs of a healthy pine. I took notes in my journal like mad, thrilled to see advanced pruning up close, standing in a Japanese garden in Kyoto. I wrote a bit more than necessary. I wanted the crew leader to see that I was serious.

After finishing my third group of azaleas, I ran over to our boss. *"Tsugi wa?"* (What next?) I asked cleverly, using one of the few

Japanese phrases I knew. The boss commanded, "*Matsu*" (pine). I hesitated a few seconds, confused. Did he say pine? Pines tend to hold court in a Japanese garden. They are beautiful when pruned properly, yet sensitive and fussy. A poor pruner could easily weaken a centuries-old styled pine, or even kill it. Pine pruning is such a complicated technique, it requires years to learn. I never expected to be asked to prune a pine in Japan.

The boss repeated his command, giving me detailed instructions as he gesticulated near a pine tree that had already been worked on, and toward one that looked bushy. I couldn't understand his specific words. He spoke to me in rapid Japanese, and I'd only studied Japanese in night school for a few years. But I felt I understood his instructions precisely: "Work on that pine, only pull needles, copy the other intermediate worker, and then a senior pruner will follow up with thinning cuts." I wondered later how I could understand the boss's instructions. Maybe, as the youngest of four sisters, I'm skilled at watching others to guess what lies ahead. Or perhaps it was because the boss demonstrated with his hands. Most likely, I suspected, I'd done pruning long enough to predict what needed to be done. I took a deep breath. I knew I could prune a pine, but I wasn't sure I could prune one in Japan, with the elite Japanese craftsman watching.

The pine I began to work on was so tall, I had to stand up on my tiptoes to reach it. I thought maybe I'd gotten the assignment because, except for the boss, I was the tallest person on my crew. I stood at five foot three. Then I figured out the more likely explanation: the pine grew far enough back in the garden that it was practically hidden from the restaurant's view. If I screwed up, no one would see. I'd been given a test.

I told myself, *Leslie, work as fast as you can.* Poised before my pine, I began at the top, pulling the needles carefully and slowly from their base—not tearing them, which would later cause stubs and make the pine look brown and sickly. I pulled more needles per branch at the top of the pine than at the bottom because the lower branches looked weak. After finishing, I again ran back to the boss and asked, *"Tsugi wa?"* I feigned nonchalance, trying not to reveal that my heart was pounding faster than my shears could cut. He looked at the pine from top to bottom, evaluating my work. I followed his eyes. A bit messy, I realized. Then I saw some gummy dead needles stuck on a lower branch. *Damn, how did I miss those?* He said nothing. He led me to another pine, less hidden.

Again, I worked quickly and ran back. The boss then escorted me past some tall bushes, over a stone bridge, across the wide stream, and up a sunlit embankment, to the smallest pine I'd seen yet, just under four feet tall. I looked up to see hundreds of well-dressed dining patrons enjoying lunch, watching me through the restaurant's immense windows, just ten feet away. *Oh, shit.* They sat on floor cushions in front of low tables, attended by waitresses wearing beautifully patterned kimonos. The diners appeared to be enjoying their view of the water and the gardeners. My boss grunted and mimed some actions with his muscular hands in an incomprehensible yet understandable way. Again, I plucked the needles swiftly and tried to forget the luncheon guests, who by this time might have noticed the Caucasian girl pruning a pine in one of Kyoto's historic Japanese gardens.

After about twenty minutes, the boss came back to review my work. When I'm nervous, I tend to overprune. I'd already realized that the pine didn't look as good as any of the other styled pines.

I just couldn't say why. One of my pruning mentors once told me, "Your pine looks like a plucked chicken." I'd become too intent on solving every problem on the tree at once, instead of solving the issues slowly, over years, as I had been taught. My boss voiced a Japanese version of "hmmph" and led me to another tree. The rest of the day, I did more pruning, clipping, and raking.

In the early afternoon, the dining guests took a stroll around the garden, and I became quite a novelty, by then a thirty-five-year-old American woman wearing traditional Japanese gardening cloth boots. Beautifully coiffed women with shiny black hair, finely tailored business skirts, and matching scarves softly inquired, "Where are you from? Is your work hard?" Many offered encouraging words, saying *"Gambatte!"* (Don't give up!) That meant so much to me on my first day.

The crew remained silent most of the day, except for the boss's pointed commands. Meanwhile, the ducks quacked overhead and various creatures flew in and out of the river. A crane landed noisily on a shallow stone. A koi harassed a napping turtle with a tail splash. Insects hovered over a thrashing waterfall. Around dusk the garden sounds softened, except for our *jikatabi*, the traditional Japanese shoes, padding softly over stones and moss. A dozen or so lanterns lit up around the garden as if by magic.

The humidity that had been steadily rising all afternoon and the dark clouds that had been gathering gave way. At first small drops plopped all over the streambed. Then it poured, thrashing the water into a roar. After thirty minutes of soaking rain, I might as well have jumped into the canal. The boss called me over to him and handed me a rain jacket. He pointed to a shed roof that he apparently wanted me to stand under, urging me to quit for the day. I put the coat over my wet uniform but ignored the shed and kept hauling debris. The youngest worker had also forgotten his rain gear. He looked doused, but no one stopped him. I wasn't going to be the first to quit, and definitely not the first girl to quit. Then the boss spotted me and repeated, rather loudly, for me to get under the shed overhang. So I sulked underneath, shivering, watching the other workers run past. Just before the men got into the truck to leave, they pulled dry clothes out of their duffle bags to change into. *Oh*. We finished at six in the evening. I felt chilled but satisfied. I had survived my first day in Kyoto's temperamental weather, alongside the crew of dedicated, traditional Japanese craftsmen.

A Seed Sprouts
in Tokyo Gardens

The living room of my childhood home looked out onto another sort of natural woodland landscape, where I climbed native persimmon trees filled with tiny fruit and buried deceased birds reverently, placing twig crosses and spring daffodils on their graves. Cardinals darted overhead as my sister and I climbed up a southern magnolia to get up onto our roof and look out over the expansive view of trees and houses beyond. Those early adventures inside an oak-forested enclave, smack in the middle of Oklahoma City, would eventually grow into my Kyoto garden journey.

I moved away from this small forest when my parents separated. During the height of the feminist movement, my mom wanted to pursue her dreams. In this new arrangement, we saw our father every other weekend. My dad must have fretted over how his two youngest would react to his absence from our everyday family life. In truth, we loved our new situation! Instead of seeing our busy father just at dinnertime, we got to spend whole weekends with him, getting him all to ourselves. I believe it was a mix of my dad's worry over the effects of the divorce and his love of traveling that inspired him to take us to a most unusual restaurant in Oklahoma City, Tokyo Gardens.

Before entering the restaurant, we'd run past a tiny Japanese garden scene, enclosed by a brick-layered raised bed. We'd look into the pond, which held plants and a hollow bamboo pole through which water trickled out into a stone basin. I didn't know it then, but the scene mimicked a traditional *tsukubai*, the spot in the tea garden where one washes one's hands clean of the stresses of the outside world before entering the tea house.

Once inside the restaurant, we'd head immediately for a side room—the *genkan*, the shoe-removal room—with a huge compartmentalized shoe shelf covering the whole wall, floor to ceiling—or so it looked to my eight-year-old eyes. Dad encouraged us to climb the wooden structure, an act that I am now sure was a faux pas, in order to shove our shoes into the highest box. After neatly tucking away our shoes, we'd enter the main room of the restaurant, the floors lined with tatami, golden reed-covered mats. I'd sit on a small, flat pillow and cross my little legs underneath the *chabudai*, a short table about a foot and a half high. Of course I didn't know any of these traditional Japanese words yet, or that I would eventually embark on a life-changing journey into the gardens of Japan. I only understood that the restaurant was as fascinating as our newly discovered father.

My dad often allowed us to order one of the biggest items on the menu, the *sukiyaki bento* dinner, which was served on a black lacquered wooden tray filled with fresh grilled meat, rice, salad, and Japanese pickles. Only upon dining in Kyoto thirty years later did I remember the delicious flavors I'd tasted at this restaurant and the scenes I had witnessed. I still crave Japanese pickles as much as I do fried okra. I once found a postcard filled with images of Tokyo Gardens—to my amazement, it looked as elegant as I remembered. This restaurant helped me develop both a curiosity about and a fondness for refined Japanese culture.

A neat and fussy child, I wouldn't eat any item on my plate that touched another, so the separated compartmental organization of the *bento* tray delighted and calmed me. Practicing on torn pieces of Wonder Bread back home, my sister and I quickly mastered chopsticks. This served me well later in Kyoto, as it's helpful to have good hand–eye coordination and attention to detail in order to work with the garden craftsmen.

Midway through the meal, hidden speakers would fill the room with traditional Japanese folk music. The waitresses, wearing stiff kimonos covered with patterns of leaves and flowers, would slowly walk down the aisles, waving fans in front of them in time to plucked instrumental melodies. My sister and I followed them with big eyes, mouths open, chopsticks poised midair. I suspect that many of these women came from Japan. They shared their culture with us generously, despite the hardships they may have endured living far away from home.

I remember a certain waitress passing our table and smiling at us on the sly—the two little girls with their handsome bachelor father. This woman's face, and her subdued beauty, still finds its way into my dreams. I wish she could have known that she inspired the younger girl, the one who hardly talked but watched her with wide hazel eyes. This shy little girl would grow up to eventually work in one of the emperor's gardens of Kyoto, swinging a razor-sharp scythe instead of waving a fan.

No one can predict what events might lead a child to her destiny—just as I cannot predict exactly how a tree will grow after my first styling. When I work on a tree for the first time, I take many factors into consideration before setting the initial pruning goal. I pull branches aside to look inside the plant's structure. I think about how that tree looks in nature when it reaches its most mature, poetic state. I rely on years of muscle memory at my fingertips, with horticulture and artistic studies in my thoughts. I refer back to an art form I call "aesthetic pruning." I'd already studied this type of pruning before going to Japan. It's based on traditional Japanese garden pruning, yet it applies well to native garden scenes and almost any style of gardening in which one desires to create the atmosphere and beauty found in nature.

As soon as I begin snipping away at the branches of any tree, the singsong of nearby birds, my endless thoughts, and the afternoon heat or morning chill slowly fade away. My mind and body focus on the tree. The plant and I dance. I have already decided on a styling goal, although the plan may take me years to fully accomplish. I remain open to new ideas as I go along. While pruning, I notice unique characteristics of the plant. These features guide me as much as my original goal. Upon finishing, I'll think, *I had no idea you could look so beautiful!* My hands tend to know more than my head can predict.

My bumpy path toward finding a garden apprenticeship in Kyoto followed much the same unpredictable route. I set goals and moved forward. I kept my eyes open so I could learn or make detours if necessary. The gentle waitresses at Tokyo Gardens watered a little seed, planted in my love of nature and beauty. Under the warm embrace of my father, the seed sprouted and began to grow. Only then could I take my few first steps down a personal path to a destination still hidden from me—toward the *uekiya*, the gardeners of Japan.

Flying into the Gardens

More than three decades after watching the mesmerizing waitresses, I stepped onto a plane bound for Kyoto. While I sat on
my thick-cushioned seat, I chatted to the man next to me. Fear
squeezed my chest during the whole surreal conversation. I asked
myself, as I smiled at him, *What am I thinking, going to a country
where I barely speak the language, looking for work?* Above the lanes
of San Francisco's Golden Gate Bridge, packed with speeding cars,
there are signs that say "NO U-TURNS!" I used to think to myself,
Who would be that stupid? On the plane I thought, *If only.*

I often wondered why I felt I had to study gardening in Japan.
If one waters a dry spot of earth, dormant seeds in the soil may
spring to life, their tender leaves pushing their way up through
the soil before they rise daringly into the open air. My interest in
Japanese gardens spread over time like these wildflowers.

I moved from Oklahoma to California in my early teens. I eventually studied painting at the University of California at Berkeley and discovered Japanese films from the fifties at the Pacific
Film Archive. I loved watching Japanese nature scenes, with
scary ghosts weaving among bamboo or old women putting out
their laundry on their home's *engawa*, long wooden porches that
looked out onto nature. I spent a year studying at the École des

----

Beaux-Arts de Bordeaux. Even in France I found myself research-
ing Japanese artists.

I took horticulture classes at a California community college,
and one afternoon I noticed a group pruning a large Monterey
pine outside of the Merritt College bonsai class. "Would you like
to join us?" someone from the group asked me. I tried scaling the
pine tree, but my legs shook as ants crawled up my shins. I hadn't
climbed a tree in a while.

A strange excitement enveloped me. I crushed some pine needles, holding onto them too firmly for safety, and released their
scent. *Something is about to happen*, I thought. I tucked a small
branch I'd pruned into my pocket. I still have that branch. The
man who was both the teacher of the bonsai class and the leader of
the pine pruning group was Dennis Makishima, my future mentor.

A few years later, while attending an Oregon conference at the
Portland Japanese Garden, I skipped out on a claustrophobic lecture to explore outside. I heard the sound—*snip, snip, rustle, snip*—
before I saw them: the first Japanese garden craftsmen I'd ever
seen in person, styling half a dozen pines with concentration. Typically, when I prune with other American gardeners, we talk nonstop, compare notes, and generally make fun of each other. Apart
from the noise of the pruning shears, these men worked in silence.
In contrast to the stained T-shirt that served as the American gardener's uniform, they wore stylish clothing: dark boots, pressed
shirts, and brightly printed cotton headbands. Their clothes and
movements hinted to me of a certain aesthetic, a particular pride
I'd never witnessed. I watched them, entranced.

After about twenty minutes, one of the gardeners looked at
me and beckoned me forward. I had been learning pine pruning

for a few years at that point, but when the gardener handed me his shears, my mind went blank. I took the tool and pruned a few branches with stumbling effort. I realized I had much more to learn. The other conference members began to show up, and I stepped back, getting lost in the crowd. Yet I'll never forget the moment the handsome young gardener placed his shears in my hand.

After the garden conference, I began toying with the idea of apprenticing in Japan. There was no set program for finding a Japanese garden apprenticeship. Regardless, I delved into my self-propelled horticulture studies in earnest. Of the rare individuals I met who had apprenticed in Japan, most discouraged me. I asked my mentor one day, "Why don't you encourage your students to study in Japan?" After all, I thought, he had apprenticed in a Tokyo bonsai company. He answered accusingly, "Why do you want to go to Japan? Do you want to be famous?" To a thirty-year-old, the idea actually sounded thrilling! But I suspected his words warned me of something I couldn't yet understand.

Learning a foreign language did not come easily to me, nor did almost any academic subject. Hence, over the years, I'd developed quite a determined spirit. I called myself a type-A wannabe. So I gritted my teeth and studied Japanese conversation at night for two years, just in case.

Luckily, I love to be still and watch nature, for a little bird brought me my biggest message yet.

It happened while I was sitting on my boyfriend's couch, watching the rustling purple leaves of a Berkeley wild plum outside the window. My thoughts wandered around lazily, like a bird I watched hopping in the plum's shade. I daydreamed about the moment I'd first seen Taylor, along the windy coastline of Point

Reyes, an hour north of Berkeley. I was busy sketching a pine on a hill when Taylor walked by, smiling at me, and I felt an instant trust in him. He asked to see some of my drawings. We ended up hiking together.

He took photos of the parched amber grass while I sketched fire-scorched pines. Walking underneath windswept Monterey cypresses, we enjoyed each other's calming presence.

After two years of dating, I felt my heart entwining with his. But I knew Taylor felt cautious. I had an active social life, hosting dinners with friends and sailing dinghies on the windy Berkeley Bay. Taylor practically lived in his darkroom and enjoyed hiking with a few friends, or alone. I admired his passion for creating beauty but did not share his reserved nature.

The bird under the plum began to poke at the soil with its beak. My thoughts strayed to thinking about Taylor and me in the future. *We could get married; we could have children.* Then another thought arrived: *If I have children soon, I'll regret never having gone to Japan.*

I spoke impulsively. "I'm thinking of going to Japan to search for an apprenticeship." Decision made, based on potential regret. After four years of thinking about it, I'd said it out loud. "Great idea!" Taylor mumbled from his darkroom.

When I glanced out the window again, the little bird was gone, having noiselessly taken flight. A week later, Taylor came up to me with a phone in his hand. "Hey, a friend of mine is on the phone. He lives in Kyoto and says his girlfriend is going away to school next fall. You could rent her spare bedroom." I took the phone hesitantly, saying, "Well, okay," already wanting to give it back.

The summer of 1999, as I headed for Japan in the swift airplane, a suitcase was stored far down in the plane's belly beneath my

----

seat, packed with enough work clothes for several seasons. A second bag was completely filled with thank-you presents. I'd read in Japanese culture books about the importance of gifts: wrap everything, and do not make too big a deal about your present when handing it over, or you will obligate the receiver to return the favor equally. I'd wrapped each gift with care, taking hours, as though this act alone would ensure my trip's success. My mother taught me how to wrap with the perfectionist spirit of an origami artist. In the fifties, she'd wrapped wedding gifts for the first Neiman Marcus department store in Dallas.

I packed garden clothes that would last three seasons: late summer, fall, and early winter. I had to bring everything—my size-nine pants, enormous compared to typical Japanese women's sizes, meant I couldn't shop in Japan. I left behind a solid pruning business with nearly fifty pruning clients, many of whom anticipated my return. I tried not to think about disappointing them. I might not find an apprenticeship at all.

Most important, I held in my pocket three letters of reference. I was told by those who'd already studied in Japan that I could not approach any garden firm without a recommendation, nor without going to Japan to request the position in person.

One letter was from a client of mine, a Silicon Valley tech innovator who lived in Palo Alto. It was addressed to a Xerox executive he knew in Kyoto who might refer me to a landscaping company that worked at his home. Rather farfetched, I thought, but worth a try. The next note was from a Canadian landscaper I'd briefly met at a Japanese garden conference, addressed to a company he'd worked with years before. I'd thought the company was based in Tokyo, so at first I hadn't even contacted him. But the editor of the

----

American Japanese garden journal *Sukiya Living* mentioned that the company was actually based in Kyoto. The letter from the Canadian man said simply: "Would it be possible for Leslie to look around the company property?" A bit more promising! Last, I held an email from my future Kyoto landlord telling me he would introduce me to his "landscaper neighbor who used to be a monk and knew the poet Gary Snyder." Most interesting, certainly. Enough hope in one pocket to buy a plane ticket for halfway around the world.

Settling into my seat, I looked forward to the airline's neatly organized *bento* box. I worried, and tried not to worry. I dreamt about men in stylish garden clothing working furiously on the pines. I imagined what it might feel like to step onto Japanese soil—fertile and dark—where my adventures could grow.

"Senteishi Desu"

Taking long strides down a path tightly packed with visitors to the public garden, I tried to keep a steady eye on the pruners working on the pines. Visitors to popular Kyoto gardens must often follow a one-way route, pushed along at a brisk pace by the crowd. Only my second week in Japan, I still watched gardeners from afar. I spotted a small bench ahead, off the pedestrian runway, and with all my courage, I stopped moving with the crowd and sat down. I tried to appear relaxed, even though I felt everyone's gaze on me. Reddening a little, I forced myself to be even more conspicuous by attempting a few crude drawings in my journal, a sure crowd-pleaser. Visitors leaned over my pages to see what the noticeably pale-skinned *gaijin*, foreigner, was drawing.

I sketched the dry garden area before me, which was made up of patterns raked into the coarse sand. The picture reminded me of a desert scene, with ribbons of sand blown by the wind. To my right stood a six-foot-tall pile of sand in the shape of an upside-down cone. The strict geometric pile contrasted with the wild-looking plants surrounding it, making it look modern and cool. I also sketched an outline of a temple hovering nearby, with distant trees filling the outer edges of my page. No need to get every detail, just the essence. The Japanese garden, after all, is the archetype of nature, just as an opera is a simplified version of a much more nuanced story.

Self-consciously, as I prefer blending in, I scraped my pencil against the paper. I'd decided to follow the advice of David Slawson, a talented and soft-spoken American landscaper and author. Slawson studied garden construction in Japan, and encouraged me to go to Kyoto. Before I'd left, he'd told me, "Draw gardens that inspire you. They will help you understand nature and recognize design patterns." *You have to sit here and sketch if you are not working in the gardens!* I lectured myself as I sweated into the armpits of my linen shirt. The only people ignoring me were the gardeners.

My bench resided in a garden named Ginkakuji, the Silver Pavilion, six blocks from the little wooden Kyoto home I planned to live in through winter. My new home felt much like the ones I had seen in old Japanese films of countryside villages, with a wide *engawa*, a deck, that looked out onto a garden. Our building, resting side by side with other wooden homes, formed a row of connected houses, one of a series on a rare Kyoto hillside. With multiple rows of houses on a hill, and a spattering of green trees throughout, from a distance the historic neighborhood looked like a well-tended row garden. Looking out from my bedroom window, I could see tall mountain ranges on the outskirts of the city. A serrated-leaf cherry branch hung close to my window. I'd stare at its mass of leaves while lying on my floor futon. Nothing relaxes me like a view of trees, so the cherry felt like a familiar friend at my window.

I never, ever wore my shoes in the house—that is, beyond the *genkan*, the house's entryway room. I loved this idea of cleanliness! When I put my bare foot on the floors, I knew for sure that no dog droppings or old chewing gum had transferred onto the floor from a shoe worn outside. I had allowed my workbag to touch the floor of the bus, so I kept it out of the main house and inside the *genkan*. Unfortunately, my laid-back landlord, raised in America, did not totally conform to certain Japanese standards. His tatami looked stained, his *genkan* was in complete disorder, and his garden held upturned pots, a barbecue, and overgrown grass. Basically, he lived in a Kyoto bachelor pad. I spent my first two full days cleaning our house in a jet-lagged daze. I used the slimy walk-in shower once, and then for the rest of my stay slipped into a spotless female-only bathhouse, a ten-minute walk away, where I'd cleanse my body of soil, anxiety, and male determination.

The familiar rooms of Tokyo Gardens, and the spirit of my dad, followed me to Kyoto. I valued my stable community back home, but my father always encouraged me to step outside my comfort zone when journeying. One time, when I was a timid young girl, climbing down one particularly steep cliff path with him, he reassured me, "If you get scared, just get on your butt and slide." That summed up my dad's spirit. Years after Kyoto, my dad lay in a hospital bed, confused from a massive dose of chemo, while I stood watching over him. He yelled out to a nurse, "My daughter Leslie— she worked in an emperor's garden in Japan!" The nurse smiled sweetly, indulging his fantasy, but I teared up. "It's true." Even lost in hallucinations, my dad continued to support me.

Sitting on the Kyoto garden bench with my sketchbook and pencil, I considered my current to-do list. First, I needed to find someone to translate an introductory letter. But I wondered how to do this in a city where I carried my address on a folded piece of paper in my pocket for fear of not knowing how to find my way home.

Second, I had to find a way to meet my landlord's neighbor, the landscaper-monk. Despite the fact that I walked past his front door mornings and afternoons, I could only guess at his whereabouts. I felt I'd spent days doing many things and getting nothing done.

From my bench I dutifully watched the Ginkakuji gardeners pruning the grove of pines. When I'd meet Kyoto locals, they'd ask me what I did. I'd place my hand on my chest, *"Senteishi desu."* They'd tilt their heads, confused. Then I'd repeat myself with a hand pantomime of scissors opening and closing to emphasize my point. *"Senteishi desu"* (I am a tree pruner). Their eyes would widen. *"Ah, so desu ka!"* (Is that so!) they'd exclaim, trying to imagine a female *senteishi* among the Japanese men who had dominated their garden craft for centuries.

I observed the *senteishi* patiently styling their trees, thinning thick branch clusters until the branches resembled a ballet dancer's elegant outstretched hands. I had been warned that Japanese craftsmen rarely teach verbally, that I was expected to observe tasks being performed, then simply try to repeat what I'd seen when asked. Like a child learning to walk, the apprentice learns through trial and error. When the muscle learns something before the brain, the lesson penetrates the consciousness more deeply. The student is corrected, and rarely appreciated. He is more likely told, "Wrong, wrong, and wrong!" until he gets it right.

I told myself I was almost a pruning student at the Silver Pavilion. *Heck, if none of my potential contacts worked out, I might sit here every day until the gardeners gave in and let me work here with them.* I'd become Leslie Buck, Kyoto garden stalker. The longer I persisted, the more seriously they'd take me. In other words, I'd begun to feel desperate.

At one point, even though the pruners never acknowledged my presence, one gardener repositioned himself at an odd angle in a way that allowed me to observe his hands and technique more precisely. He'd never so much as glanced in my direction, but I felt he had moved so I could watch his progress more carefully. *Did he do it on purpose? Did he see me watching him?* I wondered. One thing I did not predict was that in Japan, the craftsmen would observe me more often than I watched them. At Ginkakuji, on a warm and humid September day, I believed I'd found my first Kyoto teacher.

My teacher worked on his tree with serious concentration for nearly twenty minutes. He stood on the top rung of a twelve-foot ladder, pruning the highest, fifteen-foot branches. Twelve feet is a huge pine. The eight-foot ladder I used back in California had seemed quite tall a few weeks before. I watched my teacher stretch right and move left to reach every branch on the pine. Then he suddenly stopped and looked up. What next? I watched him in fascination as he grabbed a new tool out of a side pocket. He fiddled with it, put it next to his hat, and began talking to it. A cell phone! I giggled. Fifteen feet above the ancient garden, he continued to chat away. I'd discovered a modern pruning teacher in Kyoto, the summer before the turn of the century. I'd found him, not in an urgent search through the city streets, but by sitting with focus and watching.

I'd ask myself several times each day, *What am I doing here?* And I tried not to think about failure. Simply visiting gardens for three months might be fun! But this idea got stuck in my throat. I'd close my eyes and breathe deeply to clear my anxious thoughts. I focused on all the people I knew back in the States who'd be thrilled to visit Japan, to watch small birds swoop over the dry sand garden, ignoring the one-way-only garden paths. They'd savor the meditative

- - - -

pruners, the wind rustling through late-summer broad leaves. Why couldn't I?

Stop thinking and look at what's before you, I beseeched myself. A dry garden. I sketched the wavy lines of sand. Some people use the religious term *Zen garden* instead of *dry garden.* And yet dry gardens, and Japanese gardens in general, are not necessarily designed with religious intention. For instance, Japanese viewers might look at one of their gardens and think about a memory as a child near the ocean or forest, or they might be curious about the botany of the trees, or perhaps, indeed, they could have a religious thought. Japanese gardens allow our thoughts to meander rather than telling us what to think.

As I began sketching again, the sand pattern transformed in my imagination from desert scene to a deep blue rippling ocean, with seagulls crying out overhead. Often, after I've been drawing for a while, colors and objects intensify, become crisper and more vibrant, and my sight becomes magnified. The most mundane scenes become stunning. Rather than reminding me of God, whom I do try to contact in my most desperate moments, the dry garden reminded me of a tide I'd seen going in and out on the first day I walked along the Point Reyes seashore with Taylor.

I turned to the cone-shaped mound placed provocatively between the dry garden and the wooden pavilion. According to the English-language pamphlet, the monks who originally cared for the garden kept a pile of sand handy to spruce up the dry garden occasionally. Over time the pile became an object of study and beauty in itself. Generally I take garden pamphlets lightly, since they can overdirect the garden visitor's thoughts. But I felt taken by this story. *What do you think?* I asked myself. I often talked to myself out loud in my California gardens, but I kept my thoughts internal in Kyoto. The motionless pile stared back at me. And I kept staring at it, looking at its outline, its simple lines, its uncomplicated existence. It was, after all, just a pile. I looked around at the rippling dry garden, the pruners, and back to the pile. My anxiety finally began to lift, and after two hours of sitting in one spot, I stood up to join the stream of garden visitors, each of whom reacted to the garden in their own way that day.

I ran into David, my landlord, on the way home. "Want to join me for a walk?" he asked. "Sure!" I said, even though I felt guilty about putting off my to-do list. We walked down brick-paved city streets, along pedestrian paths, and past a local monastery with chanting monks. Turning into one side street, David exclaimed, "Hey, look, there's my neighbor, the landscaper Sogyu!" Heading straight toward us was a thin Japanese man in a worn white T-shirt, jeans, and sandals. As we got closer, I realized how tall he stood; his hair was pulled back into a ponytail, and he sported a faint philosopher's beard. *He looks just like a Berkeley hippie*, I thought to myself. I held an image of Japanese gardeners: functionally cropped hair and shirts with collars. Yet Sogyu looked unique, with kind, curious wrinkles that graced his eyes. He looked physically fit and healthy, with muscular arms, and was anywhere between thirty and fifty. I found him handsome. Most Japanese craftsmen glow with health and strength.

"Ohayō gozaimasu!" (Good morning!) David called out with a smile. We both bowed toward Sogyu. David bowed slightly, with each arm hanging loose at his side, a man's bow. I bowed more deeply, placing my right hand over my left, a woman's greeting. Hierarchy existed everywhere in Kyoto. I wondered if I traveled

back to the time of Emily Brontë's *Wuthering Heights*, a favorite book of mine about love touched by wild nature, if I would find as much attention being paid to cultural formality as I found in Kyoto near the turn of the twenty-first century. Despite the fact that I'd done my best to learn about a continually evolving Japanese culture before my arrival, I often felt like I wore clunky garden shoes everywhere while attempting to be a ballerina.

Just before I did my bow, I considered Sogyu's place next to me in the hierarchy. He was a man, a teacher, and a potential boss, making him my senior in many ways. Most important, as I learned growing up in the American South, he was my elder. "*Ohayō*," Sogyu responded. His bow played out as barely a dip of his head. This gesture gave me the impression that he considered himself above both David and me. The two men talked while I stood by, unable to understand any of their conversation. Sogyu rarely looked at me, even when my name popped up. I felt invisible. Having followed the children's section of *Ms.* magazine as a girl, I instinctively felt like waving, "Hello! I'm here, I'm alive!" Yet I would eventually discover that most Japanese craftsmen had quite a bit of confidence in me—more than I had in myself, in fact.

After a few minutes, Sogyu turned, looked toward me, and asked in excellent English, "Would you like to see some of the gardens I've built on the hill above our neighborhood?" "Yes!" I said eagerly and succinctly, looking respectfully at his nose, his ear, chin— anywhere but his eyes—out of politeness. As my California mentor had taught me, unless I could think of a thoughtful question or statement, it was best to just "clam it" in Japan. "Thoughtful silence shows more maturity in Japan than bringing attention

----

to yourself." Besides, an *uekiya*, a real Kyoto garden craftsman, stood before me. My thoughts froze.

David and Sogyu started up the hill. *Oh, he means now!* I pursued the two strong walkers. But I kept my distance, always staying a few feet behind the men, another attempt to submit to hierarchy. By this point I was feeling pretty good about my knowledge of how to be humble.

We wound up the hill, passing a small shrine around which an elderly man circled, reciting chants. I often saw him early in the morning when I did my daily run. I considered him my jogging buddy of sorts. I hadn't spotted him two mornings in a row and had worried, *Is he okay?* I felt relieved to see him there that afternoon, and I wondered what he prayed for so intently—loved ones, health, peace? I felt I was keeping an eye on him, but in fact I think he held me up those first few weeks in Kyoto.

Sogyu talked as he walked farther up our neighborhood hill than I'd ever gone. He pointed to low grasses. "I just removed some of the summer flowers and put in these thick grasses that will eventually give this area more of a fall feeling." Instead of changing annual flowers for color variation, Sogyu alternated the seasonal-looking plants. Each season he renovated a new area on the hill. We came upon a lovely wooden hutlike structure near the top. Sogyu explained, "We built this teahouse so people could relax while enjoying nature on the hill." David reminded me that Sogyu used to live as a monk and that he specialized in the *Urasenke* school of tea, the building of tea gardens, until he left the monastery to work more closely with everyday people.

"My company installed the gardens around this building," Sogyu said as we walked inside. I'd thought the landscape was

- - - -

simply nature, untouched. The interior of the teahouse held rustic tables and chairs, potted plants, darkly glazed cups, and teapots of brownish clay. "How beautiful," I said, stroking the top of a thick farm table in the middle of the room. "I made all the furniture," Sogyu said matter-of-factly. *Wow*, was all I could think.

Sogyu talked directly to me for the first time. "I visit a nursery tomorrow with my employees to shop for wild plants. Would you like to come?" All the sounds around me—grass swishing outside the door, birds twittering from trees, and a teahouse employee chatting to a customer—quieted in my mind when Sogyu uttered those words. Run around with garden craftsmen from Japan? *Hell, yes!* I wanted to scream, but I remained calm outwardly. I'd been warned to keep my excitable emotions in check in Japan. "That would be nice," I said, trying to maintain a Prince Charles sort of smile—kind yet detached. I'd followed the Prince of Wales's interest in California horticulture closely when he'd visited the organic farmlands in Point Reyes. Not only was he a strong advocate for organic agriculture, but he'd also expertly conversed with farmers about crop-growing methods. His devotion to plants, his desire for knowledge, and his calm, polite demeanor struck me as traits similar to those of a traditional Japanese craftsman. I sought to emulate his demeanor in Kyoto.

Later that evening, David threw a party so he could introduce the new American to some of his friends and have an excuse to drink some of the California-crafted wines I'd carried with me to Japan. He opened half a dozen fifty-dollar bottles I'd bought at an esteemed Berkeley wine shop, Kermit Lynch. The smell of fermented grapes and good food reminded me of Berkeley and all the fantastic craftspeople I know there. I watched as David's friends

----

poured the beautiful violet liquid into oddly matched glasses and realized how all familiar tastes, sights, sounds, and smells had vanished since I'd arrived in Kyoto. People sat on David's Western-style black leather couch and relaxed on the tatami floors. They feasted on Japanese beef grilled in a tiny hibachi in the backyard. I drank and laughed, while inwardly I preoccupied myself with my latest worries.

Toward the end of the party, cleaning up, I spoke to a friendly woman, a Japanese mom named Minami. I took a chance and asked her, "Would you mind translating a letter for me to a company?" I'd decided to contact the unlikely Xerox garden company just in case things with Sogyu didn't work out. My Canadian contact's company, Uetoh Zoen, had already told me it didn't have time to see me. She hesitated a few seconds, examining a glass for chips around its edges. I felt embarrassed asking her for a favor, having talked to her for only a few minutes. I remembered all the fuss my Japanese American friend had made over a thank-you note I'd written to his mother. He said letters in Japan had to be handwritten, using perfect grammar. Minami piled a collage of glasses on her tray. "Yes," she said, smiling kindly at me. "I can translate your letter." And we headed off to the kitchen together, carrying as many dishes as we could manage.

Tying the Knot with the Kyoto Craftsmen

I met Sogyu near dawn at his front door. Two of his loyal employees had already arrived. We began the day by visiting Japanese mountain plant nurseries and then working on a small pocket garden. The day ended when we loaded Sogyu's handmade drum into his truck, a gray Toyota that looked identical to mine back home, except for the steering wheel that sat on the opposite side. In addition to being a gardener, carpenter, and former monk, Sogyu was an educator and musician.

Early in the morning, in low light, I watched as Sogyu's workers silently and speedily loaded their truck with landscaping materials from a small nursery Sogyu had constructed on our hill. He propagated plants typically found in the mountains of Japan, and then mixed this stock to create whimsical *sanyosho*, potted arrangements of wild mountain plants to sell in the teahouse. Then we drove to a commercial nursery that sold only herbaceous plants, tender plants that do not form woody stems. I'd never seen a nursery dedicated to the tiny plants in wild nature. Most Americans were interested in purchasing the biggest plants possible for their gardens. I was enthralled by herbaceous plants and felt particularly drawn to the feminine native plants of California, such as bleeding heart. Often forgotten in huge landscape projects, tender plants are crucial in nature-inspired gardens. If solid trees and shrubs form the structure, or treasure chest, of a native landscape, then soft herbaceous plants act as the jewels inside: small, colorful, delicate, and ephemeral. These plants may appear unassuming, but they draw a viewer intimately into the scene.

Sogyu took us all out to lunch. His workers were as curious about me as I was about them. The first question was, "How did you come to run your own pruning business?" I told them that I'd studied horticulture, pruning, and native plants at night and on the weekend for years, and that I'd done many volunteer pruning projects my mentor had arranged. Advanced students mentored newer pruners, forming a sort of Japanese-style apprenticeship program. I said that I'd worked on weekends building a pruning business for four years, until I had enough business to quit my job as a general book conservator. I learned from Sogyu's workers that *kiku*—to ask—also meant to listen, an important skill in any Japanese company.

The restaurant's Japanese chopsticks—polished, narrow, and pointed—were difficult to handle compared to the thick, coarse chopsticks I'd mastered in Chinese restaurants. I took pains to hold firm to more than a few grains of slippery rice between my chopsticks. If I couldn't handle chopsticks, how could I expect them to believe I could handle pruning shears? I asked Sogyu's employee Kan, who I'd found out was twenty-eight years old, "How did you become a gardener?" He laughed, his smile radiating health like a shiny camellia leaf, as though this question might be harder than it looked. Speaking perfect English, Kan explained, "I lived as an exchange student in the Midwest, went to college, did a stint as a roofer for two years, discovered plants, and then joined Sogyu's company in my midtwenties." This differed considerably from what I learned was the traditional apprentice's path, where garden training began at age fifteen. David told me that Sogyu employed workers of varying ages and unusual backgrounds. He said Sogyu's workers often found him before he found them.

I turned to another employee, a woman named Shigemi, who I felt most curious about. She looked younger than my thirty-five years and had a slim build, a delicate complexion, and straight black hair. I never expected to meet a Japanese craftswoman. I listened carefully while Shigemi told her story. "I worked with antiques before gardening, so I had to memorize much information. But I found that I loved nature and plants more than objects. So plants became the new things I collect." Kan translated for her and added, "Shigemi is very good with plant nomenclature!" Speaking slowly, and choosing her words carefully, she added, "I'm most interested in mountain plants," and Kan added, "She creates lovely arrangements."

The group talked in a playful, tumbling way. Kan revealed, "The Japanese characters for Shigemi's name are special. Her name means 'growing beauty' and 'tree shrub.'" Like a proud father, Sogyu added, "Very appropriate for a skillful gardener who is also beautiful." Everyone burst out laughing over this comment, especially Shigemi. I wondered about Sogyu's comment, which instinctively did not feel inappropriate but instead struck me as wise and supportive. I sometimes felt self-conscious about my girl-gardener's dirt-stained outfit and clunky boots. Sogyu told me at the end of lunch on our way to his truck, "There are many gardeners in Kyoto, perhaps a thousand. But also, there are around thirty female gardeners in Kyoto." Then he looked at me and added, "Maybe thirty-one."

We drove to Sogyu's current landscaping job, which was at a dentist's office—and not just any dentist's office. The patients' chairs were placed around the edge of one big circular open room. Each chair had a view through a window, the sill of which brimmed with potted plants. A fairly large tea-making area took up a nook. The owner explained that she wanted her patients to feel relaxed, as though they were at home. She said that she hired Sogyu to create a natural, abstract waterfall scene in a small spot between the entryway and the street, so clients would start to feel soothed even before walking in the door.

Sogyu tied reeds and branches into neat bundles, which he then used to camouflage a pond pump. Kan and Shigemi taught me how to tie a traditional Japanese knot called *otoko musubi*, which literally translates as "man's knots." Using strong black jute, we tied *otoko musubi* knots around young camellia branches to train them onto bamboo trellises so they would not stretch too far out onto a narrow street. The knot tying took quite a while to learn, and I had the feeling that its interest lay less in function or nomenclature than tradition. The very act of folding and tightening the string bound us together in a subtle way I did not yet fully understand. I felt exhilarated working with the crew; I could barely exhale, for fear my breath might propel the day to its end. The day marked the beginning of a dream, of working with the traditional craftsmen—and craftswomen—in Japan.

Sogyu motioned for me to follow him. He pointed to a small lavender bush about two feet tall and asked, "Can you please prune it?" Lavender plants can be found all over California, but I didn't expect to find them in Kyoto, where they probably died in winter frosts. I considered the little Kyoto lavender plant my compadre, my friend far away from home, who like me was an outsider. Actually, even after seven years of pruning in the San Francisco Bay Area, I'd never worked on one lavender plant. Maintenance gardeners handled these small perennials. In my California business, I only pruned trees and special shrubs, and gave general design advice. I left the weeding, irrigation, and planting to specialized maintenance gardeners or landscapers. Treating lavenders like ornamental grasses, most California gardeners simply cut them to the ground in early spring or generally trim off the dead flowers. I pruned shrubs and trees so they'd look as close as possible to how they appear in nature. I'd never thought about how to prune a lavender in an "aesthetic pruning" way. I couldn't simply cut this one to the ground. The craftsmen might think me a barbarian! It would probably be killed by frost come December, anyway, I reasoned. Best not to hasten its departure, or mine.

So I knelt down, pulled out my pruning shears from a well-worn scabbard, and carefully removed each individual dead lavender sprout, about thirteen in all. Looking thoughtful, tilting my head this way and that, I thinned certain thick clusters of flower shoots. After I finished, Sogyu came over and said, "Good job." I grinned sheepishly. But inside I felt ecstatic. I'd pruned my first plant in Japan, a little purple lavender. Sogyu's request had given me some confidence.

Sogyu was a kind boss with high standards. He built traditional and eclectic gardens, used rocks from Bali in addition to those from Japan, and sometimes hired foreign specialists. As with almost all landscapers in Kyoto, he did design, construction, rock work, pruning, bamboo work, and maintenance. Unlike in most Japanese companies, he asked his employees to work only five days a week instead of six. "It is important to take time off," Sogyu said firmly. I thought this marked another reason he'd make an ideal boss. Traditional and alternative, casual and passionate, Sogyu's team felt like home.

The following day, Sogyu had no work to offer me, so I found my way to Shisendo, a historical garden in the densely forested hills of Kyoto that Sogyu had recommended I visit. Sitting on a straw tatami floor bathed in natural light, I followed the progress of three young gardeners pruning azaleas only fifteen feet away. Two walls of the room had been slid open to allow this expansive view. The gardeners wore khaki uniforms and had a white strip of cloth wrapped around their heads. Behind them swayed a dark mass of maple trees with undulating depth.

Pencil and journal in hand, I thought back to a brief trip I'd taken to Tokyo years before to attend an international Japanese garden conference. I'd had the opportunity to visit gardens with a young Japanese landscaper, Marcello, who taught me that Japanese gardens were for enjoying, not for simply documenting with a camera. Marcello and I often pulled out books and read while sitting on garden tatami mats. We'd write poetry, or just watch the garden and enjoy our friendship. I sometimes tell Americans who visit Japanese gardens, "If a Japanese tourist went to Disneyland, snapped a bunch of photos, and then left without ever getting on a ride, would they really have the full experience? Take the time to relax and enjoy the gardens in Japan."

I was intently writing away about all I'd seen and heard in Sogyu's company, when a Japanese man in a well-pressed, stylish

----

business suit entered the room with a huge camcorder in hand, filming. *Jeez*, I thought, annoyed. *So this is modern Japan. Can't he just relax?*

Although I had yet to feel relaxed myself, at least I was trying. The man sat down beside me, placing his huge recorder on the tatami. And then he proceeded to stare at one spot in the garden for a solid hour. I watched him watching the garden and wondered what he was looking at for so long. So I started looking more closely at the garden myself. I watched gardeners rhythmically shearing azaleas. *Snip, snip, snip.* I moved my pencil in time on my page. *Scratch, scratch.* Birds sang and a bamboo clacker softly knocked together every minute or so to scare off deer. *Tweet, tweet, clack.* I could not see it, but I heard bubbling water. *Gurgle, gurgle.* And I watched shadows play on the fine white gravel near the azaleas. Such a seemingly still scene, yet so much action took place. All the activity took my mind off my inability to predict the future and instead brought my thoughts to the present lively scene.

Shisendo looked wild, like most Kyoto gardens I'd visited. I suppose that the first time I came to Japan, I suspected all Japanese gardens might be filled with overly sheared poodle-ball shrubs, oddly miniaturized landscapes, and brightly colorful azaleas. Instead, the garden before me made me think of the wild forest behind my first home with only enough flowers to signify seasonality. Almost all the Kyoto public and private gardens I'd seen were planted with at least ninety percent native plants. Like most Kyoto gardens, Shisendo was a native garden, designed to reflect nature.

I looked up from my tatami sitting perch, at the silhouette of hundreds of maple leaves against a blue Kyoto sky. I was reminded

----

of a Yosemite, California, camping trip where I saw stars above the mountains, sparkling in a pitch black universe. Neither view could look more natural or feel more relaxing. And yet all the plants and trees at Shisendo had been meticulously styled and pruned for more than three centuries. Still, the garden looked and felt as though it had been plucked out of nature. Sadly, many Japanese American gardens in the United States are sheared by well-meaning gardeners who have no means to learn naturalized pruning. These gardens end up looking overly pruned and miniaturized. Americans rarely understand that the gardens of Japan are some of the most stunning native plant gardens in the world.

I've heard many times at Japanese garden conferences that to create a Japanese garden, one should use the plants native to the surrounding area of the garden, rather than plants native to Japan. The American Japanese garden landscaper David Slawson often discusses this concept, which is mentioned in one of the oldest Japanese garden manuals, the *Sakuteiki*, translated by Slawson and Marc P. Keane. Shisendo would look beautiful in California, but would not necessarily feel natural, given that Japanese plants can look so foreign in the dry-summer and wet-winter California climate.

When I thought back to my familiar memories of nature to gain inspiration for my California home garden, I returned, like many city dwellers, to remembrances of family camping trips. A landscaper in Japan once told me, "Leslie, do not imitate our forests in Kyoto; imitate your own forest. Landscapers throughout Japan make this mistake and copy the forests of Kyoto instead of the local forests surrounding their own area."

Hence I decided to use a scene in California nature very familiar to me: I built my garden to playfully feel like a California

----

campground on the edge of the forest, using Japanese garden principles I saw at Shisendo. I have a madrone and toyon evergreen trees, which block the views of neighboring buildings, and I planted simple white yarrow flowers that show a season more than a color. Most of my plants are found in local parks of my area, and all can be found in climates similar to Berkeley. I thought about the essence of a campground, so I have a tent, a fire pit, and a big rock for leaning against. Yet I decided against finding a black bear, so I wouldn't have too many things to distract from my wondering thoughts in nature. The tent is surrounded by a huckleberry grove. From it, I can see a meadow, my favorite spot in nature. I am just a beginner landscaper, so my garden is not designed anywhere near as well as Shisendo. But I hope that one day, perhaps after a few decades of natural pruning, it will allow me to have a calming experience like the one I felt at Shisendo that day.

I had been sitting toward the back of the room at Shisendo, and when the businessman departed he was very careful not to walk in front of me, instead taking a circuitous route behind me, even though there was barely space to walk in that area. His calm presence, and the garden's natural beauty, allowed me to enjoy a garden in Kyoto as I hadn't in a long while, with a light heart.

While the trees and wind swirled softly about me, I had time to think about my future plans. I kept wondering if I should ask Sogyu directly if I could work with him. David had encouraged me. "You should ask. Sogyu has already asked you to join him for a day." Deep down, I felt he'd make a perfect boss. He spoke English, he lived locally, he was highly trained, and I might have more chances to do landscaping. On the other hand, Sogyu told me straight out that he felt uncertain about how much work he had to offer. And it looked as though I wouldn't get to do a lot of pruning.

But when I returned home that night from the garden, David handed me a fax that had arrived from Uetoh Zoen, the landscaping company that had turned me away previously. He translated the note: "You can come to visit us next Sunday at 8:00 a.m. No one in the office speaks English." *Hmm,* I mused. *Now what do I do?* How could I figure out how to hire someone to translate? It felt simpler to ask Sogyu if I could work with him and stop looking into other situations. As my thoughts went in every direction, a Buddhist saying entered my mind: *The easy path is the right path.* But the only way I knew to contact Sogyu was by running into him on the street. I needed some advice.

I decided to call an American who had lived in Kyoto for many years. The editor of the American Japanese garden journal had recommended I contact Asher Brown while in Kyoto and ask him for advice if I needed it. Originally from the East Coast, Asher apprenticed in a large Kyoto landscaping firm. His company didn't need any extra workers, but I still called him occasionally while I searched for a position in Kyoto. Asher always offered a willing ear and encouraging words. I told him about the past two eventful weeks and ended with, "I don't see the point of traveling several hours across town to visit Uetoh Zoen if no one there speaks English, especially when there is an excellent landscaping company right next door!"

Asher disagreed and said, "Why don't I come with you to translate? It's on a Sunday, my day off." I hadn't thought of that. "Are you sure?" I didn't want to keep him from resting on his day off. Anytime I'd worked seven days in a row in California, I'd break down crying near day six. "It would be an insult not to visit Uetoh after you requested the meeting," Asher persisted. He had a point. So we made plans to meet on Sunday morning. I could at least get a peek at what Asher said was a fairly large Kyoto company.

My emotions had calmed at Shisendo, but within an hour of returning home, they were back on high alert. I'd done nothing much my first few weeks in Kyoto beyond cleaning my little house on the hill, and then, within just a few days, I'd flown to all sorts of new scenes. The transformation took me high off the ground like a butterfly, but perhaps I'd traveled too high into the clouds, away from a safe landing.

Reaching for the
Unexpected Fruit

I bought a bus map and did a practice ride to the western side of Kyoto, where Asher and I would visit Uetoh Zoen the following Sunday. I felt too shy to venture right up to the company property, thinking someone might spot me; I'd seen only one or two Caucasian faces a day in Kyoto, and I felt shy there. On my way home, I ventured into the monastery garden, Tenryuji, which I'd found in *A Guide to the Gardens of Kyoto,* my favorite Kyoto guidebook. Japanese gardens are often mythologized, misunderstood, stereotyped, or given religious connotations that aren't accurate in Japan. But this book was a rare gem in that it gave authentic explanations of the gardens and was easy to follow. I didn't know it yet, but I'd eventually work in one of Tenryuji monastery's private gardens.

That day in Tenryuji's main garden, I discovered aged, weeping cherries made up of thickly ribbed green summer leaves. I sat for a while under the cherry branches in a light mood. But slowly, loneliness crept up. The leaves I sat under would disappear in a month or two. I could sit still as long as I wanted, but the trees would keep forging ahead. I thought about how I'd rather be sitting there next to Taylor instead of a silent old tree. I had two loves: my social life and gardening. They fought for my attention. While in Japan, the gardens must be my focus.

That night I gathered a pile of items from home next to my futon to take on the tour of Uetoh: pressed work clothes, note-paper, business cards, a thank-you present, and a small portfolio of my work in California. My California mentor would show up hours before class to set up supplies and talk to eager students, and then he'd stay as late as anyone needed to answer questions. "Until the last student fell asleep," we'd tease. I felt I must prepare for my interview properly.

By Saturday night, my endless worries took over as I lay down to sleep. *Working with Sogyu feels good. Why force myself to go to this interview when it stresses me out?* I felt annoyed with my need to organize every step so exactly. I'd gone over my stockpiled items several times, set up two alarms for 5:45 and 6:00 a.m., closed my eyes, and prayed for sleep.

My first alarm at 5:45 a.m. failed. I'd been so focused on the proper wake-up time, I'd forgotten to push the "on" button. My eyes blinked open, and I tried to focus on the soft light glowing on my work pants draped over a chair. My eyes opened wide as I panicked, thinking I'd overslept. I looked at the clock: 6:00 a.m. on the dot. The next alarm sounded. I often woke up seconds before my alarm, my subconscious more reliable than my conscious mind.

I arrived twenty minutes early at the bus stop where Asher and I had decided to meet, my heart still beating more quickly than usual. I felt hyperalert. Typical for the worrying adventurer, I told myself. I sat down on the bench and, surprisingly, became peaceful. Cars whizzed by. I remarked softly, "I can't believe how relaxed I feel, I must be groggy," and the sense dissipated. "Just get this meeting over with."

Asher arrived. "Good morning!" We chatted a few minutes before he asked me, "Leslie, what would you like from an apprenticeship with Uetoh Zoen?" Well, he's taking this seriously. "You must know what you want," he added, "so that we can ask the right questions." I sat with that for a few seconds, adjusting my thoughts from wandering ramblings to serious statements. I'd actually prepared some questions, but an impetuous response came forth. "I definitely want to work with Sogyu, unless . . . unless this company offers me the world," I replied. I was tired of searching.

I felt prepared enough, but Asher felt otherwise. He insisted on looking over my questions. I proudly pulled out my list of prepared questions. But Asher wanted to go even further by arranging the questions in numerical order and discussing what our moves would be at each juncture. This seemed a little overboard, but I complied.

An hour and a half later, we stepped off the bus into what looked like a Kyoto suburb. Walking around several streets, I felt disoriented, not sure if I'd ever learn my way around Kyoto. We walked up a concrete driveway that led to a large property with buildings, sheds, carports, and trucks of every shape and size: the Uetoh Zoen company headquarters. I glanced into a shed with an open door to find a room filled with twenty or so shovels and dozens of extension ladders. Everything was neatly hung on its proper hook or stacked precisely in descending order of shape or size. I thought about taking a photo of the delicious organization but held back.

A middle-aged man in shorts and a T-shirt came out of the central building to greet us. Definitely a casual tour, I thought. I took in and exhaled a deep breath, realizing I'd barely been breathing. I'd eventually learn that standing before me was the acting director of Uetoh, Shinichi Sano, the son of the well-known, sixteenth-generation Kyoto landscape designer Toemon Sano. I bowed deeply to Shinichi and repeated the formal Japanese introduction I'd practiced in night school: *"Hajimemashite"* (Pleased to meet you). He made a slight bow in return. We sat down in a rather bleak fifties-looking office, and Asher started asking questions right away. The "tour of the company" pretext was never mentioned again by either man. This was an interview.

"We wondered if you have hired foreigners before." After a little bit of casual conversation, Asher began to ask our questions in Japanese, then translated each question and answer for my benefit.

"Hai" (yes), answered Shinichi Sano. I waited for more details. The pause grew longer. Finally, when no more information was given, I assumed that because a Canadian had given me the referral, the answer must appear rather obvious. So Asher continued, "Have you hired someone not fluent in Japanese?"

"Yes."

"Have you ever hired a woman?"

"Yes. A young Japanese woman." This response surprised me. It was easier for foreign women to break into the traditional male-dominated occupations than for Japanese women, who were expected to adhere to cultural traditions. If the company had hired a Japanese woman, then I figured they must be prepared for an American one.

Asher asked, "Have you hired anyone for a short-term period?"

- - - -

"Yes, we hired someone for two weeks, and another for eleven months." I had an itch to look at Asher and give him a wide-eyed "Is that so?" look. But he never looked my way, keeping up his momentum. Couldn't they slow down? I sat restlessly in my seat, hardly able to keep up as the men moved forward, craftsman speed.

Down the list of questions we moved. *"Hai, hai, hai."* It felt like rain after a long drought. Asher asked, "Who is the oldest and the youngest person working in the company?" I thought I heard Shinichi Sano respond, "The oldest person in the company is eighteen years old." That's crazy, I thought! They only hire teenagers? I'm way too old. I interrupted Asher and asked again, "What age is the youngest and the oldest?"

Shinichi Sano repeated, with Asher translating, "The youngest person working in the company is sixteen, and the oldest is eighty." My mistake.

All our preliminary questions had been answered. Asher looked to me intently, our secret signal to find out if I wanted him to continue with more specific questions, the ones we had categorized as "very serious." I nodded yes, very calmly. Inwardly I went back to the odd sense I'd felt at the bus stop. I realized it was not sleepiness, but a premonition. I saw this now. *Something is about to change.* The simple words had entered my head at the bus stop. But I'd ignored them, still focused on the idea of working with Sogyu. Rarely did I have such premonitions, except for that time I'd slipped the pine branch into my pocket. I didn't feel ready for the opportunity opening up before me. But it beckoned.

I once worked for a California client whose avocado tree died almost down to the ground in a frost. I wanted to chop the rest of the blackened trunk down, but she made me leave it just in case the roots were still alive. Indeed, the avocado tree came back. We waited for it to grow and produce fruit. Four years went by, six, then eight. It continued growing into a lovely tree, but never would an avocado appear. The client grew older and became ill. Both of us hoped for fruit each year, laughing about it, until my sweet client passed away. When I talked to her daughter over the phone about long-term garden plans, I noted, "We had a strong frost last month." I asked, "Did the avocado die down again?" "No!" she said. "It's covered with avocados." I thought of all the rich avocados, and then I thought of Eleanor and her lively, hopeful spirit. One never knows when a hope will bear fruit.

"What type of work could one expect in Uetoh Zoen?" Asher continued.

"We work in an assortment of gardens: private homes, temples, and public gardens." The answer proved modest, considering I found out later that the company worked all over the world, in one of Kyoto's imperial gardens, and that half the company currently lived in Tokyo, constructing a multimillion-dollar public garden.

"Would there be much opportunity to do pruning?"

"The company runs a pruning-only crew." That answer got my attention. I'd never imagined the possibility of a pruning-only crew. All my California advisors told me that I should expect to do weeding and raking but very little pruning, depending on what project the company worked on at the time. Because the company was so large, it had several separate crews with rotating members. A pruning-only crew was certainly appealing.

I mentioned to Sogyu the week before that I might look into other companies. "Make sure the companies do not work only on street trees, low-quality work in Kyoto," he'd advised me. I

----

remembered his words, so I mentioned to Asher, "Can you ask what specific types of pruning projects the pruning crew does?"

Shinichi retreated to a back room and returned with a tall stack of Japanese garden coffee table books, which he opened up. *Oh, my.* I looked over photos of some of the most pristine Japanese garden landscapes I'd ever seen, Uetoh Zoen gardens. Subtle flowing streams, fine gravel paths, and huge moss-covered rocks looked back at me from the pages. The gardens surrounded handcrafted wooden buildings, traditional temples, and stark contemporary buildings. The trees looked so naturally styled that they appeared to have been part of a forest. "The company is made up of master gardeners," I remembered my Canadian reference telling me. I suppose I hadn't believed him.

The books made quite an impression on Asher and me. We began to stumble. Neither of us had expected the meeting to go so well. I asked Asher several times, "Should we show him the portfolio now?"

"No, later." I noticed that his hands had begun trembling a little. "Should I bring out my photos?" I asked him again a few questions later. "Not yet," he brushed me off.

"Make sure to ask every question you have, until you're satisfied that you have enough information to make a decision, Leslie," Asher had warned me at the bus stop. I tried to think of any other question I could ask the man, as apparently he had decided to hand me everything I wanted: a traditional company that hired foreigners, that was okay with non-Japanese speakers and women; a company that worked in a wide range of gardens and had a pruning-only crew that would allow me to study the art form I felt passionate about.

I finally said to Asher, "Let's go to plan B." Asher's idea was that if either of us felt Shinichi was on the verge of offering me an apprenticeship position in the company, we'd have to hold him back. I'd told Asher that no matter what Shinichi offered, I couldn't say yes until I'd talked to Sogyu. Asher had explained, "If Shinichi did offer you an apprenticeship, any answer other than yes, even hesitation, would be considered an insult." So we'd devised a plan to alert Shinichi not to ask me yet. At the time, the idea sounded crazy and indirect. Saying one thing, meaning another, expecting the other person to get it appeared passive-aggressive by my Californian standards. But all of a sudden, Asher's plan not only made sense, it became necessary.

So Asher cleverly asked, "If there were another company across town, near Leslie's home, do you think that would be a better situation for her?" Shinichi responded ever so briefly, "That is a decision for her to make." Our message was successfully delivered.

Shinichi then spoke up and, for the first time, asked Asher a question. Asher translated, "He asked if you have any photos of your work." I felt pleased that we'd waited so humbly. Finally I had the opportunity to show off! I reached in my bag, conscious that my hands were noticeably shaking, and pulled out my small album, a plastic-coated book with around twenty photos slipped into clear sleeves. I'd spent weeks putting the album together.

Shinichi leafed through the photos in a few minutes, viewing the gardens and individual plants I'd pruned over the previous seven years. My gardens looked Japanese, European, and eclectic, and included both private estates and public gardens. I included native California gardens and Oakland artist Bruce Beasley's sculpture garden, with trees standing alongside twenty-foot metal sculptures. Only in the last three photos did Shinichi hesitate. One photo showed me teaching a youngster bonsai techniques at the San Francisco Exploratorium. The next displayed my mentor, Dennis, pruning a gnarled pine with his students gathered behind him. The last portrayed a small white-haired Japanese man, my bonsai teacher, Mas Imazumi, standing in front of his famous plant collection. Without my mentors, none of the other photos would have existed.

We had no more questions. I realized that seven years of work, six months of preparation, and countless kind gestures had guided me toward that very moment, the end of a brief thirty-minute interview. I reached again into my bag, pulled out a business card, and handed it to Shinichi in the traditional way, as I'd learned from my culture books: I held it on both sides with two hands, saying, "*Dōzo*" (please), and bowing slightly as the exchange took place. My card displayed a hand-sketched maple leaf, with its tiny seed, a samara, dangling from its branch. A former chef of Berkeley's most famous restaurant, Chez Panisse, had hand-printed the richly textured card. Shinichi handed me his card. "*Dōzo*." Conventional and probably factory printed, it looked dull. Yet, as I was instructed in both of my culture books, I pondered it awhile as though it were printed in gold leaf, with lots of admiring noises, and slipped it carefully into my business card holder. Absolutely no tucking the card into the pocket near my bum, much less an old wallet.

I handed Shinichi my thank-you gift, a brown paper bag of homemade chocolate chip cookies I'd baked the day before. I hoped this would let him know I appreciated his time, and that I had come as myself: a sincere, hardworking American with few

----

frills. When it seemed that at last it was time to stand up and leave, Shinichi looked at me directly for the first time and said, in perfect English, "When you want to call, I will be waiting."

Well, I thought, astonished, *no man has ever said those words to me before!* We exited the office in a trance, as it occurred to me that Shinichi, even wiser than Asher and me, had understood that he shouldn't ask me yet if I'd like to work for him. He'd even thought ahead to suggest my next step if I were interested. He seemed to understand English.

I felt exultant. Asher had forgotten his backpack, but I had grabbed it without a word. Twenty feet beyond the building, I handed it to him. "Can you believe that?" I exclaimed. "No," he mustered. Each of us burst into laughter. Asher had only a few free hours left in his precious Sunday off. So, like a craftsman familiar with a tight schedule and long work hours, he spent yet another hour with me, weighing the pros and cons of working with Sogyu's company versus Uetoh Zoen. We both felt jittery and jubilant about the amazing opportunity that had opened up. Asher headed home, and I thought the best place for me to think might be in a garden.

I ventured over to the world-renowned rock garden, Ryoanji. With its austere bed of raked sand and rocks, I thought it would allow me the space to think. I made it to the northern tip of Kyoto by bus. Most signs in Kyoto were printed in beautifully drawn Japanese script, which made them completely unintelligible to me. When I took the bus or train in Japan, I felt blind, unable to translate the signs fast enough. I memorized the number of bus stops on my map until I reached my stop. I proceeded on foot, but as I neared the garden, I began to see signs in English, directing

----

tourists: ROCK GARDEN THIS WAY and USUAL ROUTE. For once I felt certain I was on the right track.

Despite having seen so many photos of Ryoanji, I still felt my skin tingle when I first set eyes on the dry rock garden, a bed of raked sand, fifteen naturally placed rocks, and a low earthen-wall enclosure. Sadly, droves of garden visitors had arrived before me; there must have been four dozen of us jostling for a garden view.

I stood my ground, trying to examine the composition, when an excitable group of schoolchildren, around six to eight years old, all in adorable identical uniforms, piled in. The decibel level increased. The children wove themselves smartly among forty or so adults until most of them had prime viewing positions. They'd occasionally burst into uncontrollable giggles, which helped me relax after my intense morning. "*Ichi, ni, san, shi.*" (one, two, three, four). The children counted the stones repeatedly and melodically in high-pitched unison. They'd tilt their heads this way and that, looking like tiny philosophers.

The brochure said that no matter from which vantage point you viewed the rocks, one was always hidden from view. "One, two, three." I counted the rocks myself, softly, from different viewpoints. Which rock is hidden from me now? I asked myself, thinking about Sogyu and Shinichi. No matter how I felt about each company, could an additional point remain hidden? Regardless of where I stood, one rock would indeed be hidden from view, even though the scene as a whole appeared natural.

I called my mentor back home, who said he felt a pruning-only crew looked preferable but that the decision was up to me. Although I already knew which company I'd choose, his words were reassuring.

- - - -

Sogyu ended up calling me later that night. I told him about the interview with Uetoh and tried to explain as gently as I could manage about my feeling that I had an amazing opportunity to work with a company that had a specialized pruning crew. I had found the company of my dreams. And I never could have guessed that I could feel as terrible as I did right then.

I didn't quite know how to explain to Sogyu that I admired him while leaving him and his crew, my first heartfelt teachers in Japan. I'd been specifically warned not to approach two Japanese companies at once. *I should have listened!* I reprimanded myself. *Why am I so impatient?* At the end of our conversation, Sogyu said, "Do not worry, Leslie. We will work together again, in another situation."

Asher sent a note to Uetoh, asking the company formally if I could work with them. A few days later, a fax arrived from Uetoh Zoen instructing me to show up for work the following Monday with "*jikatabi* and a white towel," neither of which I understood. That evening, though I was on a tight budget, I decided to splurge and made an expensive call to Taylor for the first time since arriving in Kyoto. "Hello there, love!" I heard his clear, buoyant voice and felt at once at ease. I tried to talk but instead began to cry. It was such a relief to talk to the person closest to my heart after weeks of meeting strangers. All my years of planning had led to something, to an unexpected opportunity. "I did it," I finally said, "I got the apprenticeship." It was all I really had to say for him to understand.

Curling up later in bed under my musky comforter, I fell into a deep, comforting sleep for the first time in weeks. I no longer had to search. I needed to rest and prepare for my first day of work with Uetoh Zoen.

Stepping into *Jikatabi*

With a shaky hand, I pulled the cord to alert the bus driver to stop at the same corner I'd gotten off a week earlier for my interview at Uetoh Zoen. The new driver kept an eye on me, particularly after we had passed an international guest hostel a few miles back. To put his mind at rest, I stepped off the bus with a confident smile, then promptly walked down the wrong street and got lost. Just as I was about to venture into a stranger's driveway, I spotted a slender man in a conservative business suit waving at me from halfway up the street. He turned out to be Nishimoto, one of Uetoh's numerous administrative workers. He was so genuinely friendly that I felt I just might survive my first day with a big Kyoto landscaping company.

Nishimoto led me to the company property, where we walked past shiny compressed trucks, piles of bamboo rakes and brooms, stacks of metal and wooden ladders, coiled ropes, and more rock-setting equipment than I'd ever seen. I wanted to pull out a camera, but we walked briskly toward the building where I'd had the interview. Only this time, it was filled with men of all ages, some in khaki gardener's uniforms, others in pressed suits. I noticed the big, burly gray-haired man who would become my boss for the next three months.

At exactly seven-thirty, two lovely young women entered the room in cute pressed cotton knee-length skirts. They were the only other women I'd ever see working for Uetoh. Everyone turned to face the father of the man who'd interviewed me. Toemon Sano, somewhere in his eighties, stood as the top leader of the company, while Shinichi Sano, Toemon's son, acted as head boss. The craftsmen waited silently, wearing pressed uniforms and traditional cotton boots, with their feet spread apart and strong hands clasped. The atmosphere felt a little like a military. Toemon gave a short speech in Japanese in the tone of a pep talk; I understood nothing. He turned to me and paused. I realized he wanted me to make a speech! I raced through my memory, searching for key sentences I'd learned in class. "Hi. I like sushi," and "Where is the train station, please?" came to mind. In a last-ditch attempt to satisfy the group's expectant glances, I put my hands together in prayer, bowed, and said, "*Hajimemashite!*" Everyone paused a second to see if I had anything else to say, chuckled, and clapped, showing their friendly appreciation of my elaborate lecture. Much later I learned that the boss had told the workers that "an American would be joining the company on Monday." Everyone had assumed I'd be a man. So I was told later that when the young woman with long, wavy brown hair walked into the office, the workers had almost fainted. I guessed nothing at the time. I never could discern the men's thoughts.

Someone directed me to a shiny, clean red-and-white truck, and as I neared it everyone began yelling at me in unintelligible rapid Japanese, pointing here and there while I stood by. Once it was loaded, I was directed to the backseat of the truck, and then it went on its way, carrying four Japanese craftsmen—and one California girl.

That first day, I met several of the men who would become my familiar crew during my three-month apprenticeship with Uetoh Zoen, spanning from late summer to early winter. I call my period studying with the craftsmen a short-term apprenticeship, as normally a Japanese gardener's apprenticeship lasts up to fifteen years. Many start from scratch in the company, so they might spend the first few years raking and learning fundamental gardening duties. I had attended horticulture school, taken design classes, and started my own pruning business. Plus I'd trained with a mentor who specialized in Japanese garden pruning. So when I worked with the Uetoh crew, I had previous gardening experience that allowed me an unusual perspective on all I witnessed. I would learn much more.

I had no idea how much my coworkers were paid, but I'd heard that young gardeners in Japan received a minimal hourly wage, with food and housing benefits. Their pay may have been low, but a Japanese apprentice is paid to learn, rather than paying for classes. The longer the gardener stays in the company, the higher the pay. I noticed that some of the senior workers at Uetoh showed up in new, expensive-looking SUVs.

Japanese gardeners learn the equivalent of five American professions: landscape design and installation, rock setting, bamboo design, aesthetic pruning, and refined maintenance. Each art form could take a minimum of three years to learn, so it makes sense that a garden craftsman in Japan might train for fifteen years in a company before starting his own business. If someone considers himself a "master gardener" in Japan, someone thoroughly acquainted with and experienced in all aspects of his craft, he could well have trained 25,000 hours. The master craftsman receives the same training, but has the added experience of working as a teacher: no one can become a master craftsman without the latter.

Highest in the hierarchy of our pruning crew was Nakaji, whom we called Nakaji-san (and whom I privately thought of as "Bossman"). When addressing my boss, coworkers, and even close friends in Kyoto, I'd always attach "san" to the end of their name, a Japanese version of "Mr." or "Ms." Although I drop this formality in my writing, I'd sooner curse in front of my grandma than not add the "san" while in Japan. Even in Oklahoma I still address my former childhood next-door neighbors as Mr. and Mrs. Hartman, as I did growing up. I enjoy certain formalities that remain in the South. Formality represents my respect for elders and teachers. The effort formality takes, just a little bit of extra effort, can subtly express my love for these individuals. But if I had addressed my Oklahoma neighbor's children as Miss Louise or Mr. John, that would have sounded weird. In Japan, this would seem normal.

On this, my first morning, Nakaji, the intensely macho leader of our pruning crew, drove the truck with passionate spirit to the historic restaurant garden with the flowing canal. In the States he'd be called an aggressive driver. In Japan, he made time. I wondered about his age. Perhaps early to midfifties? He looked big and strong. He had an endless supply of freshly ironed clothes without any hint of soil stains. He wore a floppy European cotton hat and sometimes the traditional *hachimaki*, a folded cloth wrapped around his forehead, and had a preference for European black tea. He worked as long and hard as workers in their twenties, and maintained our schedule of ten- to twelve-hour days, six days a week. He ordered everyone around in the gruff, effective manner of an excellent mentor. He never spoke English, or cared to try. Our clients praised Nakaji as one of Kyoto's most talented pruners. Certain female clients practically trembled next to him. Nakaji had the power to ruin my stay in the company, and I obeyed him implicitly. He treated me thoughtfully, and although he never once gave me verbal appreciation, he challenged me day after day as though he thought I could handle the pressure—a far greater compliment. He pushed me when I had energy, eased up when he thought I might break, then continued pushing, eventually teaching me some of my most important lessons. My coworkers guarded a secret about Nakaji I would only discover later.

On the way to our first job, we stopped at a professional gardener's supply store, since Nakaji insisted I wear *jikatabi*. These were dark cloth booties, with the big toe separated from the other toes, which made me look like the cute girlfriend of the Creature from the Black Lagoon. With their soft rubber soles, *jikatabi* felt like wearing socks in the garden, so gentle on moss and spring maple bark. For standing in sharp-angled tree crotches, I prefer hard-soled shoes. But the men made it clear I could not set foot into any garden, as a member of the Uetoh crew, without wearing them. Gardeners and construction workers wear them throughout Japan. *Jikatabi* connected us intimately to the gardens. They allowed us to run on the moss without tearing it up. But mostly, *jikatabi* represented tradition. One of my coworkers, Kei, who spoke perfect English, helped me negotiate with the merchant to find a pair big enough for my "huge" feet—American size seven and a half. There were few in stock.

The coworker I came to know best, Kei, was a bit shorter than I, with considerably more arm muscle. He was a senior worker who wore a traditional headscarf tied near the base of his scalp, and although he could be very social and chatty, he was also comfortable with prolonged silence. Kei began pruning in his midtwenties after feeling dissatisfied with studying landscape architecture at a university. He liked the movie *Hair* and Beatles songs because they helped him learn English. Like me, Kei loved pruning more than any other garden art form. He helped me navigate traditional Japanese company social life and introduced me to my Kyoto American girlfriends. Kei, my saving grace, would more than a decade later become the talented owner of a landscape design and building company of his own in Japan, and also a father. I'm sure he conducted both in the same firm and gentle way he nurtured plants.

As the Uetoh truck moved toward the historic restaurant garden, I still had no idea where we were actually headed. The company property was on the western edge of Kyoto city, so I knew we were going toward the center of town along a major river channel I had biked along a week earlier. I figured we'd mostly work at the gardens of private residences, so it confused me when we made a quick left onto a concrete path normally reserved for pedestrians. There wasn't a garden in sight for blocks, as far as I could tell. All I could see was an impressively neat and clean homeless person's encampment under a bridge nearby. I thought, *Okay, we'll start out slow today.* Kei saw me looking under the bridge at a homeless person's sizable bonsai collection, and explained, "In Japan it is not shameful to be homeless." He said homeless people in Japan had free access to decent government housing and healthcare, but they chose to live independently, with pride. I didn't know a single gardener back in the States who didn't struggle with the cost of housing and healthcare. Most simply couldn't afford the latter. I wondered if the Japanese homeless were an urban version of mountain hermits. I admired the men under the bridge, their ability to enjoy seclusion, and their independence.

Just when I had decided we'd be working in a concrete jungle, one of the guys jumped out to open a tall metal gate. As we entered the lush garden property of Ganko Takasegawa Nijoen, I felt as though I had entered the magical estate of *Willy Wonka and the Chocolate Factory*.

Sixteen-year-old Masahiro closed the gate behind us, and soon handed me my first pair of *karikomi*, the shearing tool that I could hardly manipulate but he handled with ease. Always sporting a baseball cap and large square-frame glasses, Masahiro looked shy and awkward, slumping his shoulders as though he'd just finished a growth spurt. No one could get lower in the hierarchy than Masahiro, save myself. As the youngest apprentice, he had to come in before the first worker was scheduled to arrive. This meant every morning, he showed up at the company property, sometimes at dark in winter, to wash down the work trucks with bare hands, occasionally with buckets of icy water. He could not leave until the last office worker departed. I'd heard he most often arrived before six in the morning and rarely left for home until nine or ten.

Even though I officially sat below Masahiro in the hierarchy, I was American. So between the two of us, I left first. Everyone ordered Masahiro around. The men often ignored me. To make matters worse, he grew up in the countryside, so others made fun of his traditional manners. The men were often curious about my American habits. Yet along with Masahiro's youthful naïveté came an almost spiritual devotion to his craft that only someone so young, with no distractions, could hold. He stood taller than most of the men, with high cheekbones, and I'm sure he eventually grew into a handsome man. Full of maternal instincts at thirty-five, I felt protective of picked-on Masahiro. I sometimes pitied him. Eventually I'd hope to emulate him.

The pine I examined at lunch, which led to my pine-pruning assignments on that first day, had been pruned by Daisuke, the crew's most advanced worker. Daisuke held a certain authority, the self-assured swagger of a natural leader. His headband, displaying a modern print, made him all the more fascinating. He and Nakaji worked steadily on pines the whole day while lower-level workers cleaned up after them. He slept with a white towel folded neatly over his eyes during each break, leading me to wonder if he had an active nightlife. Soon he disappeared from our pruning crew; I believe he went to work for Uetoh in Tokyo on a high-profile public garden installation.

That first morning, I'd decided to leave my raincoat at home, thinking, *It's so clear this morning, it'll never rain!* Considering how drenched I was by the end of the day, I never tried to predict the weather again. Mother Nature held more surprises for me in Japan. At the end of my first day, we returned to the office—Japanese gardeners return to their company property before heading home, even if that means crisscrossing the city several times in one day. As soon as I jumped out of the truck, the company leader called me into his office. He asked in English, "Do you work rain days, or do you want rain days off?" I weighed my options: Should I act all macho and work like the guys, six days a week, rain or shine? Or should I be sane and take an extra day off here and there, precious time I could use to visit Kyoto's gardens or just

----

get to rest? I responded in English so he'd understand: "Yes, I work in the rain."

After all, the last person added to the crew was born in Oklahoma, raised in California, the granddaughter of a dirt-poor, landless tenant farmer grandmother, and the daughter of a feminist. Because of my American birth, I was addressed in the company as "Leslie," never "Leslie-san." At the end of the day, I'd throw my full body on the debris pile to punch it down, but mostly to prove my enthusiasm to the men who had more muscles than me and carried larger loads. I worried constantly about holding back the crew and about what they thought of me. But I worked boldly and with determination. As the youngest sibling to three bossy older sisters and daughter of a strong Southern mom, I could handle the obedience required when working inside a strict hierarchy. I knew how to quietly observe their successes and my mistakes, but also how to occasionally step out and take my own risks.

I felt I might survive these intense craftsmen using my feisty spirit, clever strategies, and a penchant for humor in the face of defeat. I was used to being a slow learner, an anxious adventurer. My worries never stopped me from pursuing goals close to my heart. Upon setting foot in Japan that humid summer, I'd hoped to meet the gardeners who, like me, felt devoted to nature. My first day working with the Uetoh Zoen craftsmen, I felt like a lighthearted California gardener, but the men saw in me a craftswoman in training.

Garden Bling Keeps
the Garden Clean

As if in response to my pledge to work "rain or shine," the rain fell like a mountain waterfall outside my window all night. I wondered if I'd still go to work in the morning, given that Asher had told me his company didn't work in heavy rain. I snuggled under my down comforter, feeling as though I were sleeping on a warm beach. I really didn't want to get out of bed. Around six, I departed my cocoon, gathered my workbag, and headed out. An office worker named Tanaka had offered to pick me up, and I didn't know how to call him to cancel. I layered my outfit with plastic rain gear, the only thing that lasts hours in pounding rain, and stepped outside just as the rain finally slowed to a drizzle. I shuffled to my designated pick-up spot on the street corner. A thin sheet of water on the pavement reflected the image of a person suited up in camouflaged gear with just a bit of sun highlighting my navy blue fleece hat. "I really look like a dork," I mumbled, standing next to a man waiting for the bus in a business suit. He'd retained his dignity, refusing hat, denying coat. The Kyoto crowd proved resilient. Just before Tanaka drove up, a woman came rushing down the street toward us with a floral apron wrapped around her skirt, looking toward the man next to me intently as though she had some emergency to report. She bowed to the man in the suit and pulled a folded white handkerchief out of her apron pocket. He placed the handkerchief in his left shirt pocket with a little corner exposed. They smiled at each other and she left. Not a scene I would ever expect to see at a California bus stop, but it made me feel once again keenly self-conscious of my bulky outfit.

Tanaka pulled up in an expensive-looking car. Getting a ride with him meant that I could sleep in forty-five minutes, so I felt lucky. But when we arrived to the company property fifteen minutes after my normal arrival time, I saw Nakaji and my whole crew standing at attention next to the fully loaded truck. I'd arrived a bit later than when I took the bus the day before. Nakaji's stare followed our car until we stopped. All at once, the crew jumped in the truck; I ran into a side door left open for me, and we sped off. I decided to go back to taking the bus.

I resumed shearing azaleas in the historic garden, blanketed by a misty drizzle. Fine droplets came from hundreds of feet up in the sky and shook the river, spanked the camellia leaves, and bent the ferns, which looked like weary backpackers, yet did not disturb the turtle on his rock. I tried to relax my arms, sore from using the *karikomi* the day before. I had already written several pages of new garden terms on a damp red pad in my knee pocket, right next to my dictionary. My garden bling included a dictionary, shears, a saw, and a floppy sun hat. I had a distaste for my bulgy pants and the pressed cotton shirt that was bubbly when tucked in. It was not just because of my outfit. I'd inherited a small stature, tiny waist, and curvy hips from my beautiful Aunt Mimi. Still, as a ballet dancer in my teenage years, I was chagrined at not having my mom's stunning tall, model-thin look. When I arrived in Kyoto, I

----

found myself glancing at waiflike young Japanese women on the streets, and I began to feel overweight. While in her thirties my mom became an Oklahoma delegate for George McGovern and chauffeured Warren Beatty in the backseat of our family station wagon. She wore beautiful outfits. In my thirties as a gardener, I wore khaki pants and sported an oversized duffle bag I'd found on sale at Berkeley's REI outdoor store. My work outfit did have its pluses; it meant I could pump the handles of the *karikomi* for hours with the wide stance my loose pants allowed. The plants and birds remained nonjudgmental.

Before leaving for Kyoto, I'd asked Yuki, a pruning friend raised in Japan, if it would be interesting for my Japanese crew to see a typical American gardener's outfit. She looked at me in my stained jeans, torn Berkeley Bicycle Coalition T-shirt, and Cal Sailing Club baseball cap, and responded, "There is a saying in Japan: You stub your toe on the nail that sticks out of the floor." So I left my American outfit at home.

Uetoh Zoen intriguingly mentioned in my acceptance letter to bring "a white towel" with me. My first day on the job, I noticed that some of the craftsmen wore a thin white terry cloth towel, about the size of a hand towel, wrapped around their heads. I debated wearing one myself. That night, I tried one on at home, looking in the mirror. Trying to re-create what I'd seen the men do, I folded the thin towel in half into a triangle and tied the ends into a knot at the back of my head. I thought about conferring with Kei first: "Do you think this towel on my head looks stupid?" But I decided against it. Not only was the question insulting, but he was a guy; he just wouldn't understand. Working on pines my second day, I finally took a chance and tied on my bright white turban top.

No one said a word. Whether they thought *She's a serious worker!* or *Duh, she doesn't know how to tie the gardener's knot,* I'll never know. The towel protected my hair completely from pine sap, which had gotten terribly stuck on my ponytail the day before, and it kept raindrops from sliding down my face—a great idea overall. Still, I prayed an American tourist wouldn't walk into the historic Kyoto garden and discover the California gardener with a shower towel on her head.

After several days of work, I discovered many brilliantly designed Japanese garden tools. I'd rake up thousands of azalea snippets with a *kumade,* a light rake made of bamboo. We'd also use a *tekumade,* a two-foot-long rake used in tighter areas. Although we never worked on miniature gardens, the tool reminded me of playing miniature golf with my sister on an Arkansas course that integrated native rock and plants. I loved the dings and scratches on Uetoh's tools. The men would regularly repair their tools, and the scratches meant that other craftsmen had used the tools before me. What artist wouldn't want to paint with Mary Cassatt's original brush or take a photo with Imogen Cunningham's vintage camera? It wasn't as though tools were sacred to the craftsmen, at least as far as I could tell. I suspected that concern for tool longevity was based more on economic sensibility than on tradition. In contrast, running to Target for a not-so-cheap plastic rake, having it break, throwing it into a publicly maintained landfill, then buying another isn't very cost effective or environmentally friendly. Each nick in the bamboo or scratch on metal reminded me that another had toiled before me. I felt inspired by my predecessors. One late workday, Nakaji threw an old pair of pine-pruning cuffs—a thick material covered in cotton, used to protect his

----

wrists from needle pricks—into a bonfire. I snatched them out to reuse them, resulting in a laughing fit from Bossman.

At the end of the day, we swept large swaths of moss with a bundle of fine bamboo twigs, gathered into a *hōki*, or broom. *Hōki*, handcrafted by bamboo artisans, can cost more than one hundred dollars. Japanese garden bling look as though they'd last forever. To sweep the smaller piles, we grabbed what turned out to be my most treasured Japanese tool item: the *tebōki*, a hand broom. This small broom sweeps every last grain of dust off a jagged small stone without disturbing moss or lichen. It is handy for furniture, sculptures, stones, steps, or even cobwebs around the edges of fences—garden-loving Californians would go crazy over this tool. I can't find it anywhere in the States.

We'd sweep small piles of leaves into a *mi*, a dustpan, but this wasn't just any pan. The *mi* was a two-foot square, flat on one side and deep on the other, with no handle. Perfect for picking up a tiny pile of dust or a bucket full of leaves, the pan was super light and coveted by high-caliber California landscaping friends. The *mi* was made of thick plastic, like a Frisbee, which made sense for a much-used and abused tool. I've seen some made of woven bamboo, but that kind would last about a week with these guys. In California I'd brush up the last bit of dust with my hand, scraping and tearing my gloves prematurely. I'd toss the debris into a tarp, where it would trickle out on my way to the truck.

In Kyoto, if I needed to move a pile of debris, the men would give me a *baron bukuro*. Years before I apprenticed in Japan, my mom bought me an expensive Smith and Hawkins tarp that looked like a four-foot-wide bowl, with sides standing two feet high. It was rather ineffectual for a pruner's eight-foot-long tree

----

clippings, so I finally gave it away. Little did I know she'd bought me a *baron bukuro*, a clever tarp that securely holds weeds, dirt, leaves, and accidentally swept-up moss that the new girl wanted to hide from the boss. Typical. Moms know best, even when it comes to Japanese tools.

In Japan, cleanup is so civilized that the men hardly looked dirty at the end of most days. Granted, some days we all needed to visit the local *sentō*, bathhouse, on the way home. Gardeners work with dirt, after all. The curator of the Portland Japanese Garden, Sadafumi Uchiyama, once told me that a professional gardener has such good attention that he is most often not dirty at the end of the day. I didn't think I'd ever be able to manage this type of professionalism.

Locals took notice of me raking with the *kumade*, but not because they saw me tearing up the moss; I hid that part. Seeing a white face in the garden must have been as new to the Japanese as seeing towels on people's heads was to me. Many people continued to approach me. I'd marvel at how many ways there were of asking, "Where are you from?" in Japanese, resulting in confusion and embarrassment in both the inquisitor and interviewee. I loved acting as a foreign ambassador but worried about my poor language skills and about chatting away while my team sweated. The white towel camouflaged my brown hair, reducing interruptions somewhat. But I discovered that if I didn't look up, no one would approach. If I looked at someone directly and smiled, the paparazzi descended.

At lunchtime, Nakaji yelled out in English, "Half time!" to signal the start of break. So I decided to try my American wit and inquired, "Where are the hot dogs?" Nakaji quickly asked Kei what

----

I'd said. Kei translated. Bossman wanted to know, "Does the American girl want a hot dog? Hasn't she brought enough for lunch?" I tried explaining the football connection, but in the end poor Masahiro had to escort me to a nearby store, forgoing his entire lunch. Looking back, the dutiful walk became precious, because it was the only time Masahiro and I got to talk in private during my whole time with the company. Masahiro actually knew English but must have felt too shy to use it in front of the others. He asked me in a shaky voice, "Do you like Madonna? What other music do you listen to?" His soft, stuttering, grammatically correct questions made him appear even more sincere than usual.

All morning, I enjoyed sweeping with a traditional *hōki*. I wanted to experience every aspect of being a Kyoto gardener! But by lunch, I heard my inner thoughts whine, *This is fine for a while, but I don't want to do it all day*. I wasn't used to doing maintenance back home. I rarely had to weed, fix irrigation breaks, or even fertilize. I left these tasks to regular maintenance gardeners. I came to the garden only a few times a year for design consultation and pruning, and I've always appreciated the maintenance workers my clients hired. But after my first few days with the proud Kyoto pruners, I began to wonder if I subconsciously felt that cleaning was beneath me. Sogyu had told me that raking was an important first step to becoming a *senteishi*, a tree pruner. Despite this humbling logic, I'd find myself grumbling, then chiding myself for grumbling. No matter how hard I worked, the men worked twice as fast.

After returning from the hot dog expedition, I sat on a wall next to Kei, devouring my lunch while Masahiro cleaned up. Kei turned to me hesitantly. "Do you have any engagements this weekend?"

Oh, definitely, my Kyoto social calendar is booked! I thought, but instead I said calmly, "No, I'm doing nothing." I had been told by my apprentice advisors to expect my coworkers to act distant, never to invite me out. Kei continued, "I have some American friends I would like for you to meet. I am having a small party at my house this weekend if you would like to come!" *Oh, my God, I'd love to go! Thank you so much, Kei!* I replied in my mind. "Yes, I'd like that," I said with composure. It was torture keeping my giddy personality inside. At the end of lunch, Kei asked me how I knew David, my landlord. I hesitated, then gave in to my honest nature: "He is good friends with my boyfriend in California." I silently sighed. *Well, that secret is out.* I enjoyed being in a foreign city for a little while with no one knowing anything about my life. Apparently the news was hot. Only five minutes after arriving back at the office, Tanaka's carpool left for home with one of the office girls in the backseat with me. In perfect English, she asked me, "Does your boyfriend have a job?"

All the Twigs
Work with Speed

Many strangers in Japan reached out to help me with unconditional generosity. Soon after I began working for Uetoh, a Kyoto café owner I'd met only once asked me with concern, "Are you okay?" I'd never admit to a stranger that I felt homesick or anxious, but it showed. Her question alone helped me feel better. I knew someone was looking out for me. My weekly bathhouse visits allowed me to feel the warm companionship of other women, and eventually I found a regular dinner spot where a cook fed me nutritious nightly meals to keep me nourished.

I was taught never to prune an old, diseased, or weak plant. If I see a weak tree, such as a camellia or lemon with yellowing leaves and burned edges, I tell the client we must first nurture the plant before we can do any strong pruning. We give the yellowing plant some acidic fertilizer so its leaves can green up and resist sunburn—the green of a leaf acts as sunblock. We make sure it is getting enough water, but not too much. We add nutritious compost around its roots to feed the soil, making a nice home for worms and bugs that dig, poop, fertilize, and aerate the soil in a healthy way. In Kyoto I needed weekly nutrition, in mind and spirit, to keep up with the intense Kyoto craftsmen. The bathhouse cleansed my psyche, and the little restaurant fertilized my body. I could not have successfully completed my apprenticeship without the people who reached out to me with nurturing actions and words.

Driving in Kyoto traffic with Nakaji, I did not feel this same sense of Kyoto nourishment. Our morning commute sometimes mimicked a high-speed car chase with Michael Douglas in *The Streets of San Francisco*. My Kyoto landlord explained that when Japanese get behind the wheel, the expectation of polite behavior disappears. The lines of the road can be crossed even while those of the hierarchy could not. The car allows citizens to let off steam—lots of it.

Kei acted as chauffeur one morning while Nakaji sat shotgun. Nakaji stared down cars in front of us that were, in his opinion, going "too slow." He'd express himself in a tortured tone; I guessed he was saying, "How could they go so slow!" Our truck moved like a fat turtle among a sea of sleek koi, weaving through tiny streets toward our garden job. Kei would speed up, then slam on the brakes. I held my breath. We aggressively tailgated a gleaming Mercedes while Nakaji ordered Kei, "Go, go, go!" The only problem was, the driver ahead, with a neat bun of gray hair peeking up over her seat, couldn't move any faster because the car in front of her had stopped. My coworkers appeared poised to jump out of the seats, turning to Kei, then to the sidewalk, and back to Kei again. Nakaji instructed Kei to rev the motor while the car stood still. I dubbed this maneuver "the Zen of driving with Nakaji." I put aside my usual urge to fit in and searched for my seat belt. I found it, dusty yet in perfect condition, stuck way under the seat.

To Nakaji's approval, we gained speed the last few blocks of our drive. The truck brakes came to a squeaky stop alongside a private residence. The men piled out of the car, grabbing ladders, while I mentally kissed the ground. Anxious to stay out of the way, I stood aside dumbly. I took advantage of the moment to look at our new job.

A large earth-tone plaster wall allowed a glimpse of the top of a grove of trees and a house. Peeking inside the front gate, I saw a pyramidal cryptomeria, Japan's version of a California redwood, silhouetted against a fat maple. Cryptomerias remind me of the redwoods because of their tall trunks and drooping green branches. Unfortunately, they release clouds of pollen in the spring, causing allergic reactions. The gravel path meandered through the trees toward a front door. Camellias, ferns, and various woodland plants, covered in morning dew, lined the path. These trees could grow up to forty feet or taller, but were kept at around fifteen, just high enough to look natural without overwhelming the house.

Awkward Masahiro, tripping over his feet, rushed past me, heroically hauling a huge metal ladder in each hand. Nakaji tailed his young worker, giving directions. Then Masahiro ran back, faster this time without the ladders, and picked up a small wand attached to a liquid-filled container that was perched on the back of our truck. I had my suspicions. He flipped a switch, causing a loud machine to start up. An arc of liquid sprayed out of the wand, and Masahiro directed it up to the treetops.

Yes, I thought as a sterile mist passed my nostrils, *pesticide*. The garden looked vibrant and healthy, with no visible leaf damage from potential damaging insects, bacteria, or fungus. "Why use it, and why so much?" I wondered. Man-made chemicals quickly and effectively eliminate pests for busy homeowners, but they also poison the people the garden benefits.

Both my father and my stepmother died of cancer, diagnosed three weeks apart. Their house sat next to a peaceful lake where swans made their home. Their outdoor storage closet teemed with pesticides and herbicides, which perhaps contributed to their illness, perhaps not. But pesticides are a proven contributing factor to cancer. Pesticides, in addition to killing bugs that are harmful to the garden, kill soldiering bugs that naturally keep away these bad bugs. By wiping out the soldier bugs, they eliminate the antioxidants of the garden. My living Oklahoma relatives don't get to see what I found magical as a child near streams, lit-up fireflies flying in circles in darkness as though they are riding invisible Ferris wheels at night—except for one family friend who recently began seeing fireflies in his backyard, after he stopped using pesticides for several years.

Watching Masahiro, I was appalled. I expected more from the nature-inspired craftsmen. After a few minutes, my Berkeley political spirit awoke. I placed a cowgirl red bandana over my mouth in silent but visible protest. A bit anxious, I stood far away from the group and for once did not run to the boss to ask for instructions. Masahiro sprayed trees over his head for a good fifteen minutes without face protection. Before he'd even finished, the men began pruning trees under a post-shower drip of sticky pesticides. I asked Kei, pointing to the wand, "Pesticide?" even though I knew perfectly well it was. "Yes," he responded calmly, "a pesticide. It kills all the bugs, including the good ones," and walked away. I realized then that maybe some contemporary Japanese craftsmen did understand the benefits of organic pest management.

Nakaji yelled out something, and I asked Kei what he'd said. He translated with a smile, "Nakaji said, 'Get to work, all my little twigs!'" Our group nickname reminded me of a lecture I heard at a Zen monastery. At a cold morning lecture at Green Gulch Farm, along the fertile coastline of Marin County, a female abbot explained how, on its own, a twig breaks easily. But when you take a bunch of twigs and tie them together, a strong branch results, one with power. I wondered if Nakaji meant that all of us little twigs worked together as a strong team, or that we were all individual little twigs, each easily snapped. Nakaji signaled to have me follow him to a corner in the garden. I had done such a miserable job on the previous day's conifer, I thought for sure he'd given up on me. He pointed to a large pine. I pulled hundreds of cool, sticky pine needles quickly, with no stop for a sip of water, hardly taking a breath.

I kept an eye on the men's pines as they transformed what looked like thick green porcupines into stylized garden swans. Japanese black pines can be pruned more vigorously in Kyoto than San Francisco because they love the Japanese climate. San Francisco has warm, dry summers; perfect weather for beachgoers. Yet Japanese black pines prefer Japan's blazing hot, humid, rainy summers. San Francisco winters are mild, with few freezes. Japanese pines are no California beach bums; they like Japan's winter cold snaps. In the Bay Area it can rain all winter long. The Japanese pines dislike the water pooling uncomfortably around their roots, and they refuse to pull liquid up their capillary tubes to their needles, where they'd otherwise use this water in a Japanese summer to help create food and strength. With too much unwanted winter water during their dormancy period, Japanese pines yellow in the Bay Area. They look and feel weak. As a result, we have to prune pines with less detail than in Japan.

In the Bay Area I spend quite a bit of time determining pine strength. On a strong Japanese black pine, such as one I prune in Orinda, an inland Bay Area city, where summers are hot and winters chilly, I can prune out up to forty percent of the branches and needles. On a weak Japanese red pine in San Francisco's Sea Cliff, a historic garden belonging to a woman who owned one of the city's first Japanese restaurants, I only prune out ten percent. The summers in San Francisco can be particularly cool and the winters almost warm, so I clean out the dead needles and do a little thinning and almost no needle pulling. Pine pruning is infinitely complicated, and must be altered for each microclimate. The most experienced pine pruners in America are skilled bonsai artists who understand the strengths and weaknesses of individual plants in the varied regions of the United States. I'm constantly assessing the strengths or weaknesses of pines back home, so I easily adapt to new situations—like Kyoto, for example. The Kyoto craftsmen pruned the Japanese pines with clear determination. Never having observed Japanese pines pruned in their own climate, I'd never seen them pruned with such styling prowess as I saw Nakaji doing across from me in the garden that day.

After several hours of focused needle pulling and watching, I began to tire. In fact, at the start of the day, I'd noticed that my muscles ached. My initial excitement about working with the craftsmen the first few days faded as I noticed that the men's pace never let up. I felt tired at the beginning, middle, and end of the day. I'd collapse each night onto my futon and fall into a deep sleep, only to receive seven hours of sleep a night instead of my normal nine to ten that I got back home. Asher said I'd get used to the intense schedule after a few weeks, but I thought I might just

----

have to get used to working under the influence of exhaustion. So when a grandmotherly woman peeked out from our client's back door, carrying our morning tea on a tray, I almost hugged her. Her traditional offering was the first of hundreds brought out for us workers, three times a day, mostly by women working inside the home. We never knew what type of drink and food might show up on a magical tray: rice crackers, French pastries, or even Twix bars. To drink, we'd most often receive green tea, but we'd also be served soda or even liquor—just once. The tray from grandma held a ceramic teapot with strainer, tiny cups, a tin of shriveled green tea leaves, and a thermos of hot water—all for making tea. She brought out an additional tray of savory warm Japanese dumplings and huge crisp Asian pear slices. I was hungry, but I didn't dare grab one of the dumplings until someone else delicately took one first. This wasn't a "guests take the first bite" situation, as it would be in Oklahoma.

I pretended to examine a pine but instead slyly eyed Masahiro, who was patiently opening the tea tin, sifting tea leaves into the teapot strainer, pouring hot water into the steeping pot, and handing out the dumplings as he waited for the tea to steep appropriately. He filled small ceramic cups with grassy-smelling bright green tea and gave a cup to each person before settling down to enjoy his own. At the end of our break, Masahiro picked up the leftover cups, plates, and pear cores, gathered them onto trays, and handed them over to our client, who appeared at that very moment. Masahiro bowed as he delivered the tray, saying, "*Sumimasen*" (I am sorry). Everyone chimed in. The elderly client bowed slightly to him, saying in a raspy voice, "*Hai*," and grasped the tray with her wrinkled hands from the soft hands of Masahiro.

I was delighted that grandma said so little during this exchange. My California clients could never have maintained such silence; nor could I, for that matter. My clients would have explained to me how to make the tea, that the fruit was organic, when the dumplings were made, and by whom. That said, my California clients have served me homemade cookies and cake, martinis with a Meyer lemon wedge and Sonoma wines, espressos or black tea with cream and sugar (my favorite), and occasionally dinner. Probably the martini wasn't such a good idea. I had to quit early and return the next day. Never drink and prune.

The minute the tray was handed back, we twigs resumed our positions. I asked Nakaji what to do next. He responded, "*Matsu*" (pine). I asked, "*Ha mushiri?*" (Needle pulling?) which was rather obvious, but I wanted to show off the new word I'd learned from Kei. He looked at me blankly and walked away. I thought, *Okay, needle pulling, stupid*, and ran back.

After an hour or so, Nakaji returned and began working on the pine next to me. He pulled out his shears, pruning a few branches instead of just pulling needles, and motioned for me to do the same. I squinted my eyes and looked over for confirmation. Nakaji had just motioned for me to do fall styling, probably the most advanced and difficult pruning in the garden. A warning from my mentor came into my thoughts: "If you weaken a pine, even just one branch, the whole tree can die." Nakaji's willingness to have me work on the pines perplexed me. So, another test, I assumed, tensing up. Tests make me feel like a deer in headlights.

My arms moved heavily. I pruned clumsily and watched Nakaji on the sly as he deftly styled his own pine. I could do this before, why can't I do it now? Searching for courage, I thought back to the first time I'd ever styled a client's pine, four years earlier.

Somehow, early on in my career, I'd managed to secure a pine-pruning account in the wealthy Berkeley Hills, with very little pine-styling experience. I worried that I'd ruin my poor first experiment, my soon-to-be "pine Frankenstein." I looked over the pine, which was thick as a bear, wondering how I'd transform it into a multibranched focal-point tree, as the client had requested.

I decided to say a prayer, a rare occurrence. I walked back to my little Toyota pickup and got an orange and a cookie from my lunch bag and placed the two items on the ground near the base of the pine. I felt I needed to make a symbolic sacrifice in exchange for the tree's willingness to face my pruning shears. Taking a look around to make sure no one was watching, I kneeled before my offering, closed my eyes, and whispered, "Please protect me from screwing up this tree. Guide me in making the right decisions so that this pine might shine in the front yard for all future people driving by to appreciate." I stood up to get my tools, and turning around I saw her. She had leaf-shaped deep brown eyes. Standing just eight feet away, a motionless gray deer stared at me intently. I'd never seen a six-foot-tall deer that close up, and I haven't since. They roam the Berkeley Hills but take off skittishly if you get within thirty feet of them. Deer love to eat roses and other flowers, so not many Berkeley homeowners welcome them. But I admire them. They know how to survive on very little nutrition, moving from garden to garden to do so. A pruning friend commented later, "The deer probably just wanted your lunch." But at that moment, I felt nature had given me a signal: "Go ahead, I'm looking out for you. I'm watching." The big-eyed deer ran off. The pine's crisp, geometric needle clusters stood out beautifully after having been pruned from a lump of green into a detailed form that looked like an open, older pine, just on a smaller scale. The client was well satisfied.

I looked over at Nakaji's tree with all its detailed styling, and then back to my own feeble attempts to open up the pads, pine branches that are distinct and thick. Either his tree was inherently more beautiful, or I was overdoing it. Sure enough, Bossman came over and looked at my tree from top to bottom, burst into laughter, and walked off. Silent, defeated, I tried reassuring myself, *You're not in Japan to be number one. You're here to learn.* This pep talk lasted about as long as it took to say the words. I'd been warned that in Japan no detailed corrections would be given. I'd have to keep trying new ways of doing a task till I got it right. Learning through trial and error is a lengthy process, compared to American-style instruction and critique. Some musicians call it "muscle memory"; I call it letting the lesson sink into your bones. Working on my poorly styled pine next to Nakaji, I felt keenly that I had let my American teachers down.

I kept sneaking looks at Nakaji's pine. He looked back at me several times and said in English, "Normal pine!" I repeated his words in my mind for encouragement: *Just normal pine, Leslie!* Normal to him, maybe. To me, incredible! I studied the pine he'd been working on. A hundred tiny connected branches on Nakaji's thinned-out pine looked like a human body exposed, with veins smoothly flowing throughout. My branches looked decent from a distance, hopefully acceptable to the client, but up close, the connections looked like the erratic skid marks of a drunk driver.

I closed my eyes before each new assignment. "Please let this pine turn out better than the last." I prayed for a sign, but none arrived. Each time I finished one tree, decently enough but not great, Nakaji would point to the next. Pine after pine I pruned in the private Kyoto garden that day.

At breaks I continued to study the men's work and to take notes. After several days of watching me, Masahiro pulled out his own plant identification book and studied trees during what few precious minutes of break he had left after serving tea. I believe I may have inspired this break-time study hour. The men teased him, shouting out little comments as he flipped through the pages, searching for answers.

I continued styling pines on and off during my apprenticeship with Uetoh, understanding I had much to learn about pine-styling techniques but also realizing that we had an excellent pruning program set up back home. Because Californians use so many different kinds of plants, we have the opportunity to learn how to prune plants from all over the world. Japanese tend to use almost exclusively native Japanese plants in the majority of their gardens. Therefore, they are masters at pruning Japanese pines. As I pruned in the Kyoto gardens with joy and fear, I sensed my California mentor watching me over my shoulder. "Don't blow it," he whispered.

By lunch I felt tense from all the concentrated effort. I needed to relax, but one thing needed to be taken care of. So, after great resistance and inner debate, I hesitantly asked Nakaji, in as soft a voice as I could manage, and in expert Japanese, as this was an important sentence to me, "*Otearai wa, doko desu ka, kudasai?*" (Can I please use the restroom?) At the restaurant, the garden had a bathroom for outdoor workers around the back. I hadn't thought of what might happen at a private home. In California, clients offer me the use of their indoor restrooms before I even bring it up. Half the day had passed in the small Kyoto garden, I'd had morning coffee and first break green tea, and I'd yet to see anyone enter the home. I saw no tall shrubs or fences for the men to hide behind. How do the craftsmen manage, I wondered. I'd held off, but now I was feeling some urgency.

Nakaji grumbled and looked annoyed. He got up from his lunch with a begrudging shrug, walked heavily across the garden, and knocked gently on the client's door. He talked at length to our client, who I assumed was the daughter of the grandmother, in what appeared from a distance to be dramatic, apologetic sentences with lots of hand movement and polite, submissive body language. They kept looking over at me, and then continuing their conversation in earnest. Several times I heard him use the Japanese phrase "*Amerika-jin*" (American person). I blushed but held firm. This was a bigger deal than I'd anticipated.

Finally Nakaji turned and nodded. I had gained approval for my remarkable errand! I tried to hold my head high as I passed Nakaji, even though I couldn't think what I'd do in the remaining weeks. Nearing the front door, I mentally rehearsed the three ways of apologizing I'd learned in my Japanese conversation class at Laney College in Oakland. One at a time, I said them to the sweet homeowner as I moved through her house. "*Sumimasen*" (sorry), I said while taking forever to remove my complicated cloth booties, which had at least fifteen clasps each, while sitting on the front doorstep. Of course no shoes were allowed in the house. I knew that. "*Gomen-nasai*" (pardon me), I said, walking through the small kitchen. I figured that even if the client questioned my ability to display a craftsman's manly toughness, at least she'd consider me polite. *"Shitsurei shimasu!"* (excuse me, please) I called out rather ironically while making the home stretch past the living room, with the bathroom door just in sight.

I was curious to see the home's interior. Brief glances revealed that most rooms, except the kitchen, were covered with the traditional tatami flooring. Yet in the living room I spied a black leather couch and in the dining room a tall Western table and chairs. This client appeared to be as interested in Western design as Americans were in Japanese style. Once we reached the bathroom, our client, looking like a friendly American mom with a Mary Tyler Moore–style bobbed haircut, patiently demonstrated to me how to use the bathroom's modern features.

She pushed a myriad of light switches, which worked the sink, the toilet, and more. Then she showed me how to flush the high-tech Toto toilet, which used so many different buttons, it resembled a computer filled with water. I wished I had taken out my pad and taken notes. Last, she placed her hands under the faucet. Wow! A motion sensor–activated water faucet! Evidently I had stepped into a modern Japanese household. The switches blinked, the toilet beeped, seeming to say "Hello, Leslie" when I opened the lid. I felt a bit like Bambi popping my face out of the edge of the forest, only to discover a freeway of beeping horns and fast cars. I eyed the door nervously.

After the hostess left, I sat down, a little sweatier than when I'd entered. Yes! Behold, a heated toilet seat! Where do I sign up? I sat there for a while, in an utter state of anxiety and comfort, and reviewed my situation. I could give up all liquid intake, or torture myself asking Nakaji if I could use the bathroom every afternoon.

- - - -

"You could act like the men and suck it up. Or you could be a woman and check out Japanese interior decor." My dedicated side chimed in, "You're not here to look at furniture. You're here compliments of this generous company, so don't bother them." My sensitive side responded, "But it's unhealthy not to drink all day. I'm already thirsty! I need green tea for energy." "Quit being such a baby. Be like the men!" "I'm tired. You're mean."

My inner debate finally ran out of steam and I turned my attention to what was in front of me. There was a cool little built-in bookshelf just across from the toilet. The homeowner had filled it with Japanese books, organized by color and size. I didn't understand a single Japanese title. But there on the bottom shelf rested a lone book in English. It had a paper jacket around it, whereas the rest of the books were hardcover. I sighed, "Finally, something I can understand in Japan!" I read the title: *Don't Sweat the Small Stuff*. Ha. I sat there a bit longer, my heartbeat normalizing as I giggled. I considered the message and decided that maybe it would be okay if I asked to use the bathroom once a day.

For the late-afternoon break, gigantic slices of peeled sweet apples were handed out. No one grabbed, even though I felt tempted. Each person picked up one slice at a time and calmly took delicate bites. After seven hours of hard physical labor, I had to rein myself in. *Slowly, Leslie,* I commanded, resisting the urge to stuff the delightfully juicy slices into my mouth, one after another.

When grandma came to retrieve the tray, I happened to be the only one in sight. So when I picked up the tray as I had earlier seen Masahiro do and handed it to her with a deep bow, repeating, as I had heard Masahiro say, *"Sumimasen"* in as gracious a manner as I could manage, grandma just stood there with her mouth open, staring at me without bowing, seemingly unable to respond. She must not have seen me earlier and did not know what to make of me. Or maybe elders didn't have to respond! I bowed again, with a kind, respectful smile, and backed away a bit. Being from the South, it's hard for me when people don't chitchat, especially older folk, who are frequently talkative to anyone who will listen. Silence, where I'm from, is a sign of anger or arrogance.

But she was my elder, and my mom had taught me to always respect one's elders, to "be seen and not heard." At least that part of my culture I think I have in common with Japan. Grandma never said a word to me, and I tried not to sweat it. I gave her one last bow and scampered off to join my crew. On our way home, Kei sped and slammed on the brakes, and Nakaji raised and lowered his voice. I noticed Masahiro had also found his clean seat belt. He'd buckled it securely.

A Seasonal Garden
Is About to Change

My first week I saw more types of *hashigo*, ladders, than I'd ever imagined existed. We used handmade *hashigo*, aluminum *hashigo*, four- or fifteen-foot *hashigo*. Pine pruning required attention to detail, so the men needed to get up close to the branches. But given that bark shows off age and beauty, climbing on the trunks is discouraged, if not forbidden. Ladders allow for access to the pines without mishap. I watched as a four-legged ladder was transformed into a flat extension ladder with a few snaps. Uetoh Zoen made their own tripod ladders by hand. The tall poles were fashioned out of bamboo canes, and the horizontal rungs out of thick cut branches. These ladders looked rickety but held surprisingly firm. Sometimes we tied a thick length of bamboo into the crotches of two separate pine trees, making a walking bridge, or we'd lean extension ladders against the bamboo to reach a difficult spot. If I had to work on a part of the tree where there wasn't a branch to walk on underneath, the men would make a walking branch with a ladder and poles. They could tie ladders into trees in seconds, using elegant twisting knots. My knots resembled huge lumpy things, requiring time and effort to dream up. Nakaji loved making fun of them.

One day, Nakaji pointed toward a twenty-foot-high pine for me to work on—it was taller than a two-story house! My eyes must have widened, but I tried to recover with a confident glance over to the fifteen-foot extension ladder on the truck. Running to the car I thought, *How am I going to carry that?* I coached myself along the way. *Well, I know you've never used an extension ladder before, or any ladder over eight feet tall, but between here and the tree you'd better figure it out!* I grabbed the thick metal ladder, so heavy I could barely hold it, and ran, or rather hobbled, over to the pine. I calculated I'd need about six ropes, given the number of branches on the tree.

I grabbed eight from the truck, to be safe, and was about to climb up when Nakaji came over, looked at my mass of ropes, and yelled, "*Dame!*" No one had ever brought up this word in Japanese language class. I guess they hadn't expected us to work with Bossman. But I understood its meaning the first time I heard it. Depending on the tone, it meant "wrong," "*wrong,*" or "WRONG!" I tried to ask formally, "Where should I tie the ropes on the tree?" But in my effort to speak Japanese quickly, I left out the "where" and must have sputtered, "Should I use a rope?" Nakaji erupted into laughter. Yet he understood, for he pointed to the exact spots on the tree where I could tie the ladder. Mysteriously, two knots sufficed to secure the entire twenty-foot ladder.

As I stood on *hashigo* for hours at a time my first week, I had to twist my body this way and that to prune the pines. The men endured regular discomfort in order to work as quickly as possible, allowing themselves few interruptions for adjusting their ladders.

Overthinking each cut while pruning usually produces inferior results. Just as when one is learning a language, there is a point when one's sentences flow better by not translating word for word and instead speaking as quickly as one can so the subconscious can join in. I couldn't yet work as fast as the men, maintaining such detail, but I would try.

The last day of our six-day workweek, I found myself in a stylish private home garden. Looking forward to my precious Sunday off, I pruned away in the middle of the garden on a blessedly short pine from a shrimpy four-foot ladder. Two L-shaped walls of the house framed two sides of the garden. A forty-five-degree fence framed in the other sides from the street. One wall of the house held a few windows. The second wall was closed up with beautiful sliding cedar shutters. A circular dry stream filled with gray river pebbles surrounded my pine, and a boulder-strewn dry waterfall rested off to the side. The landscaper had hidden neighboring homes with maples, camellias, nandina, and azaleas, so I felt completely surrounded by nature. The men pruned with vigor and in silence. I could hear only snipping shears, rustling plastic tarps, and energetic birds, observing us from the trees above.

Then I became aware of a different noise: the wooden shutters behind me sliding open with a soft rumble. I looked over toward them, yet the shutters remained closed. I searched around to locate the sound, and the ladder I stood on began to move gently, then more decidedly, as though I were standing on a pine branch being shaken out to clean dead needles. "Earthquake! Duck and cover under a chair or table," said a warning drilled into my memory from California earthquake-wary schools. Should I hide under my ladder? The shutters clacked forcefully against the house. For a surreal thirty seconds or so, the earth rippled beneath our feet. I looked toward the men for reassurance. They continued to prune. I wanted to run but just clutched the ladder tight, knowing there

----

was no fighting Mother Earth's power. Not one craftsman took his eyes off his tree as the ground shook. *Just keep going, Leslie*, I reassured myself. The movement stopped short, and I went back to work without a word—a complete victory for me. I practiced my impenetrable Japanese gardener façade, though I did raise my eyebrows a bit. I mean, no buildings fell, no one was hurt, so what was the big deal?

Nakaji came over just before lunch to examine my pine. I had pruned the top with more detail than the lower branches because the top looked stronger and could take the stress of more cuts. The top now looked styled, and I could see rough bark through elegant branches. I'd left lower, weaker areas more full, and pulled fewer needles there. Hence, the lower areas looked fluffy and green. Tops are not always strong, or lower areas weak, but this particular imbalance often occurs. Overall, I thought I'd done a fairly good job, considering I'd removed fifty or so fresh pine shoots, and hundreds of needles, while maintaining a cohesive overall look. I awaited Bossman's feedback.

Nakaji lifted a few branches with his muscular brown hands to examine a few small branches deep inside the pine. I hadn't missed them. He looked the tree up and down. He finally advised me, in English, "Do more pretty." Sigh. I looked at the branches he had just pruned on a nearby tree, then mine, then his. It was a "which part of the picture looks different from the other" kind of situation. I finally reasoned that perhaps I wasn't shaking out enough old brown needles, making my branch pads look messier. I had left maybe two to five brown needles out of fifty or so per pad. Nevertheless, as I paid attention to such minute details awhile longer, my tree looked better. I had to slow down quite a bit to make this adjustment. Kei, on the other hand, was pruning like a machine—half robot, half artist. His big party was set to occur that night, and he looked determined to finish the project on time, by six. In fact, the office secretaries, knowing he worked late, would arrive early at his house to prepare food and stay late to clean up. I found this kind of outside support for the hardworking craftsmen quite common. Gardening was one of the last Japanese traditional crafts requiring years of physical hardship. I think others understood this and supported the men (and one woman), allowing us to train and have a semblance of a social life.

At lunchtime, Masahiro handed out steaming teacups in descending order of the hierarchy as fast as he could, while others ignored him. This was not a practice in humiliation; just what was expected of a beginning apprentice. The timing of our breaks remained steady, exactly at ten in the morning, at noon, and at three in the afternoon. All craftsmen took their breaks at the same time across Japan, including the carpenters who constructed buildings for the tea gardens, bamboo craftsmen who wove together our rakes, and even potters who molded the cups we drank from. The tea tray connected us all.

There was more unpredictability to come that day. In the morning, the tray arrived bearing green tea and Twix bars. This made for a funny break from the subtle handmade desserts we'd been served for a week. I was raised on *Masterpiece Theatre*, and I simply loved English tea trays. Kei told me that, in the past, housewives served lunch as well as tea to the gardeners. Times had changed.

On our third break, an even more unusual food item appeared. The men gathered in a silent circle around the tray, staring at a new arrival, mystified. They tilted their heads to get a closer look at one

----

of the more unusual trays it seemed they'd ever received. On a black lacquered tray, painted with tiny pink flowers and golden leaves, sat six hot dogs, tiny wieners stuffed into baguette buns.

One of my top childhood memories from Oklahoma was tasting homemade ketchup at a fourth-grade friend's birthday picnic in the park. Rhoda was the only black girl in my very integrated class who dared to invite her shy white classmate to her party. I remember sitting at a picnic table and biting into a hot dog Rhoda's mother had given to me. Flavor exploded in my mouth. I stopped eating the hot dog for a moment to savor the taste, a big deal for a nine-year-old. It was one of the first moments I can remember when I noticed that a simple ingredient could be improved if one spent time developing it by hand.

But that day in the private Kyoto garden, the hot dogs held no appeal. A stale line of ketchup trailed the top of each. All of us felt disheveled and sappy from the pine work we'd labored on all day. The air hovered humid. There were six of us, one hot dog each. Nakaji, Kei, and Masahiro, the brave ones on my crew, nobly ate their hot dogs. I ate mine, of course. Two workers wouldn't touch the tray. Normally we'd clear the tray, but with two hot dogs left, the situation looked truly dire. I felt guilty, suspecting this snack had arrived because an American was part of the crew. I reflected on how much effort the client might have taken to find them. I forced myself to eat one more salty dog, but I just couldn't eat the last.

At lunchtime our new client gave me a tour of her house, introducing me to the fine art of viewing the garden from inside a stylish Kyoto home. Much of the house was furnished with Western furniture. There was one special room in the back where the family did

----

prayers and entertained guests. It was the garden-viewing room. The floor was covered in clean tatami mats, a gold-lined prayer altar sat in a corner, and a *chabudai*, the same kind of low table I'd seen at the Tokyo Gardens restaurant, rested in the middle. A cubbyhole shelf had been built into the wall near the entryway. On this little shelf sat a bowl filled with fresh chestnuts that were just popping open their bright green thorny summer jackets, with three orange persimmons resting next to them. The homeowner said that this fruit display, directly across from the altar, was created to remind visitors of the current season, late summer.

Along the wall facing the garden, she showed me how two separate horizontal lengths of sliding shutters, one on top of another, opened to allow a view to the garden. These were the shutters that had clattered during the recent tremblor. She opened the lower section and showed me how the guests, as they entered the room, could see a hint of the garden through the long, low opening. This low opening made me think of flirtation. With less than half the garden revealed, the guest might sense an atmosphere of mystery and feel a subtle desire to see more. The homeowner invited me to sit down on a floor cushion in front of the table. As I did, I could see a bit more of the garden and the low pine I'd been working on. Then she slid open the remaining shutters, inviting me into full conversation with the garden. The landscape came together swiftly—waterfall, stream, hill, pines, and maples. Not only was the scene intensified by the gradual opening of the shutter's frame, but my feelings were heightened as well.

She mentioned that every season, the color red appeared in her garden: bright red azalea flowers in spring, deep red ilex berries in summer, great swaths of rust-colored maple leaves in fall, and scarlet camellia flowers in winter, striking against a snowy back-drop. Japanese gardens rarely emphasize color; this was unique to her garden. But I find that female clients love flowers. Her use of color in every season may have appeared more acceptable because each flowering plant symbolized a season. In the Japanese garden, a client would be more likely to spend money on styling the maple tree, which changes each season, than they would on buying flats of colorful annuals. The season ended and began again in this private Kyoto garden, but a consistent color theme made the landscape timeless, combining the past, present, and future for the viewer.

I've had a few California clients call me, panic-stricken, saying, "My tree has died!" only to have me rush over and inform them, "That is a maple tree; the leaves fall off each year when it goes dor-mant. It's alive." I think their lack of plant knowledge compared to that of the typical Japanese homeowner was not a product of igno-rance but of different values. Where do most Americans spend more money: on the kitchen remodel or on the backyard? Working for Uetoh that year, I saw homeowners willing to spend a fortune on yearly gardeners. For many Americans the garden is an after-thought, but for many Japanese it is an integral part of the home. My hostess, with her rumbling, double-tiered shutters, made her home feel much larger in a way I'd never seen before. Just before I left, she said her garden was about to change. How true, too, for my life in Kyoto.

The day progressed very slowly, as we workers had the evening party in mind. The hill pine dissolved from a short, stocky Christ-mas tree to an open, stylized silhouette against a deepening blue sky. I cleaned up as fast as I could. According to our plan, one of the workers would drive us directly to Kei's small apartment, where we'd change into our party clothes.

The craftsmen knew how to work their tight schedule. We began our elaborate cleanup routine with gusto. First we piled cuttings into the *baron bukuro*, the round tarp, and carted them off to the truck. Kei switched on a blower that efficiently, and loudly, rounded up the debris. Finally we picked up every last remaining stubborn needle and leaf by hand and began folding the tarps, a signal that the evening's excitement, away from plants and sweat, was about to begin. I'd survived my first six-day workweek in Japan. I rarely drank, but I thought, *I'm going to stay up all night and get blasted.* The disciplined schedule took its toll. I felt like I deserved a break from reality.

Nakaji yelled something, and we all looked up. He pointed at the pebble stream surrounding the pine hill, to our tarps, and to the truck. His voice went up and down in consternation. He bent down, pushed pebbles aside impatiently, picked up some pine needles, and threw them off to the side with disgust. Apparently, a few pine needles had gotten into the dry pebble stream. Kei briefly instructed me on how to push aside the pebbles, a square-foot section at a time, brush out dirt and needles from the concrete bottom, and then return the rocks to the clean stream. This took three of us, working desperately quickly, about an hour to complete. Believe me, I didn't leave a single pine needle behind. The work proved tedious and annoying. But when it was done, the stream did appear to sparkle, exquisitely transformed. I'm a clean freak, but when it came to Nakaji, I'd met my meticulous match.

We zoomed off to the festivities. In front of Kei's apartment door, I removed my muddy work boots and placed them next to a mosaic of high-heeled pumps, stylish tennis shoes, and leather boots. Kei's apartment looked tiny and was packed with smiling faces. Uetoh secretaries had lined a table with trays of food. We walked into a combined kitchen and living room. Someone led me through a bedroom the size of a walk-in closet to a bathroom the size of an airplane restroom with shower squeezed in so I could change out of my filthy clothes. The floors were made of traditional tatami, but Kei's furniture and large computer table had a decidedly modern flavor. I found a cookbook by Jamie Oliver on the kitchen counter, and, on Kei's narrow balcony, a collection of potted herbaceous plants. I'd never met a man who grew tender woodland plants.

I was thrilled to meet two American women my age, who would soon become my closest Kyoto girlfriends. Maya had lived for many years in Berkeley before coming to Kyoto. She edited and translated formal Japanese art books. Jennifer, from Wyoming, had completed a formal multiyear apprenticeship in Japanese art restoration. It was explained to me that Kyoto life for an American woman could be lonely because Japanese men were shy at first and unaccustomed to treating women equally, as we American women had come to expect. Both women had wise, open-minded Japanese male friends and heartfelt, dedicated careers that held them in Kyoto.

A young American man, Aaron, introduced himself to me. He studied landscape architecture at the University of Kyoto. Impressive, I thought; I still could speak only a few Japanese sentences. I thought about Taylor, wishing he were there with me, looking into my eyes, asking me how my week had gone. "Uetoh Zoen is one of the top landscaping companies in Kyoto," tall Aaron stated. At least he looked right at me, instead of politely off to the side, as all my coworkers had done over the past week. "They're maybe in the top ten percent." "Really? Wow. Cool!" I said, enjoying my ability to use American slang for the first time in weeks.

Feeling relaxed, surrounded by familiar-looking faces, I discovered the true advantage of tatami flooring as the evening wore on. Some people went home near midnight, but many slept over. If anyone got tired or drank too much, he or she could just grab a pillow from the bedroom and lie down on the tatami to sleep out the rest of the night. I felt a strange temptation to get completely drunk so I could escape from all the formality and respect to my seniors I'd had to adopt over the past week. I just needed a break for one night before facing another six-day workweek. Did my drinking coworkers feel a similar stress? I wondered. Late into the evening, we talked and laughed. One young Japanese man in a business suit lay down in the middle of the floor with his coat bundled up as a pillow. Another young woman lay next to the drink area, near fresh crumbs and empty beer bottles.

Near midnight I lay down under a kitchen table, where I slept warmly and soundly, next to a toaster oven that had been placed on the floor because of lack of space. Sometime near dawn, I took a sleepy, and a tad nauseated, survey of the room. Light spread out over the tatami, turning guests a dreamy golden hue. Aaron snored loudly, flat on his back, with his huge legs and arms outstretched as though there could never be enough floor space for him. Across the tatami, I spotted Kei, who, despite being one of the most intense workers I've ever encountered, slept curled up like a kitten, with his head resting on a traditional rice hull pillow. These were my new friends, who would support me throughout my Kyoto journey.

Surviving Masahiro's Island

The following Monday morning, Nakaji stuck to Masahiro like a mosquito for hours, issuing a steady stream of loud commands. If Masahiro didn't do exactly as he was told, which invariably happened with the fledgling gardener, Nakaji would keep increasing his decibel level: "Here! *Here!* HERE!" Whoa. Masahiro remained unperturbed. He'd never storm off and quit, as most of my American friends would do if their boss used that tone with them. One of my Japan advisors explained to me, "You'll be lucky if your boss yells at you. That means you're being treated like one of the guys, not an outsider." Masahiro reminded me of Gilligan on my favorite childhood television program, *Gilligan's Island*. Gilligan is always attempting to carry out orders from Skipper, and there's always some obstacle in the way. Following each critique session, Masahiro would bow his head repeatedly, saying, "*Hai, hai,* Nakaji-san." Masahiro's persona was a mixture of youth, naïveté, and hopeful intention.

Masahiro spent ten hours that day cleaning up after me while I pruned. He didn't seem to mind. Once, when I tried to haul my own debris, he shook his head and wrestled the tarp from my arms. I suspected he thought I wasn't strong enough, so this goaded me on to haul an even bigger tarp load the next time. Never baby a woman raised by a feminist. I finally gave up after one more tarp wrestling match and let him do his noble duty. Gilligan faced his destiny with absolute determination. I just didn't get it. What drove him? How long would I last in his place?

The morning's stomp-and-command drama took place while four of us worked on pines in a monk's peaceful courtyard garden, one of the enclosed gardens of a larger monastic property of Tenryuji. Blankets of moss sat at our pine's feet, with all sorts of green shrubbery and trees as neighbors. Nakaji decided to move on to Kei. *"Hai, hai, hai,"* Kei responded with a firmer, deeper voice, and with plenty of enthusiasm. I pulled pine needles like the dickens, reflecting on the fact that I was the only one left who hadn't been yelled at. I waited my turn while my hands were tearing at the sticky, waxy toothpicks, and I tore some in my haste. Finally, I saw out of the corner of my eye Nakaji changing course, heading in my direction.

Mind you, Kei and I were sitting on bamboo poles, fifteen feet up in the pines! The men had tied narrow logs between the trees, and extension ladders rested against the logs to allow us access. Not only could we reach complicated branches with ease, but Nakaji could reach us from pine to pine without ever setting foot on the ground. I saw him cross the log between Kei's tree and mine like a seasoned tightrope walker. I followed him out of the corner of my eye, trying not to appear like I was watching. He was coming closer and closer, the pole creaking under his bulk, when I saw that just behind Bossman, Kei was waving at me frantically with his shears, trying to get my attention.

With his eyes and hands he was telling me to remove a certain branch that was near my right arm. I had wondered about this branch earlier. It shaded another branch underneath it considerably. I often identify my pruning students as "aggressive pruners" or "gentle pruners." I fall into the first category. If I need to cut out a branch to keep it from shading out a more desirable one, I won't hesitate. The higher branch that Kei was motioning toward looked boring—straight and stocky. The beautiful branch beneath grew slender and sinuous. Toward the top of the pine, a smaller branch with more interesting curves made sense. Logically, I should cut the bigger branch, before it shaded and killed the smaller and more interesting one.

"Some must die so that others may live," said my native plant teacher, Stew Winchester, inadvertently quoting Winston Churchill when describing the oldest trees on earth, the bristlecone pines in California. These pines live as long as five thousand years and thrive in the scorched, remote mountain ranges of California's eastern Sierra. Nature recognizes that plants have limited recourse. Apple trees, for example, drop a certain number of apples in spring to allow the rest to thrive. The pruner must also remove certain trees or branches so others can survive.

"Here, then, is a disadvantage of great old age: persist too long and eventually the very ground you grow in will wash away!" said Ronald Lanner of bristlecone pines, in his book *Conifers of California*. The branch Kei was motioning me to cut could have been a hundred years old. Do I dare? Did I understand these two old branches well enough to decide which is worthier? I hesitated, my shears hovering over a straight old branch covered in poetic fissured bark.

Nakaji still hadn't reached me, and I tried to make up my mind. I stifled a giggle watching Kei's pantomime and awaiting my approaching doom. I made up my mind and cut the branch—but only in half, as a compromise—seconds before Nakaji reached me. He crouched down a foot away, yelled his disapproval, forcefully grabbed the big branch I'd sawed only in half, and chopped it off at its base with one clean snip of his pruners. Nakaji was strong.

He yelled something in Japanese at me, and motioned for me to remove another branch to my left. I was taking a second to reposition myself when Nakaji, staring at me intently, yelled the same phrase a bit louder—actually, way louder—while pointing aggressively to the target branch. I had a realization. When my Japanese boss says something, I need to do it fast! I got off pretty light with only one reprimand, yet I felt a certain pride. Yelled at for the first time! Whoopee! I rejoiced in my head, giving Nakaji a high-pitched yet firm, "*Hai.*"

After my reprimand, I tried to stay more focused on my pine. But after about twenty minutes or so, thoughts distracted me. While pruning pines, I'd cover just about every possible subject in my mind, except the branch in front of me. Most days my thoughts swayed toward my boyfriend. *Why hasn't he emailed me more?* My landlord's archaic computer system took time to work, so I checked emails only on Sundays. Taylor had written just twice since I arrived a month before. *Was he working late developing photos, taking hikes in the hills, or spending time with a new friend?* Each scenario demanded to be imagined in detail. We had a disagreement right before I left, and I'd tried to replay the difficult conversation in my head in dozens of ways since. I did not realize it yet, but despite the fact that I thought about Taylor a lot in Japan, I would have almost no contact with him during my apprenticeship. *The pine*, I'd correct myself. *Focus on styling the pine or you may be*

----

hauling debris tomorrow like Masahiro. Occasionally, I'd look over at Kei's pine. Reality dawned. My pine paled in comparison to the exquisitely stylized work of my coworker. Drat.

Just before lunch, trying to make cuts while focused instead on thoughts and subsequent emotions, I noticed that Kei behind me was pruning with hardly any noise. I admired his smooth technique. Then I heard a funny sawing sound. I turned around and saw Kei slumped over a branch, asleep and snoring gently, fifteen feet up in the air! So I wasn't the only one lacking in proper sleep. I quickly decided to vigorously clean my tree before Nakaji came around. With poles attached, if my tree moved, so did Kei's. He woke up and began pruning again within a split second. We had to stay alert together to avoid the mosquito's bite.

Trying to stylize the pines that fall day in the monk's garden was like uncovering an intricately woven basket hidden inside a haystack. Pines grew so much stronger and thicker here than in California. In spring, pines send up a long, thin shoot that looks like a candle. In late spring, the candles open up into a cluster of needles, called a whorl, that radiate from one stem. A California pine's candles only grow about two to four inches a year. In that same time, Kyoto candles grow a foot and a half! Hence spring styling in Kyoto looks dramatic. To top this off, the men paid incredible attention to small details. Kei told me, "I leave fifteen to seventeen needle pairs per whorl at the tops of pines. As I move down, I prune out fewer and fewer needles." I had a hard time believing his exact needle count, so I climbed up one of the monks' pines and counted the needles myself. Sure enough, despite the fact that Kei worked like a Cuisinart, every top whorl indeed held fifteen to seventeen needle pairs. A professional pruner must think about that day's finished look, the next year's growth, the growth five years from then, and, on top of this, way into the future. I felt beaten.

I practiced counting needle clusters for a while and felt I'd gotten it when I looked over at Kei's tree. He was hardly styling his tree at all! In fact, he was leaving his pine as thick as I normally did in California. In contrast, my pine looked way more stylized and overpruned. If I pruned a tree too much back in California, my bonsai teacher Mas would tell me, "Your tree looks a little cold." Bonsai teaches the aesthetic pruner how to hold back, to humble oneself, so the plant has some say. Working on bonsai is perfect training for the landscape pruner; if I even slightly overpruned a two-foot bonsai tree, there wouldn't be much left! I looked around the Kyoto monks' garden and saw that the men were leaving the styled pines thicker and fluffier than I'd seen them do in other gardens. I must have missed out on instructions earlier in the day. Some clients just like the pines thicker, sometimes the scene calls for a thicker tree, or occasionally the client just doesn't want to pay for super stylized pines. "Why didn't Kei say anything to me!" I moaned, frustrated. I'd done as I was told yet continued to fail.

Clouds loomed most of the day, and just after lunch it began to rain, then pour. *Boom!* Lightning struck nearby. Light flashed on the darkened pines, and yet the men continued to work. We worked for four hours in the downpour without a break. My thick plastic rain suit kept me protected, except for the water and sweat dribbling down my arms. I felt chilled, but as long as the men kept going, I would too. Near four o'clock, Nakaji came over one more time to yell at me. Three feet away, he had a lot of reprimands and corrections to give, his lips moved energetically, but I couldn't hear a word he uttered with all the rain and thunder. I did my best to yell loudly, "*Hai! Hai!*" and tried to do something really fast that looked different. My cloth *jikatabi* shoes got soaked, but eventually Bossman motioned me over to the truck and handed me a pair of plastic *jikatabi* rain boots. Stoic Masahiro wore his soaking shoes till dusk.

Changing into the rain boots in the dry car while the men continued to work, I hung on to a few precious moments of protection from the crazy men outside, the relentless downpour, the thunder crashing around us, and the lack of anything I'd ever known. The car became a haven where I could hear my thoughts and encourage myself to continue. The new shoes felt good thanks to a cherished extra pair of dry socks in my bag. I hung out in the warm car a few seconds longer than needed, then headed back out.

Surprisingly, I look back on that day at Tenryuji as a peaceful one. Birds chirped early in the morning, then hid out somewhere during the rainstorm, probably cleaning themselves delightfully. They may have liked their impromptu shower in their Kyoto tree bathhouse. The monks served us individually wrapped *mochi*, small balls of pounded rice filled with sweet bean paste, lightly dusted in rice flour. We also ate *mochi* on sticks, dipped in a sweet dark brown sauce. I called them *mochi* shish kabob; the men called them *dango*.

While drinking steaming hot tea during the last break, under the shelter of a wooden temple building, I placed a soft, flour-dusted mochi ball against my cheek and thought about how I must have felt as a baby while nursing. I'm certain this was not the traditional way to handle mochi, but it felt good! Kei said that when people visited the monks they brought food and drink offerings, which the monks passed on to us. Thank you, monks and monk visitors! The monks left the trays discreetly behind a special sliding door. As we tended the garden, we could hear their rhythmic, monotone chants and drumming coming through the walls of nearby buildings, pulsating through the rain. Their prayers surrounded us: *clip-yell-chant-pound, clip-yell-chant-pound, clip-yell-chant-pound, strike.*

Communicating in Silence

"Otsukaresama!" the men shouted to the other male workers who strode assuredly through the office door each morning. The exact definition of this phrase eluded me; perhaps it was a mix of "Good morning!" and "Welcome back!" and "Dude!" I never quite knew the exact meaning of the word, nor did I use it. I just left it for the men. But any time I heard it shouted, I'd still feel the excitement of an old friend returning home. I learned this phrase by witnessing the interaction directly, without verbal explanation, and in this way I learned many things from my crew.

Uetoh employees returned that day from the Tokyo landscaping project. Unfamiliar faces showed up in the office. Everyone began talking at once. Uetoh builds gardens throughout Japan and in countries around the world, including Germany, the Americas, and China. Sometimes they design the gardens and then build them, and sometimes they just do the installation. I explained to Kei how in the United States, landscape architects are given more societal respect and pay than installation crews, who often have little aesthetic training. Kei explained, "It is not considered shameful to be a garden builder in Japan." He continued, "First a landscape architect designs the garden. Then the builder of the garden makes changes to the design as the garden is installed. The two have equal skill, control, and pay."

- - - -

One of my clients in California had a plan made of his garden by a famous Japanese garden landscape architect, but then chose to hire an unskilled construction crew to build the garden, following these plans. The garden cost him almost a million dollars, and it looked as though children had overseen the piling of rocks. I felt so sad looking at that garden. If he had a limited budget, he should have done the opposite and hired a skilled installation crew who understood plants, rock placement, and the overall design of a garden, and skipped having the landscape beautifully drawn on a piece of paper. A simple sketch could help homeowners on a tight budget. Of course, larger, more prestigious gardens need both talents working together. But the skill of the garden builder is the basis of landscaping a Japanese garden.

After dozens of bows were exchanged, the craftsmen caught up on news while running equipment to the trucks—all while taking side glances at the American. I felt even more the odd one out than usual. I clambered into the truck next to Kei, wondering how the men could keep up their high-spirited banter at seven in the morning. As we left the company property and sped onto city streets, the men gradually became more silent, until they sat as quiet as churchgoers. *Praying to the god of safe driving?* I wondered.

In fact, the craftsmen preferred silence most of the time. The ongoing friendly chitchat between my American gardener friends and me did not exist for Japanese craftsmen. They seemed intent on trying to outdo each other in pruning, speed, and effort, with hardly a word exchanged. That quiet morning, as we moved along the streets of Kyoto, chilly air seeped into the truck and nudged its way through my two layers of fleece sweaters. I'd arrived in Kyoto at the tail end of summer, and early autumn coolness had silently caught up with me. Slanted fall sunlight extended long, crisp shadows onto garden paths. The colors in trees and flowers, previously washed out by summer's brightness, intensified and deepened as we moved into November. Kei bumped into me occasionally when the truck swerved. Our accidental contact reminded me of how little human connection I'd had of late. Like many of my Southern relatives, I'm used to hugging friends and touching people's arms when I talk to them. None of this could I do in Japan. I had to sit up straight and never speak of my emotions. I felt lucky to find a friendly coworker like Kei. I relied on him to help me navigate the craftsmen with his translation skills, and, as a result, he'd become a familiar face amid foreignness. Yet I noticed that Kei was particularly silent that day. I wondered why but let it go. Most of the time, working with the men, I felt both surrounded and alone. Regular friendly chitchat existed only in my thoughts.

As soon as we arrived at the monastery, everyone ran off to their various assignments. If I'd studied the language more. I' have known what to do. Nakaji gave instructions while ' Then he gave more detailed instructions while Kei put his shoes on. Kei always waited till the last minute to slip on his *jikatabi*, even though he could have done this in the car. I waited against the car's warm hood until I heard some movement and found Masahiro behind the truck, untying ladders. He looked up nervously as I approached. I asked him in rudimentary Japanese, "Me . . . take the ladders off . . . the truck?" He responded rapidly with multiple unintelligible sentences. I stared at him. *How hard is it to say yes or no?* In my thoughts, I waved my mental shears threateningly at him. I attempted to translate his words and figured he'd said, "I'm just untying ropes right now. We'll take the ladders off later." So I went back to leaning against the front of the truck to stay out of his way.

Then Masahiro jogged past me with a ladder in each hand. *Well, does he want me to help or not?* I vented. I reached for a ladder to follow him, but the young apprentice turned around, ineptly thunking a ladder against a tree trunk, and shooed me away. He mimed for me to stay put. Stoic Japanese gardeners can be trying.

He continued to run past me, back and forth, unloading equipment. I grew impatient and felt tempted to glare at him. *Don't do it, Leslie,* I lectured myself, trying to be mature. *You're not supposed to show anger.* Even furrowing one's brows in confusion looks like out-of-control anger to someone in Japan. Instead, I averted my eyes each time Masahiro passed. I figured that when visible methods fail, resort to passive-aggressive behavior. Bossman popped his head out of the bushes, ordering me, "*Matsu!*" (pine). I tried to follow him, but he'd already disappeared. I returned to my companion, the truck.

Finally Masahiro turned up and signaled for me to follow him. I stomped impatiently down the path behind him. He led me to a big pine, which I examined. A tall extension ladder rested in a crazy position against a trunk almost two stories tall, with all kinds of ropes securing it in a way I never could have figured out. I realized that while I'd been having a meltdown by the truck, Masahiro had been prepping my ladder for me to climb safely. He'd probably been ordered to do this task by Nakaji but didn't know how to tell me. Poor Masahiro, caught between a commanding Japanese boss and an equally commanding American woman. The young pruner mimed for me to prune the pine, something I figured he was dying to do himself. Regretting all my previous thoughts, I

----

put a pleasant look on my face and responded, "*Hai!*" He wished me "*Gambatte!*" as proud as a Boy Scout who'd just earned his ladder badge, and ran off. While in Japan, I thought *gambatte* meant "good luck." Only later did I learn it meant "don't give up," which is a much more craftsmanlike way of thinking.

After I'd completed the upper branches on the tall pine—quite poorly, in my opinion—Nakaji grunted and led me over to another pine with a beautiful extended lower branch of six feet. This pine stretched its limbs out on a small hill, like a dancer on a raised stage, accompanied on either side by sizable rocks sunken in the earth. It faced a large living room window just four feet away. *Is he crazy?* I thought, looking from the pine to the close proximity of the window. The pine was clearly the garden's masterpiece, the focal tree. No matter how poorly I felt I'd done on one pine, Nakaji would offer me another one, even more challenging.

I was instructed to work on the lowest, most elaborate branch first, so I took a deep breath. After I'd done a fair bit of thinning, Nakaji came over to inspect. For the first time in a month, he decided to give me detailed feedback. He gestured wildly, pointed to particular areas, going on for a while, while I stood still, unable to understand his words but knowing I'd completely messed up. I couldn't resist my desire for an interpretation of his critique, so I looked around for Kei. "Kei, Kei!" I discovered him hiding behind a shrub across the garden, close enough to have heard. He hesitated as though he didn't understand, then shrugged and walked over to where Nakaji waited impatiently. No turning back now.

I placed my yellow dictionary into his hands with an encouraging, appreciative look, and he opened it in search for words. I waited apprehensively, excitedly. I'd never received direct feedback from Nakaji. "Nakaji said," Kei spoke with clear enunciation, "your pine looks as though it were blown by the wind." *Hm*, I reasoned, *blown by the wind could mean good or bad*. After all, there is a tree style in bonsai called *shakan*, windswept. Then Kei flipped through the dictionary, to the back, then the middle, his face constricting with concentrated effort. "I have it," he said. "Tortured," he proclaimed. "Nakaji said your branch looks tortured. Blown by the wind and tortured."

Kei and I looked straight into each other's eyes for a few seconds and burst out laughing. I had to appreciate his honesty. When I was twelve, I baked my first homemade bread. I asked my sister how she liked it. My sister took a hammer and hit the loaf, hard. I can still hear the *bang! bang!* as the hammer hit the hard-as-a-brick loaf while we both laughed uncontrollably. Her attempt at humor in the face of complete failure still makes me smile. The pine branch looked equally dire, but the message had been delivered with poetic grace. No wonder Kei had been resistant to help. I cringed inwardly as his words sunk in.

Learning pine pruning through trial and error felt like physically wrestling with an idea for a while before taking it on. It took longer than it would have had Nakaji just given me a few sentences of explanation ahead of time, but the lesson stuck; it became entrenched in my being. I might also ask myself how I've learned about the most intimate matters, such as sex. Through a book? Or by trying, failing sometimes, and trying again until it felt right for me? Trial and error is an intimate learning process.

Once when I tried to ask the curator, Sadafumi, a question about gradual pruning to encourage atmosphere at the Portland Japanese Garden, he hesitated a second, then told me, "Leslie, in Japan we so rarely teach verbally, we often don't even know how to give feedback. One cannot expect to find good teachers in Japan; an apprentice must instead be the good student." I tried to hide my disappointment over Nakaji's "tortured pine" remark, so I maintained a "no biggie" look on my face. No frown, no smile. I looked over the previously fluffy pine branch, and indeed it looked bare. Back to the drawing board.

With American instincts, I asked Kei how I could improve. After much head tilting, he said I'd pruned the branch too flat instead of leaving it fluffy and mounded. He also said I wasn't pruning gracefully enough. One of the lessons I teach my beginning pruning students is, "Follow the line of a tree from trunk to outer branches. The thickness decreases gradually, from coarse to fine. Make sure that as you prune, the remaining branches transition gradually and gracefully." Kei's branches looked like a river with a delicate network of connecting streams. My branch looked like a choppy ocean on a day when the wind kept changing directions.

Kei suggested that I take out larger branches rather than pruning out many little ones. He abruptly cut off advice time by saying, "Anyway, Leslie, you must understand that Nakaji speaks in an old-fashioned, thickly accented dialect. None of us can understand him most of the time." He walked off. I took that to mean, "Don't ask me for any more translations." Nakaji led me over to work on a pine far in the back of the garden. I held back my tears, still trying to see failure as an opportunity to learn. It just felt hard to be wrong every day.

When the announcement of morning tea came, I could have kissed the mossy ground. We sat in a covered bench area while Masahiro brought over tea and a plate of large round purple plums.

I curiously picked one up to inspect. I tried to do so slowly so as not to appear greedy or impatient. I'd had enough of standing out for one day. I tasted the plum. It was not a plum, but a huge grape with seeds! Wow, the power of genetic selection. I asked myself, *Just how do the guys eat grapes and handle the seeds? Hold on a few seconds, Leslie, and watch*, I thought as I sat back quietly, eyeing them closely.

Bossman, definitely the manliest man on the crew, with the creases and wrinkles of someone who has lived life in earnest, popped the grapes one at a time into his mouth, chewed them up, swallowing the fruity part and spitting the seeds and skin out forcefully on a newspaper placed between his spread legs. *Hm, I* cringed inwardly, *I don't think I should do that.*

I watched the next senior worker, Toyoka. I thought he might be a good role model. Toyoka, new to the crew that day, was fairly tall and slender and surprisingly strong. He spoke with a beautiful clear voice that did not insist on your respect but assumed it. The men looked up to him. He was the calmest and most polite gardener I'd ever met. Toyoka slowly peeled the grapes one by one, eating the naked fruit peacefully and then gently spitting the seeds into a cloth napkin folded neatly in his hand. Okay, that seemed more doable, but peel the grapes? I'm a delicate woman, but a hungry delicate one! And I didn't happen to have a cloth napkin. The other guys followed suit, peeling each grape before eating it. I couldn't believe my eyes. They worked as hard as soldiers, and then peeled grapes while sipping green tea from tiny cups. I felt it was precisely this ability of theirs, to manage both the most delicate and the most physically demanding tasks at the same time, that enabled them to build and maintain the highest-quality gardens in the world.

- - - -

I had to make a decision, and soon. I began peeling the grapes one by one, as if this was totally normal to me instead of something my sister and I did as kids for fun. Then I popped them in my mouth one at a time, chewed them, and swallowed the whole thing, without spitting any of the seeds out. I learned how to do this while living with a Dutch family one summer on a sailboat on the Côte d'Azur. You just separate the seeds from the fruit in your mouth with your tongue, swallow the seeds first, then enjoy the fruit on its own. Tasks are carried out so traditionally in our crew that the slightest diversion got instant attention. I figured there was no harm in encouraging the "there goes the American doing another weird thing" reaction. They did stare at me but said nothing. Either they refused to react, or they knew I was up to something. Of course while this cultural interaction took place, not a word was spoken.

Usually at break time, the men conversed a bit. But that day, when the men had returned from Tokyo, the crew was quiet, even at break. Masahiro just sat staring ahead at nothing, and Toyoka slept with his colorful cloth headband over his eyes. Bossman took his shoes off before lying down and put them neatly by his side. Kei smoked his cigarettes despite my icy stares. I'd already delivered my California-style "stop smoking" speech the week before. Calmness had overtaken our group. Kei hadn't addressed me the whole day except to talk about the pine, not even to say hello in the morning. I worried I'd said something to offend him, but tried to think positive thoughts about how great it was to learn through observation. But I still wondered about my new friend's distance.

I hoped that perhaps Toyoka's presence had calmed our group. He not only pruned with grace, but he also related to others with a certain gentleness. Toyoka addressed me as "Leslie-san." No one else addressed me this way, and I noticed the difference. Each time Toyoka said "Leslie-san," I felt as though he offered me something important, something hard to place. He did this without ever speaking a sentence to me that I could understand. Toyoka did not speak English. He'd get my attention, mime his message, or speak in slow Japanese. His usage of one word, *san*, meant more to me than I could have predicted.

Continuing to prune pines after lunch, I shook branches hard to make them rustle and opened and closed my shears midair, making lots of clacking noise, so Nakaji would think I was busy at work. I was actually looking away from my branches to observe the men's pruning techniques. If I was failing so much, I needed more time to learn. I watched how Toyoka pulled his pine's needles with precise, smooth, almost soundless motions. Kei worked quickly and skillfully, but with a bit more macho yanking. With my needle-pulling style, because I was trying to keep up with the men, I probably looked like a contestant in a hot dog–eating contest, trying to eat as many as she could in a short period of time, no matter what it took. So what if I left a few half-torn needles behind; I could clean them up later!

I kept close track of the time that day. How much longer till lunch? Finally, my watch showed it was noon, the moment when everyone drops their shears and heads for the tea tray. I looked up to see Masahiro still pruning. How odd. *Why doesn't he stop?* I whined inwardly. If one person didn't quit, no one could. *Now I'll never get my snack.* I sulked over my pine, which had prickled me so much that an itchy rash had developed along my wrists. Then I noticed the men beginning to gather around Masahiro. I dared ask

----

Kei a question: "What's going on?" Kei responded, "Masahiro has been allowed to prune his first tree."

We watched in silence. Masahiro's hands shook as he tried pruning a few small branches in his insecure yet fiercely determined way. He'd had six months to observe the men's pruning while he swept, raked, and poured tea. He made one cut after another without a single specific instruction on how to do it. One after another, the men walked up to him and gave suggestions. Nakaji, eight feet away, barked his critique without moving from his spot. Precious, rare suggestions were offered. I watched silently, chastising my rumbling stomach to quiet down. I realized that despite loud commands, occasional teasing, and predictable morning reprimands, the crew in fact deeply cared about their youngest apprentice. Would we respect doctors as much if they did not endure a difficult residency where they practiced their healing work with a stressful schedule, under the eye of demanding mentors? After a brief, humble lunch, we picked up our shears and recommenced work at a furious pace.

Toward the end of the day, we did our normal fanatical cleanup routine. We raked the garden, swept the rocks, and blew leaves off the paths. Sure, the blower ruined the garden's peaceful lull, but it moved those leaves quickly and satisfied the men's need to operate a mechanized toy. We picked up every last pine needle by hand. On top of that, we cleaned up a gravel area around a sitting bench, per Nakaji's request. All he had to do was point and grunt. I knew instantly that the area wasn't up to his standards, that I would have to grab a bucket, move the rocks aside, square foot by square foot, dust the ground, and replace the rocks. For some reason I wasn't allowed to push all the rocks in one huge pile, sweep the area, and then replace them. "No," the grunt meant, "do it the traditional way!" As the last bit of the day's light faded, Nakaji commanded me to find my camera and snap a close-up photo of our handiwork. The camera made a loud click as the men gathered behind me closely, helping me focus on my important task. They had spoken but a few words to me that day, yet their silent lessons follow me to this day.

Working under
the Tree of Thorns

One Monday morning at a company pep talk, I stared at the elder patriarch of the company, Toemon Sano, while everyone else listened with their head bowed and feet separated in the at-ease position. Toemon looked to be somewhere in his eighties. Several years after I returned to California from Kyoto, I met a California landscaper who'd studied decades before with a younger Toemon, who was at the time an active leader of the company. The landscaper, a young man himself at the time, had asked Toemon why he'd taken the time to train an American. Toemon replied that, with each generation, fewer Japanese enter the physically challenging traditional craft of landscaping, and he hoped that foreigners who showed an interest might learn this art form to keep it alive. "Please share this knowledge with others," Toemon had told the California landscaper, who related this to me during a phone conversation. A tingling sensation moved down my arms to my center, where resolve waited, patiently. I never spoke directly to Toemon, but his message reached me anyway.

Later Kei told me that Toemon had said, "It is unusually warm for this time of year" and "Today would normally be the first day of frost." *Good news*, I thought sarcastically, *it's not actually as cold*

124

as it feels! I worked that week in a fleece hat, long scarf, and double gloves. Bossman teased me about my hat. He wore a thin cotton shirt. Toemon also said it felt like earthquake weather. Great, more tremblors while standing on the ladder! Then a worker stepped forward to give a short speech thanking company employees for donating money, equivalent to about three hundred dollars, for his grandmother's funeral.

We worked one last day at the temple garden, which had grown cool and humid in the mornings. Moisture penetrated my cloth boots as I ran over the squishy moss carpet, making me feel particularly chilly. The senior crew members pruned trees while Masahiro and I hauled debris to a hidden area behind the garden. The company's youngest apprentice stopped several times to instruct me on how to cut the debris into smaller pieces in order to keep the piles compact. His idea made sense, considering we only had so much space to pile the branches. But it modeled a common mistake of the inexperienced gardener. Rather than spending time tediously cutting already pruned branches, one can simply stomp hard on the pile and reduce its size in seconds. I tried to ignore Masahiro, as the men were pruning furiously and we had to move quickly to keep up. On the third lecture, I decided to obey him just to avoid another one. As I cut up branches into tiny pieces to please Masahiro, Nakaji walked by. He yelled at me, pointing to my pruning shears, and jumped on the pile of branches to show me how to reduce the pile efficiently. Masahiro happened to be in another part of the garden during this demonstration.

Eventually, Masahiro was asked to prune a tree and join the senior crew. This meant I had to clean up after everyone. The tree Masahiro climbed was huge, tangled, and more than twenty feet high, covered with fat glossy green leaves and fruit resembling lemons. I would later find out this was a yuzu tree, a richly scented, traditional, and coveted Japanese citrus. I felt jealous of Masahiro and ill spirited in general. I didn't mind the advanced workers getting to prune, but Masahiro was less experienced than I was. He'd worked only six months as a gardener, and I had seven years behind me. He had pruned his first tree only the day before. Yes, I knew that, according to Japanese craftsman hierarchy, he had seniority because he'd arrived at the company six months before me. He was supposed to prune while I cleaned up. He could tell me what to do anytime, as could anyone else who'd entered the company before I had. Yet I couldn't help but resist. It seemed stupid to do something wrong. It felt unfair that Masahiro should get to do more advanced work when I could do it better. I eventually tried to turn the situation around in my mind by transforming myself from debris girl to power girl. I carried big loads to show the men how much I could carry at once and walked as fast as I could. That way, I breathed hard and sweated a lot, but Masahiro didn't have time to instruct.

Words from my pruning friends back home occasionally worked their way into my thoughts. I imagined hearing my California mentor's stern voice: "You're lucky Masahiro didn't start instructing you on day one!" Dennis warned me to expect to have several bosses who would contradict one another. He said that obeying multiple senior workers would allow me to learn a variety of methods and would teach me how to remain calm in the face of frustration—a handy practice for those who adhere to the American motto "The client is always right." Later that day, Dennis's voice came into my thoughts again. In his fatherly way, with a sigh, he said, "Just do your best, and then some."

- - - -

I also heard Van's voice. He had been a boyfriend of mine for far too brief a time. A forest ranger in Yosemite, Van shared my dream of apprenticing in Japan. He died two years before I came to Japan, when his car crashed into a tree. After years of sobriety, he had succumbed to a one-night drinking binge, and was gone. Since then I had been determined to go to Japan for the two of us. Van was always committed to doing a little more than his share of the work. At his memorial, a Buddhist nun who'd known him said, "Van would always go the extra mile in whatever he did." I imagined us standing together, watching Masahiro up in the tall tree he was pruning.

We're here! I exclaimed to Van in my thoughts. *Isn't it amazing, even if Masahiro drives me crazy?*

Well, Van reasoned in his soft voice, *Masahiro has been working pretty hard the past few days. Come on, let's go haul some more branches.*

The last friend who joined my thoughts was Dick, a pruning buddy and landscaper. He spoke fluent Japanese and was called "Mr. Dick" in Japan. "I can't bear to correct them!" he'd muse. Dick was twenty-five years older than I, but often seemed younger in spirit. He never complained and hardly ever got tired, making me feel like I whined a lot over nothing. Dick ran beside me today, even though my crew couldn't see him. *Hey,* he said as I carried a huge tarp of debris on my back, humoring me in between breaths. *At least we're not up there, doing what he's doing.* We both looked up at Masahiro, who was busy pruning the tangled citrus tree.

Masahiro's persistence in correcting me was worrisome. I believed the men told Masahiro to give me corrections, right or wrong, because he was my *senpai*, senior worker, and I was his *kōhai*, junior worker. Learning how to mentor others is a key part of becoming a master Japanese craftsman. Masahiro surely would have bossed me around from my very first day if I had been Japanese. But perhaps my teenage boss just didn't know what to do with a thirty-five-year-old American woman.

In part, I worried that if I got put in Masahiro's slot, Nakaji might start yelling at me every morning. I wasn't sure if I could handle it. Indeed, as my time in the company increased, the boss did treat me more firmly.

Kei told me that the company had hired its first female Japanese gardener a year before I arrived. He said the men had decided to treat her as a "regular apprentice" and that "she cried every day, for a year, until she quit and got married." Is he warning me? My paranoia increased with my exhaustion. I felt I needed to hold my ground with Masahiro or I'd be the next one walking down the aisle—with a long garden tarp as my bridal veil.

I tried to do what Masahiro said. After all, I was in Japan to learn new ways, not to teach others. I'd make exceptions only when Masahiro told me to do something absolutely ridiculous. I'd hesitate just a few seconds before doing the task. I'd tilt my head to signal I was thinking about his words. I'd procrastinate by looking in my dictionary. Or I'd pretend I didn't hear him at first. I figured that obeying him eventually would be enough. I'd stomp on my pile of twigs, and then, after about six reminders, I'd prune it into a million pieces. At least while he got to prune the tree, I didn't have to obey him.

Two advanced workers took off that afternoon, so only Nakaji, Masahiro, and I were left. I realized I'd never get to do any pruning. I'd been running the debris hard for an hour, hoping for some extra time to do something more interesting. I felt defeated. Even hot coffee delivered by the monks, a real treat in green-tea country, did not lift my spirits.

Late in the day, the sun tilted against the trees, pushing clumpy dark shadows over the temple garden. Masahiro worked up in the citrus tree, getting prune-by-yell commands from Nakaji. The boss's voice boomed over the temple garden. Way up in the tree, Masahiro frantically tried to keep up with the torrent of directions from below, yelling, "*Hai! Hai! Hai!*" every few minutes. I sulked in the back of the garden, jumping hard on the pile of broken branches in frustration. Then, I heard nothing. The silence continued. I looked up. Erratic footsteps came my way. Masahiro appeared out of some shrubs and quickly walked past me with a distant, cold look on his face. His arms, exposed in short sleeves, were profusely bleeding, gashes all over them. His shirt was stained with red splotches. What I didn't know yet about a yuzu tree was that its coarse branches are covered in large, sharp thorns. It dawned on me that while Masahiro had the seeming privilege of a pruning assignment, Nakaji had given him the worst job; thorns had stabbed him at every turn.

I heard muffled noises coming from the bushes. I realized my young coworker had gone behind the debris pile to cry. I didn't feel sorry for him, though. I admired him. My tedious complaints looked ridiculous in comparison to his determination. Nature does not always play the soft role that so many weekend gardeners rightfully and peacefully enjoy. For full-time gardeners, the midafternoon sun can be brutal when the branch you have to work on doesn't happen to be in the shade, and plants carry thorns and sticky sap that attracts dirt and sometimes causes infection. So why was Masahiro determined to help make the thorny tree look more beautiful? Was his sacrifice because of a simple desire to acquire skill? Masahiro worked harder than what was necessary for him to learn. No matter how tired parents feel, they take time to read to their children at night, the adults often falling asleep first. I saw Masahiro working with heartfelt purposefulness that day, the sort of love and care that a young parent feels for his child.

Red-faced Masahiro walked slowly past me again to return to his tree. His shoulders slumped a little, but he held his gaze purposefully forward. When I saw him coming, I rushed to climb atop the debris pile and cut the branches into small pieces like mad. How could I have thought of Masahiro as my competitor? We worked as a team, the two lowest workers. We sacrificed for each other, for the garden. After he'd climbed back up the yuzu tree, I ran over and made a show of hauling the largest and thorniest branches I could find.

Slowly, the light faded to dusk. I ran debris loads while the men pruned in earnest. Warm, sticky sweat slowly trickled from my scalp down my face. I didn't stop to dry it off, or take time for sips of water, as I would have done in California. I needed to support my team. I jogged to and from the debris pile a bit more slowly than I had earlier in the day, but the bright citrus and busy craftsmen, my vibrant companions, kept me engaged. Nakaji's and Masahiro's voices echoed in the garden. My footsteps pounded down paths that had filled with dark shadows. The birds joined in with their dusk singsong, egging us on to walk the last mile.

Owning my own business over the past few years, I realized, had allowed my ego to grow too big, too fast. I was the boss of a business that had built up fairly quickly, making me feel quite proud and independent at an early time in my career. I pruned only small trees and plants, and rarely had to weed or get my hands in the dirt. I offered design advice to help the garden develop gracefully, and seemed to have a knack for dealing with all kinds of clients. In general, I was paid well and my clients offered only praise. True, I strived to do the highest-quality work for every garden. But most of my clients couldn't tell the difference between good and excellent work. My mentor warned his pruning students to remain humble. "In America you are some of the best pruners. In Japan you are beginners." I had become like a plant that had been given too much fertilizer. When a plant is overfed, it indeed grows fast. It will burst out with fresh, green, vibrant foliage. But while a heavily fertilized plant will grow big, it tends not to flower.

Shifting Perspectives
in the Landscape

Rain pounded the truck's front window as we splashed through drenched concrete streets. I wore a raincoat, plastic *jikatabi*, and my anti-dribble terry cloth tennis cuffs. I'd sweat in my sealed plastic suit, but a fleece sweater under my coat would wick the sweat away from my skin. Over time, moisture would line the inside of my rain jacket, but my skin would stay fairly dry. Expensive polyurethane breathable rain gear lasted about ten minutes on a gardener's rain day. I noticed that two of my *senpai* still wore their thin cloth *jikatabi* in the rain! "Why don't they buy plastic rain boots?" I asked Kei. Knowingly, he responded, "To make excellent gardeners."

We worked along a wide hillside garden. A building looked up the gently sloping hill, while evergreen trees screened surrounding neighbors. Upon our arrival, I traced a cross over my heart and muttered a few prayers to "His Mostly Ignored" for our safe passage, given Nakaji's driving speed. The first thing I noticed was a fifteen-foot dead pine tree, completely brown, in the middle of a mostly green landscape. Early in the morning, the men moved as quickly as ants whose hills had just been toppled, surrounding the brown tree with ropes and digging tools. I had to quickly assess the situation, guessing three steps ahead so I was in the right position, with tool in hand at the right time. Working with the men was a codependent's dream job! The company hierarchy kept the momentum going. No one stopped to discuss a plan. You do as you're told, or guess and accept the consequences. Kei started up a chain saw. I eyed his traditional boots made of thin, soft cloth near the spinning blade.

The men grabbed ropes and frantically moved around the pine to pull shrubs out of the way. I attempted to tie away a wide aucuba shrub when Masahiro ran over, saying, "No, no, no!" waving a three-foot rope he held in his hand to let me know he thought I'd used the wrong size. His rope looked too short to circle the shrub, yet obediently I dropped my hand, stood back, and let him tie the shrub his way. Sure enough, his cord failed in length, but he kept trying to tie it in different places, each attempt more unsuccessful than the last. If anything goes wrong while the ants are marching ahead, it throws everyone off, like a multicar freeway crash. With Masahiro's inability to tie one shrub, everyone else screeched to a halt.

Toyoka rushed over, yanked the original long rope out of my hand, dangled it in front of Masahiro's face, yelled at him in earnest, and then tied the shrub exactly as I had intended. I felt triumph wash over me along with a splatter of rain against my cheek. Much to my astonishment, Masahiro turned to me, bowed deeply, and said in the most humble manner imaginable for a sixteen-year-old, "Gomen-nasai, gomen-nasai" (Sorry, sorry). He'd never apologized to me directly before. Sure, I felt more experienced than Masahiro, superior in my gardening knowledge. But he did the most painstaking jobs, worked faster and longer, and never complained: he was a young Japanese craftsman. I still felt like an

American pruner who practiced gardening in Kyoto. My intense satisfaction at being right melted into a puddle near his muddy *jikatabi*. I marveled at how he could maintain such maturity in the face of humiliating failure, with yells coming from every direction. I renewed my vow to obey him when expected, knowing I'd break it soon enough.

Masahiro climbed the dead pine to tie a rope to its top and then scrambled down. A second later, Kei sliced the base of the tree with his chain saw while the three of us pulled on the ropes, conveniently keeping the tree from falling on Kei. The tree crashed to the ground, sending a thousand brown pine needles in every direction. I said a silent "thank you" that the pine did not fall on my new friend. All this occurred before 8:00 a.m. And Masahiro and I would pile eight truckloads of debris into the bamboo grove in back of the garden before lunch, in the rain. I normally fill my truck bed one time on a California pruning day.

As the day progressed, Nakaji yelled from various locations as he tried to keep his litter, scattered all around the property, under control. Most of the time, it was raining so hard, his booming voice came across as though over a bad phone connection. There was no real way to stay completely dry. I tried to be strong like the advanced workers and ignore the chilly clamminess inside my suit. I prayed for lunch. Kei began softly singing a variety of Beatles songs. "Yesterday, all my troubles seemed so far away," he sang in tune just out of Nakaji's earshot.

Between Nakaji's booming voice and Kei's soft humming, I had a little time to consider the design theory of contrasting elements in the garden. I looked around. The advanced pruners were drastically opening up a huge row of backdrop trees on top of the hill, while

----

Masahiro and I tediously sheared long azalea hedges down below. Contrasting elements help heighten drama and direct the eye toward certain highlights in the garden. The choppy backdrop trees might be ignored, which is all the better, as a neighboring building might lurk behind them. But pruning the azaleas into a clean form may draw the eye into the central area of the garden and cause it to hover on the most tended area. If both the azaleas and the backdrop trees were pruned in detail, the viewer would not know where to look. My clients often want all their plants finely pruned. It's hard to convince them to leave some plants less tended. I ask them to consider a Rembrandt portrait. He painted faces with such detail, one can see wrinkles and creases in the lips. And yet the hair of his sitter might be a thick, dark brushstroke fading into a black background. The contrast in these paintings emphasizes the personality of the sitter rather than a potentially distracting background.

Backdrop trees I liken to the chorus in an opera. So that we can hear the power of the soprano, the chorus sings more generally as a group. My mom studied opera in her youth and commented, "I respect the chorus. The prima donna could not shine without them. They play an important role, yet with little applause." In the general pruning of backdrop trees, the art of restraint holds as much importance as skillfully detailing the azaleas.

Many years after I returned home from Kyoto, Kei came to visit me in my Berkeley Hills home. He offered to prune the California native garden I'd created in my front yard. He spent a few minutes on my California redbud and even less time on a pink-flowering currant, and then devoted three hours to pruning a non-native boxwood shrub off to the left of the garden, hiding trash cans, into a refined rectangle. I'd always just left it general and messy. I asked him afterward, "Why did you spend so much time on that ridiculous hedge when the focus of the garden is the native plants?" He said, "Step back, Leslie. Take a look at the scene. Now that the lines of the hedge are so symmetrical and clean, don't you notice the wild beauty of the native plants more?" Like a beautiful frame around a naturalized landscape painting, the clean boxwood hedge did make the native scene look more wild and powerful.

I tried to focus on my azalea hedge while Nakaji's voice boomed nearby. I thought I'd try Kei's trick and sang, "There are places I remember, all my life, though some have changed."

Nakaji yelled, very close by, "*Dame*, Leslie, *dame!*" and I saw him pointing at me from down below. He made a "slice your head off by the neck" hand gesture and pointed to my hedge, I assumed instructing me to lower a particular lump in the hedge to my right. I hesitated, daringly so. I knew I should obey Nakaji, yet I felt that pruning off the sizable lump would create a gaping hole, revealing a bunch of deadwood from the internal part of the shrub. Sure, azaleas sprout back from hard pruning, but I'd never prune a plant so hard that the viewer could see exposed deadwood. If such a reduction was needed, I'd lower the plant slowly, year by year, allowing internal green sprouting to occur until a desired height was reached. I pruned the azalea as far as I dared, with only about a quarter inch of green leaves left to hide a tangle of brittle, dead branches. Still, Nakaji came closer and yelled in Japanese, "Not enough!" He made dramatic hand gestures, motioning for me to cut it lower. I looked at it, and then at him, but held my shears midair. Nakaji stormed off, motioning for me to follow him.

I ran over to where he stopped, far away from my hedge, near the bottom of the hill, just in front of a large viewing window. He

----

bellowed, "*Mite!*" (Look!) I took in the scene. At the top of the hill, a long row of generally pruned trees made up the backdrop, and a series of even longer azalea hedges formed the midsection of the garden. Then I saw it. My azalea sat toward the middle of the other surrounding hedgerows. When looked at from afar, it had a big lump in it, unlike any of the other hedgerows surrounding it. It ruined the lovely, repetitive lines of the azalea hedges together. My mentor's voice popped up, "When deciding how to prune a plant, stand at the viewing point, not the easiest place to stand." I had failed to remember a basic lesson. I had forgotten that the azalea, and each individual plant in the garden, played a small part in a cohesive scene, viewed from the lower building windows. I also surmised an additional reason the men had choppily opened the thick backdrop trees all morning. On a sunny day, the gaping holes, small from a distance, would fill with dappled light, creating an enchanting effect, like lights streaming down on a stage. Up close, the easiest place to stand, the cuts looked brutal, but from the viewing point, the stubs remained invisible. I returned to my shrub and sliced off its hunchback, creating an ugly gaping hole that was invisible to viewers down below.

After I'd smoothed out the rest of the azalea shrubs, I proudly ran over to Nakaji, who stood next to a corner of the building, and asked good-naturedly, "*Tsugi wa?*" (What next?) He pointed to a small area of large, rounded pebbles next to the corner of a building and signaled me to push them aside, rinse them off, and put them back. He liked clean pebbles. The only problem was that the rocks lay beneath a gutter's spout. In the pouring rain, water flowed out of the spout like a mini Niagara Falls. "*Hai!*" I'd decided in the span of a few seconds that even if I'd get wet, I'd clean those rocks better

----

than any male Japanese gardener ever could. I concentrated on my task, cursing a little while water poured onto my head and clothing, and continued to work until I worried that everyone had forgotten about me. Nakaji came over near lunch and looked down. I'd dug a two-foot hole, removed dirty pebbles within a large concrete drainage ditch, and built next to me a small pyramid of clean rounded stones. Nakaji looked at the hole, the pyramid, and then me with a startled expression. "Enough!" he exclaimed. "*Hai!*" I responded, drenched, with a smile, and began filling the hole with the clean pebbles.

On days when everything seemed like a struggle, I gave myself tidbits to look forward to. As I stood under Niagara Falls, I promised myself, "You can go to the *sentō*, the Japanese bath, after work. There you will soak in the warm Jacuzzi and sit in the hot sauna!" Further on into my apprenticeship I pledged, "You can read a mystery book instead of studying Japanese" or even, "You can go to your room and cry as much as you want; just don't do it in front of the guys!" This was my last-ditch effort to keep the men from seeing me cry when I got really frustrated, which happened only twice. I wasn't even close on that long azalea hedge day.

During lunch the rain finally let up. While we drank hot green tea and ate lunch, the skies began to clear. I dried my hands and took a moment to show the men photos of my pruning work back in California. They seemed most interested in the two photos displaying my teachers. Toyoka pointed to my mentor, Dennis, standing in front of a group of about fifteen pruning volunteers, and said in surprising English, "He has a shiny head," noting Dennis's receding hairline. Everyone laughed. I think this was their way of appreciating someone older and wiser. They took a quick look at my

----

bonsai teacher, white-haired Masahara Imazumi, in his backyard, surrounded by his famous bonsai plants. The craftsmen mused over Mas's bonsai landscape. "That's in Japan, right?" I responded, "No, it's in California!" But they kept repeating the same question. Nakaji asked many questions, and Kei graciously translated, even though I worried he'd rather nap. "Where do your mother and father live? Do gardens in America have Japanese pines? Have you been to the Grand Canyon?" Nakaji laughed at all my responses.

Despite my desire to spend the rest of the afternoon chatting with the men, at 1:00 p.m. on the dot we got back on the garden track. Nakaji led me to a small camellia shrub and gestured at me to prune it. The deep green plant was only waist high and stretched hardly wider than my hips. As opposed to a thick hedge, the camellia was see-through, but the outline was a bit messy, covered in small, thick, glossy leaves. It was *Camellia japonica*, the same plant found in gardens all over the United States. Thousands of hybrids have been carefully imported, propagated, and distributed in America for more than two centuries. I'd met a famous Japanese American nurseryman, Toichi Domoto, while pruning old pines on his property with several other volunteer pruning students. Domoto gave a fascinating oral history interview to the UC Berkeley Bancroft Library. But he didn't talk much the day I met him. He just watched us working on his huge styled pines from his porch chair, in the shade.

The reason I've never forgotten one of the smaller plants I ever pruned in Kyoto is because, besides the pines, this was the first plant I'd been asked to naturally prune by Nakaji. "Sacrifice, and you'll get the reward," my Japanese American teacher regularly told us. Perhaps because of my extra effort cleaning the stones under the drainpipe, Nakaji decided to give me a special project. Pruning the

- - - -

camellia allowed me a chance to show off the pruning techniques I'd learned in California.

There are general pruning tricks to keeping a plant looking natural while styling, such as pruning at intersections of branches bigger than a chopstick, rather than leaving unsightly stubs. Another trick is to prune anywhere along a smaller branch, just above leaf buds, to spur on reactive growth and create a thick hedge effect. Another is to study the poetic version of any given plant or tree at its mature height, untouched. Camellias grow generally in a rounded, mounding form, with strong horizontal branches pulled down by masses of leaves. Camellia branches thin out when mature so that light gently penetrates their canopy. The little Kyoto camellia seemed to sparkle as I reached down, my sharp shears ready to trim its dainty branches. I am not the only one showing sacrifice; trees tolerate quite a bit of risk in allowing me to trim and slice them year after year.

I pruned only a few branches to lighten the foliage of the little camellia and neaten its rank outline, even when I still left its form naturally undulating. Light penetrated its rich canopy, creating a dappled effect on the leaves and then fell onto the moss below, shimmering.

My Japanese crew worked so hard and so long for a monthly salary, acting as though life would be unworthy to them unless they displayed a willingness to sacrifice their comfort and time every hour of the day. I completed the shrub in about five minutes and returned to shearing. But I remember the tiny shrub and the effort it took to get to it.

Toward the end of the day, Nakaji reached a new world record for yelling. Evidently we still had plenty to do. I heard heavy footsteps headed in my direction, and I upped the pace of my pruning shears to a mad frenzy. Nakaji's voice commanded my attention: "Leslie!" I jumped and looked up to see him glaring at me, pointing to the back of the garden with his amazingly clean white glove. He took off, and I had to run to keep up with him. We came to a group of camellias. My eyes darted around, searching for a problem before the command could be given. Nakaji stood over a camellia shrub with unusually delicate leaves, a half-inch wide, and white flowers with only about five petals to each flower, a single-petal camellia. He snapped off a small-leafed branch with a blossom on its end and held it a half-inch from my nose.

I'm not blind, you know. I can see it! I thought, staring at the branch. He said, ever so gruffly, in English, "Tea." I realized then that the branch was *Camellia sinensis*, whose young leaves are used to make both black and green tea. For years I had been trying, without success, to find one of these plants in East Bay nurseries. Nakaji held the flower not for me to see but to smell. He waved the flower under my nostrils impatiently. I took in a deep whiff. Sure enough, it smelled sweet and familiar, strikingly similar to the Darjeeling tea that he and I enjoyed. "*Tabero!*" (Eat!) he commanded anew. I obeyed, taking a nibble. Eww, bitter! I had to spit it out fast. Nakaji laughed and laughed, tossing the twig back into the garden. I guess he couldn't resist his little joke. *Camellia sinensis* is not edible. We looked into each other's eyes for a few seconds and smiled. Then I ran back to continue shearing before Bossman could order me to do something else.

On our way home, Kei told me that Nakaji, who worked just as hard and fast as any twenty-year-old craftsman, was not in his fifties, as I'd assumed. He was actually seventy-three years old! Well. He did act gruff and stiff at times, and also wise and strong.

- - - -

Kei added that Nakaji worked every Sunday in the gardens of his personal clients. My eyes must have widened at this point in the conversation. Kei looked smug, and I could sense him thinking, "You'll never fully comprehend the Japanese craftsman." I decided to skip going to the bathhouse, even though I felt crusted in dried, salty sweat. I walked directly home, my body heavy with fatigue, and fell onto my futon, soon entering a deep, sweet sleep as I did after most long garden days.

Shearing with Emotions

I always felt safe with Kei in the driver's seat. The two of us had been instructed to drive over early to work at a temple, Sainenji, while the other men worked at another project till midday. Kei's compact features remained still, except for the back-and-forth movement of his head to check the mirrors. I had the unusual opportunity to sit in the front seat, with a panoramic view of Kyoto's streets. I looked in every possible direction, my torso twisting right and left, sneaking glances at the new man in charge. I wanted to ask a million questions, but I resisted, allowing Kei his concentration and peace.

I'd lived in Kyoto for two months and had finally begun to feel accustomed to my routine. My muscles felt firmer. Between eating out nightly and using the bathhouse for all bathing, I'd pared down household chores to sleep, breakfast, and lunch prep. I tried to quiet thoughts of casual dinners with Berkeley friends or seeing Taylor on my porch playing the guitar, waiting for me to come home. In general, my heart had sunk into hibernation mode. I enjoyed the familiar companionship of the quiet, hardworking craftsmen. Sharing work with others felt as intimate as sharing words. So with few sentences spoken, I'd grown close to the men. My landlord often got home late, and I enjoyed the silence in my Kyoto house when I got home, as it allowed me to fall asleep quickly. I had little energy to think of anything besides trying to keep up with the craftsmen in the increasingly cool Kyoto gardens.

So I was quite surprised when Taylor called one night and said, "I found a ticket to Kyoto in a few weeks. Should I come for a visit?" "Of course!" I'd said instinctively. Kei and I drove toward the temple garden the day before Taylor's visit, and I worried that I should have waited until after my apprenticeship ended to have my boyfriend come out. I'd been warned by my mentor that if I took vacation during my apprenticeship, it would set me apart from my Japanese coworkers. But that sounded to me like a male workaholic's suspicions. I felt passionate about the gardens and passion for those I loved; the two held equal weight.

I called my new American friend Maya, who had lived in Kyoto many years, for advice. "Do you think it would be such a big deal if I took a week off for a visit with my boyfriend? I would have time to tour other gardens. Would the crew really care?" I asked. "Yes," she replied bluntly. "Such a request would be unheard of for a Japanese worker," she had to add. Damn. I'd never worked so hard and felt like such a quitter. Yet how could I say no to my boyfriend's desire to see me halfway through my stay? I missed him. I tepidly asked the head of Uetoh for permission to take a seven-day holiday and forged ahead with my plans, hoping the men would understand. I wanted to see Taylor, and I also needed some time off to mentally prepare for the winter's approaching chill.

The cold, which was increasing daily, had me freaked out. It was one thing to write to friends about pruning pines in a lightning storm, watching soap operas on the built-in Japanese sauna television screens, or sipping udon noodle soup covered in locally picked wild mountain vegetables. It was another to bother my friends about the cold numbing of my hands and feet every morning. My thoughts began to sound like a scratchy broken record: *Why can't Masahiro leave me alone? When is break? Why doesn't my boyfriend call?* I never once heard a complaint from the men. Even my banal curse words—Darn. Shoot! Fudge.—had to be held in check. Maya had explained to me that Kei got only twelve days of holiday a year. I heard he'd asked for a week off right after my holiday request and that the supervisors had said no. I once asked the men gamely, "What is your favorite holiday? New Year's? Some other particular holiday?" They laughed but wouldn't respond. Finally Kei translated for Nakaji, who said, "You silly girl. We don't care about the holiday's meaning. We love New Year's because we get our longest vacation of the year, a full five days off!"

In California I worked in the gardens four days a week, did office work on Fridays, and always took a full weekend off. Plus, I allowed myself a four-day weekend once a month in addition to a month or so of vacation a year. *I just need some time off*, I reasoned with myself, feeling guilty about my Kyoto holiday. I couldn't feel sure, but I sensed the men becoming more distant as my holiday approached. For weeks, Kei still remained fairly quiet around me. What did he and the other men think? I could not guess, nor did I feel comfortable asking. I anticipated Taylor's visit like a child waiting for Christmas.

I continued to ponder Kei's silence. I asked Maya if perhaps I'd offended him by asking too many questions. She reassured me. "Japanese men," she explained, "become quiet as you get to know them." Yet I suspected otherwise. "Any other reason you can think of?" I prodded her. "Leslie, silence is comfortable to Japanese men. Kei feels you are becoming a friend, so he is becoming more himself. He'd only talk to you a lot if he considered you just a polite acquaintance." That made me feel better for about an hour. Then I'd slip back into paranoid thoughts: *He's definitely giving me the silent treatment. He's mad.* In my family, silence meant anger. Silence equaled the unspoken message, "You pushed me too far" or "I'm upset about something, and you have to figure it out."

Over the past few weeks, I had noticed my thoughts straying more and more toward Kei. It seemed natural for us to get along. We both obsessed about nature and our gardens. We'd both attended college and studied horticulture. We knew by heart Helen Reddy songs—he to study English, me because I was a child of young hippie parents. Despite our academic backgrounds, both of us had chosen to do physical design work. We loved pruning, touching the plants directly. We both understood the monetary and physical sacrifice of working on behalf of nature.

I thought back to the day when Kei showed me his small patio filled with thirty or so delicate woodland plants, known as accent plants in bonsai. "I like pruning pines," he'd explained to me, "but I most enjoy working with the plants that grow in the mountains." That was the moment when I felt I'd found a special friend. I had never met a man, particularly someone so macho, who loved tender accent plants, often placed in bonsai shows next to specimen bonsai to help viewers imagine a certain time of year or a particular scene. Kei's two-inch-tall fern in a misshapen tiny pot might have suggested a wild woodland scene; a cluster of fresh grass in a half-inch-high pot, a meadow. Tiny

----

flowers suggested springtime. The pots of his plants were so small that Kei would have had to care for them carefully, watering them sometimes twice a day.

As the weeks passed, I realized I was thinking about Kei more than what was usual for a woman with a boyfriend she loved back home. I told myself at first that I was thinking about him only because I was lonely. Yet the more I tried to shove thoughts of Kei out of my mind, the more they found their way back. A forcefully pruned plant reacts with taller, stronger, more numerous sprouts. Only with skillfully selected, delicate cuts will a plant's reactionary tendencies diminish over time.

Yet with my boyfriend's imminent arrival, I had to face something I'd been trying not to think about. Just before I'd left Berkeley, Taylor asked if he thought we should leave open the possibility of dating other people while I lived in Japan. At the time, I'd fallen into tears and said—in an unhelpful, angry sort of way—absolutely not, that I loved him. He assured me that he loved me too, and that he'd asked only because he wondered if I needed some space. Then he'd gotten upset that I'd gotten angry, and I'd left the next day with both of us feeling out of sorts. It was not the farewell I'd pictured. I'd tried to eliminate that conversation from my mind over the past eight weeks in Japan. But just like with weeds, when we try to ignore them, hoping the more desirable plants will take over, they just get bigger and spread.

As I wondered about Kei, I occasionally felt justified in thinking, *Fine, if my boyfriend wants to bring up dating other people, then I'll consider it.* I was afraid of being alone, and I felt so tired and confused. The day before Taylor arrived, I sat on the edge of a garden fence between two starkly different gardens, one I knew well and another hardly at all, not knowing how anyone felt about me. In my loneliness at the time, I could hardly admit this to myself.

I found it a little odd that Nakaji had sent Kei and me off to work alone together at the temple garden the day before my boyfriend's visit. Why did he choose this day in particular? Had he also noticed that Kei had grown particularly distant with me ever since I'd mentioned my boyfriend was coming? He was older and wiser than either of us. I understood Nakaji's commands without him speaking a single sentence in my language. I could almost guess his daily directions. Could he do the same with me?

Once we arrived at Sainenji, Kei, my boss for the morning, let me take a few minutes to look around. The property stretched wide. It grew lush with strolling gardens and private courtyards. It offered burial grounds and buildings for relatives to relax and meet. Kei told me later that visitors wandered about the gardens after funerals, and that the monks lived in some of the buildings, looking out at private courtyards from inner rooms. He instructed me on how to prune the dead tips off hundreds of slender reeds inside a small courtyard garden surrounded on three sides by four-foot-deep *engawa* decks.

One could open the sliding doors of particular rooms and look out over the *engawa* into the courtyards—much like sitting on a dock and looking out onto a lake. The monks and their guests could feel the presence of the garden this way while still being protected by a roof. I'd never had a chance to sleep in a room with *engawa*, where the walls could be opened up completely onto the garden. If the monks slept this way, could they feel the early morning dew? Feel the drop in temperature just before an evening

----

shower or see with perfect clarity shooting stars while snuggled under covers? I had no idea if anyone ever took advantage of the opportunity to open up the walls at night, but I liked the idea.

In the courtyard, we worked amid pines, camellias, azaleas, reeds, and ferns. It felt like a soft, wild forest, with sheared plants formalizing the scene. No one plant was allowed to grow too big and dominate the space or shade out smaller plants, nor were any plants pruned so tightly that the scene looked miniaturized. The courtyard felt like a lovely spot in nature, even though every section of it was maintained carefully, probably pruned and cleaned once or twice a year.

Japanese garden pruning is a unique combination of the pruner's skill and the plant's spirited growth. A proficient pruner not only learns pruning and horticulture but also studies how plants look in nature. The pruned garden plant should reflect the same species in its native habitat. It should not look like a made-up form or an animal. I love biking past a certain hedge in Berkeley that is regularly clipped to look like a squirrel. It always makes me laugh. This pruning technique is called topiary and has little to do with aesthetic pruning.

To encourage a natural look in the garden plant, the aesthetic pruner nudges the plant toward its natural form but doesn't force this look in a harsh, manipulative way. I might want a tree branch to lean a certain way—for example, toward a front door to guide the garden visitor down the front path. But if the plant keeps growing away from the door because of sunlight in that location or an out-of-control irrigation system, I might change my mind and let it grow into a tall overhead tree. As a pruner, I am the silent assistant to the plants, not their demanding style-maker.

CUTTING BACK

I once pruned a small pine at the Berkeley cooperative Cal Sailing Club. I spent four hours, along with two fellow volunteers from my pruning club, pruning and styling a five-foot tree that had previously been styled for years by an infamous Japanese windsurfer. The next week, I happened to be sitting on some steps right next to the pine when a longtime member of our club said, "You know, I've never noticed that pine before. But it just looks beautiful." I remained silent. An aesthetically pruned tree will shine, but it will never appear just-pruned.

My morning task in the Kyoto temple felt rather mundane. I snipped off the browned tips of hundreds of reed plants to allow the viewer to focus on the green, the living. As my fist closed on the handle of the pruning shears to cut one reed, my eyes would already be searching for the next. This process helped me maintain maximum speed and focus. Then I'd find myself wondering about what Taylor and I could do next week, wishing Kei would work nearby so I wouldn't feel so alone. The pruning helped me keep my mind on the garden, and each physical snip allowed for a certain emotional release.

Finally at lunch Kei and I sat together in the truck with a pile of individually wrapped monk snacks between us. We listened to the radio as we sampled our green tea and sweets. When we'd both consumed enough sugar, I pushed the pile of leftover snacks toward Kei so he'd take them home. Then he pushed them toward me. I felt guilty about my vacation tomorrow, so I pushed them back. Kei looked at me sternly and once again pushed them over to my side. He won. I didn't want him mad at me. And Kei was the boss.

A radio DJ kept up a frantic monologue on the radio, pretending in a funny accent that he was a crazy Japanese housewife. We couldn't stop laughing. I found myself thinking how much I'd miss Kei the following week. I felt I needed to say something to him, like, "You are an important part of my life now." Nakaji had given us this precious opportunity, after all.

"I'll miss working with the crew," I said. It was all I could manage. It was my apology to him, just in case he was secretly upset about the visit. Silence ensued. The monks brought us bright green tea in handleless ceramic cups. I swirled the powdery green residue from the tea in my beige cup. It reminded me of our frequent tornados in Oklahoma. My father would watch the news on the television set upstairs, prepared to join the rest of the family if the weather map showed a dangerous funnel moving too close to our part of town. Scared, I asked my mom why Dad didn't join us in the tiny cellar. She responded, "He's protecting us." I sipped my chaotically spinning tea. It warmed my spirit a little. I thought about how, despite Kei's silence, he remained my closest friend in Kyoto.

After lunch, the rest of the crew joined us. I was determined to refocus on my work and away from my emotions. I spent the rest of the afternoon shearing hedges all around the property while the men worked with vigor. In general, I disliked shearing, a process of making hundreds of tiny blunt cuts that spur the plant into reacting with three hundred tiny shoots, creating a shrub. I preferred gentle pruning to reactionary work, even if purposeful. I mentally tried to deduce why *tamamono*, the rounded sheared shrubs common in Kyoto, existed in Japanese gardens at all. *Aren't the gardens meant to imitate nature, not Disneyland?* I'd quip in my head. After having visited dozens of gardens in Kyoto, I'd observed that,

----

151

contrary to popular American belief, most Japanese gardens were not sheared. Certainly, there existed some *tamamono* in almost all the gardens I visited, but always in moderation. The question remained: were sheared plants an inherent element in the Japanese garden palette?

And why did Americans think Japanese gardens were completely sheared, miniaturized landscapes? I believe this misunderstanding arose in part because sheared, miniaturized gardens do exist in Japan. When American tourists come to Japan, they look for and find what they expect: the most intensely sheared gardens of Kyoto. They take photos of these landscapes because Americans tend to be drawn to what is fascinating, not subtle. They'd pass by the subtler gardens, which look like common forest scenes. Then they bring home photos of sheared gardens, the branches held up by posts, stone lanterns, and metal statues of cranes—anything that looked interesting. The misconception that Japanese gardens are contrived, rather than some of the most natural-looking native landscapes in the world, continues. Photos of naturalized gardens often look boring. Everything is green.

On the positive side, *tamamono* bring elegance, formality, and a soothing quality to gardens. When viewed in person, they look more natural than in photos. I've wondered if they might be used to represent distant plants, as one might find in landscape paintings. Artists often blur the plants in the background of paintings to create an illusion of distance to the viewer. Sheared azaleas might mimic this effect, making a plant in a small garden appear distant.

Many consider the beauty of an azalea to lie in the flower. By shearing the azalea, the pruner is creating more reactionary sprouts, and therefore more flowers. One might theorize that the desire for a flower show is the purpose of shearing.

Almost without exception, my eighty or so California clients that I visit once a year or so feel more comfortable with loose, natural pruning than with formal shearing. They want their garden to look as though it comes straight from the forest—a relaxed, free California feeling. Yet most lack the powerful drama of the gardens I witnessed in Kyoto. I shear only one shrub in California. One of my clients, Maggie, whom I've known for more than nineteen years, serves me tea with cookies each time I visit her. She mesmerizes me with her stories of living in Japan during the World War II reconstruction period. She felt such admiration for the Japanese people she met there, who showed "graciousness and resilience in the face of hardship." For her I pull out my stiff American pruning shears and neatly trim two of her English vase-shaped hedges as requested.

After pumping my arms on my millionth *tamamono*, I came upon a hedge that was horribly flat and square instead of rounded. I had already worked myself into a sour mood after so many hedges, and this square shrub grated on my nerves. It stood next to a gray utility shed way in the back of the garden and looked like a Tinkertoy. I pruned it nice and flat. Masahiro came over and corrected me. "No, no, Leslie, no." Unlike Kei, who was self-assured, Masahiro spurted his commands out, sounding frantic and desperate.

He spent nearly five minutes explaining that I had incorrectly pruned the square hedge. I needed to prune it into a "square shape," going so far as to outline the shape of a square in the dirt with a stick. *Thank you, Masahiro, for the visual prop!* But I'd already pruned it square. I looked up the Japanese word for square, *shikaku*, in my dictionary, and repeated the word to him, emphasizing my understanding of his instruction, even though I'd already understood ten minutes earlier. But each time I began shearing it square again, he'd begin drawing square shapes on the ground anew. Finally, I could stand it no longer and went off in search of Kei. Maybe he'd understand.

I felt so annoyed at this point that when I found Kei, I did what I'd never allowed to happen. I let a bit of anger slip out. Not at him specifically, just toward Japanese craftsmen in general. I said, "If the Japanese really want to shear hedges so perfectly, why don't they use electric hedge trimmers like American gardeners? They are faster and easier to handle." I thought this was a doubly clever statement given that *karikomi*, the traditional handheld hedge shears, were not only slow but such a bitch to maneuver with their wobbly handles. Kei, understandably, appeared peeved by my interruption.

After talking to Masahiro for a while, he admitted that Masahiro had indeed gone too far in his need for the square shrub to look perfect. But because one shrub had been pruned so exactly, the rest of the hedges in the area had to be done the same way, by everyone in the crew. He told me this in a way that insinuated that all the extra work was my fault. Then, in his masterful fashion of appearing calm outside even when he was agitated, Kei pointed to an azalea shrub, told me I hadn't pruned it well enough, and walked off. He completely ignored me the rest of the day and would hardly even look at me.

I felt horrible. I hated the anal square shrub. I felt angry at Masahiro, but mostly I blamed myself. I knew I'd gone too far with my friend Kei. No one ever expressed anger to anyone above them in the hierarchy. And I'd done it on the day before I was about to get seven days off in a row, more than he'd ever had in his whole time with Uetoh. And the day before I was to meet up with my California love.

Soon the whole crew joined us, and indeed the whole area apparently needed redoing. The afternoon of the last day before vacation, the angry god of "thou shalt take no extra days off as a Japanese gardener" had arrived. No one said a negative word or teased me about my impending vacation, which made me more suspicious. They just sheared furiously until afternoon break as though we were competing against some invisible team on the "Iron Garden" show.

Toward the end of the day, Nakaji told me firmly to shear a huge, round azalea *tamamono* near the front entrance to the hospital. "Prune just a little," he said simply in Japanese. I took this to mean, "Don't take too long on this one." I worked quickly and debated internally whether I'd done a good enough job. But I reminded myself, "Do as you're told," and whipped through the area. Bossman returned to inspect. He looked intently for a few seconds, and then went into a crazy reprimand, yelling loudly, gesticulating dramatically, grabbing my Japanese hedge trimmers and pruning the azalea much more neatly than I'd done in my haste. He hesitated only to glare at me silently and wait for me to respond.

I stared back, dumbstruck. I'd never been yelled at that forcefully and loudly. I felt less than emotionally prepared that day. And I'd tried so hard to do the right thing and yet apparently had done it wrong. I tried to look respectful, as Masahiro did when he got

----

reprimanded. Yet I couldn't understand how I could have so misunderstood him. Worst of all, I began sensing in the back of my
mind that maybe the worst scenario had arrived. I felt my temples
tighten and restrict. I felt on the verge of crying.

Jennifer, one of the young American women I'd met at Kei's
party, had been through a much lengthier Japanese apprenticeship
than mine, studying fine art restoration for years. She said she had
decided that, no matter how hard things got, she would not cry in
front of her boss. When Jennifer told me this story, I had decided
that, as another woman, I needed to model her inner strength. I
tried to focus on how being yelled at was considered a compliment
because it meant I was being treated like everyone else. Still, while
I began pruning the shrub over again, very carefully this time, I had
to focus very intently on the smooth slicing noises of the *karikomi*
blades in order to keep my emotions in check. This is a compliment,
Leslie, *slice*, a compliment, *slice*.

Then the men showed up to help me finish the azalea. They acted
as though they just wanted to help so we could leave on time, the
sun sitting near the horizon. Yet squeezing back tears, I suspected
they felt sorry for me. *How dare you help me!* I thought. *Just because
I'm a woman, and an American, you think I can't handle Nakaji yelling
at me.* Even though this was true. I wanted to keep up with the men,
but they appeared determined to show I never could. I wanted to
tell them to go away, but I knew that humiliating tears would spill
out if I spoke one word. So I kept silent while they clipped furiously
beside me. As the last tiny lump on the smooth azalea was snipped,
I made one more effort to keep my moist eyes from spilling over by
promising myself that I could go to the bathroom and cry as much
as I wanted right before we left. "Just hold on," I told myself.

As soon as everyone began loading the trucks, I casually walked—like it was no big deal—to the one place no crazy Japanese male gardener could find me: the women's bathroom. Earlier I had found this particularly fabulous female-only bathroom with a heated toilet seat. Warmth, comfort, solitude. While I occupied my comforting seat, it occurred to me that if I did cry, I'd have red, puffy eyes when I returned to the group. So I altered my strategy. *Just wait till you get home tonight to cry.* I couldn't sit there too long, or it would be obvious I was upset, so I reluctantly jogged back to the men.

With the truck finally loaded, the sun setting behind a sleek, sheared background shrub, Nakaji decided to hose down a path leading to the front door of the temple entrance. I wondered if I'd ever get home that night. We stood watching for quite a while. Five minutes passed, then eight, then ten. I silently willed him, *Please finish so I can take my vacation, please.* He watered one square-foot concrete spot for literally five minutes. I looked at Kel, who stood next to me, still as a mannequin. I turned my head toward him slightly and gave him my best big-eyes, "I can't believe he's so slow" expression. He whispered, "This is Nakaji's me-di-ta-tion," placing slow emphasis on the syllables, speaking ever so close to my ear. We smiled at each other. After about fifteen minutes of brutal, enforced patience, Nakaji gave Masahiro a terse hand signal while still keeping his eyes on the end of the hose. The youngest apprentice, who had his eyes fixed on Nakaji, his hand hovering over the water spigot, flipped the knob to the off position in a split second. We sped home.

By the time we returned to the office, I had only three minutes to catch the bus, five blocks away. So I bolted without saying good-bye to everyone. With the bus stop in sight, I slowed down to ease my labored breath and heard something behind me, sounding like, "Essie, Essian, Leslie-san, Leslie-san!" I turned and saw Masahiro far away, running toward me, trying to catch up with me. It turned out that one of the seniors had instructed him to chase me down and tell me I had been offered a ride home.

He had run full speed for four blocks to carry out his assignment. Masahiro insisted, between gulps of breath, with hand signals, that I should walk back slowly, while he'd run back to inform the driver he'd found me. I obeyed willingly for once, defeated and exhausted from my own sprint. I walked back to the office calmly. My week off from the determined craftsmen had finally begun.

Songs from
the Emerald Opera

Ka-klunk, ka-klunk went my shoes down the gray stone steps as I sprinted with anticipation toward the city bus, carrying me back to Uetoh Zoen. My Kyoto holiday had passed by as quickly as it took to get to the bottom of the stairs. For an ever-so-brief week, I got to wake up to the glowing sun on my indigo futon cover instead of darkness. I could feel the warmth of Taylor's cheek pressed against my shoulder as he slept, and witness brilliant, scarlet cherry leaves outside my window. One morning I saw a delicate bird staring at me from a silky smooth cherry branch; we looked at each other, both allowing ourselves a moment to relax. I savored Taylor's sandy smell, his curly hair, even his coarse day-old stubble, all so different from the clean-shaven craftomen.

Taylor had already returned to Berkeley, and I knew we'd probably hardly communicate again until I returned home in two months. Working at craftsman speed sapped all my energy. Taylor made me laugh so hard for a week with all his American antics, overslouching in his chair and pretending he would step on the tatami with his dirty boots. Yet I sensed, and wondered if I imagined, a distance between us. I felt tired a lot rather than excited to run around with him all over Kyoto, and Taylor seemed to walk slower than normal too. He seemed fine to anyone who didn't know him well, but I noticed he rarely had any interest in deciding where to go or what to do together. By chance, I managed to secure a ticket so we could visit the very garden I worked in my first week back with the Uetoh craftsmen, one of the most spectacular estate gardens in Kyoto, Shugakuin Rikyu Imperial Villa. I'd felt so excited to take Taylor there to show him the beautiful estate. But he was so caught up in taking photos that he stepped off a path and destroyed some lovely moss on a rock, and then smashed the lower limb of an innocent azalea. I cringed, hoping our tour guide hadn't seen, and then cringed for cringing. Taylor didn't know how long it took for a garden to grow.

I hoped for a moment to have a quiet talk during our Kyoto visit week. I took him to my local homemade tofu stand where the lady smiled particularly sweetly at me. We visited a real pub from Ireland: Irish craftsmen-carpenters had been hired to transport the building, piece by piece, to Kyoto. We ate at a traditional Japanese restaurant where a female chef prepared homemade stock next to our table with leftover fish and vegetables on our plates. We snacked on feather-light pastries from the French bakeries; Japanese took their training in France seriously. Every few days we'd step into a steaming bathhouse, even though we had to separate here, to retreat into the male and female tub areas. Of course I had to give Taylor strict instructions on how to clean himself properly, three times, before entering any tub or sauna. I simply could not find the right time to talk about any of my concerns. I'd wanted to keep things light for his trip to Kyoto. When we said good-bye, he told me, "I love you." I couldn't really hear him because he spoke to me from behind a closed taxi window. We hardly communicated again while I was in Kyoto. I held on to that image the rest of my stay, repeating it in my mind, as though the tree I stood in felt unsteady and I needed something extra to hang onto.

Within five minutes of arriving back at the office, the crew shot off toward Shugakuin, the emperor's garden. Packed into the work truck like a row of logs, the men and I rode to my most anticipated project yet. The men sat stiffly, with excellent posture, caught in their own reveries, never glancing at me. I felt loneliness creeping up, a heaviness in my spirit. We approached the sublime villa of Emperor Go-Mizunoo, a broad estate positioned at the base of a pine-covered mountainside, the garden my father never stopped dreaming about. Three hundred and forty years ago, the emperor, savvy not only in politics but also in calligraphy and art, oversaw the design and construction of his garden. He built it as a refuge for retirement, combining rice fields, lakes, mountains, buildings, bridges, roads, trails, and plants.

I shivered on first sight of the tall mountainside surrounding Shugakuin. Temperatures had dropped that week, and I'd come down with a cough. Yet nothing would keep me from working in one of my favorite Kyoto gardens. Shugakuin both intimidated me with its exclusiveness and enveloped me in its romantic, poetic tones.

I'd visited Shugakuin years earlier with Marcello, the young gardener I'd met at a garden conference. The two of us had approached Shugakuin, as did all visitors, by walking up a dirt road running between sunny rice fields with farmers working on either side. The harvest added to the drama of Shugakuin, allowing the visitor an imaginative, historic setting as they approached from the rural countryside rather than from a concrete parking lot. While Marcello and I strolled toward the central lake, insects sang, imperial koi splashed in the lake, and birds flapped their wings over a maze of paths.

I wore a breezy skirt and carried an open umbrella to ward off the sun on that hot and humid day. Women farm workers along the path called out to us. I looked at Marcello questioningly by tilting my head. I'd learned to tone down my speech and emotions with my Japanese friend. He understood, and said with a grin, "They ask if we are married." I felt self-conscious but certainly not offended. Marcello was a handsome young man of Japanese ancestry, raised in Brazil. The joyful women, like all the elements of Shugakuin, assisted in creating a magical atmosphere of wild beauty and fanciful imagination.

Although Marcello and I remained shy friends, I believe neither of us could escape the romantic entanglement Shugakuin placed on its visitors, past or present. The emperor and his friends would have walked on the same garden paths at night to watch the moon's reflection on the lake. They would have strolled along the same curve of the water's edge and perhaps floated on the lake in sturdy wooden boats. A boathouse still stood, rotting, its roof covered with moss.

When I first heard that our pruning crew would work at Shugakuin, I thought I'd misheard. After all, Shugakuin was one of Kyoto's more prestigious gardens. Visitors have to ask permission a year in advance from the Imperial Household Agency if they want to walk through the gardens, although foreign tourists can attain entry in less time. I'd asked Kei about Shugakuin, and he confirmed that we'd work there, although he warned of the dangerous nature of the work, which I didn't understand at first. He'd said that Shugakuin had initially barred me from working there, hinting at security concerns. But Uetoh had persisted, and I'd finally been allowed to join the men on their imperial excursion.

Through vibrating truck windows, I spied Shugakuin from the worker's entrance road rather than from the tourist path. I felt thrilled. I noted that pines on the mountains surrounding Shugakuin were sixty feet high, and some maples in the central garden reached twenty to thirty, much taller than the trees we'd worked on at private homes. The height of the pines reflected an old Japanese forest in its mature grandeur. Yet every square inch of the property, from rice field to landscaped estate to mountainside, had been cared for, pruned, and maintained for hundreds of years by imperial gardeners.

Ron Herman, an American landscape architect who trained at length in Japan, designed the largest traditional Japanese private estate garden in the United States, for a North American contemporary emperor: high tech billionaire Larry Ellison. Mr. Herman had based a portion of Ellison's traditional Japanese landscape design on Shugakuin. Both emperors' estates represented nature, wealth, and power, in that order. Also, the construction of both properties allowed the training and employment of hundreds of woodworkers and garden craftsmen. The construction of Ellison's estate created a subculture of high-end Bay Area artisans who specialize in Japanese design, construction, and furniture building—a subculture that persists today.

Speaking loudly over the truck's rumbling engine, Kei teased Masahiro about the dangerous work ahead. "Someone's gonna get hurt," he said in English, for my benefit. Young Masahiro tried not to look anxious. I asked with a stiff smile, "What?"

----

refusing to let the men recognize my first-day-back-at-school anxiety. Encouraged, Kei described with a sly look how we'd be using razor-sharp traditional Japanese scythes called *uchigama* to prune in the garden that day, and how past gardeners had cut themselves while learning to handle them. Masahiro became even quieter. A small patch of sweat formed on his long cheekbones just beneath his glasses.

Before entering the gardens, we had to check in with security, three guards in crisp uniforms in a plain stucco-walled room with a high ceiling. I leaned against a cool plastered wall, out of the way, while the men handled things. I wondered how many American women had been allowed to prune in Emperor Go-Mizunoo's 340-year-old estate. I may have been the first. Panicking, I realized I had forgotten my passport. *I've blown it*, I thought, *after all the trouble the company went to!* How could they allow a foreigner into the garden without proper identification? My pulse beat quickly as I tried to adopt what I imagined was Kei's most self-assured stance. Stare ahead, eyelids slightly droopy with boredom. I tried to remain still, especially my hands, which I kept clasped in front of me in an attempt to look humble. A guard sitting at a small wooden desk with an expressionless face looked over at me, nodding to motion me forward.

He asked my name, as he had each worker. I glanced down at the huge ledger book in front of him, two feet wide, one foot tall. Dozens of names were written on each page in beautiful, stylish swirls of Japanese calligraphy, except one. Glaring at us in the lower section of the right-hand page was the name Leslie Buck in boring roman lettering. Instead of looking at the obvious, the guard put his finger on the top of the first page and traced the names down slowly with his finger. Everyone in the room stood so still, I could hear the faint brushing of his skin against the page as he moved his index finger down. He continued on to the next page until his strong brown finger stopped at my name. I resisted the urge to say, "There it is! Right there!" I'll never forget my number: twenty-one, the year that one reaches maturity, becomes an adult in the United States. He grunted his approval. He never asked for identification.

The security guard mumbled something to Nakaji, which I understood as, "Make sure she's careful!" Bossman smiled encouragingly and laughed. I giggled softly with them, smiling sweetly, praying I wouldn't accidentally behead anyone in my favorite Kyoto garden.

We finally drove toward the central part of the estate and went deep into a tall cryptomeria forest. *Cool! We get to drive on the road of a real emperor*, I couldn't help but think. The air was chilly and moist, despite the warm sun just outside the tree canopy. I spotted a small wooden structure, dark under the thick ceiling of branches, a gardener's shed. It had a little chimney with smoke coming out of it. *Nice!* I thought. *We'll get to meet some of the imperial gardeners!* I'd only seen them from a distance on my previous tours. I felt so excited I could hardly contain myself. We didn't come close to entering the building. Instead, the men set up camp on the wet, mossy, cold ground near the truck. My first day at Shugakuin with Uetoh, poignant and filled with poetic beauty, felt particularly chilly under the trees there, furthering my illness.

Sliss, slash, sliss, slash. The men pressed and slid their shiny metal blades against porous flat stones. I tested my scythe blade. It was plenty sharp. But the men kept sharpening their blades, so

I did too. I stroked the metal against the stone repeatedly, dipping the blade and stone periodically into a bucket of water to wash away built-up grit. I watched and copied the men who tested their blades by gently slicing them against their thumbnails, leaving fine crisscrosses on the nail. I'm not sure what the scratches revealed, except my overlapping levels of fear, but I figured if I did it enough times, I'd unravel the mysterious technique.

Years later I learned the secret behind this sharpening method from a friend who sold scary-sharp kitchen knives made by small craftsman groups in Japan. I hesitated buying one of Sazuki's knives. She showed me how to sharpen my pruning shears after tolerating my dull kitchen knives for years. She stroked one side of my blades ten or so times with a sharpening stone, maintaining a steady, level stroke. Then she turned the blade over to feel for a slightly raised bur with her thumbnail, just as the craftsmen had. She said, "The bur proves the blade's sharpness. You must feel it along the full length of the blade, or continue sharpening." Next she turned the blade over to the bur side and made a few passes with the stone to smooth it off. She cleaned grit off the stone under her kitchen sink faucet. Although she used several grades of stone, she said I could use a single diamond metal file instead when sharpening my garden tools for ease. My pruning shear blade glinted, just like my coworkers' blades at Shugakuin.

I spied Masahiro's hands trembling while both of us stood back and watched the older men demonstrate the use of their *uchigama*. Shugakuin gardeners had used this tool for more than three hundred years to shear the hedges here. I wondered, *Why not improve this project by using electric hedge shears? Maybe the power cords wouldn't stretch far enough?* I watched the men, deducing that if anyone let go of their scythe while swinging it like a baseball bat, the spinning blade would propel across the garden like a Frisbee, literally slicing open anyone in its path. Now I understood why Shugakuin security hesitated to let a visiting foreigner work in one of Japan's high-profile gardens, with tourists walking about. I pondered my new responsibility.

Nakaji, much to my relief, took me far away from the others. He swung my scythe a few times, then handed the blade back to me. He positioned himself right in front of me, just ten feet away, and motioned for me to give it a go. I hesitated and gave him a questioning look, allowing him time to move off to the side. But he held his ground and waved his hand impatiently for me to begin. So I took a deep breath and began my practice swings. *Swish*. Nakaji stared. I got in a few good swings out of a dozen. Nakaji's unflinching gaze showed confidence in me, and I transferred that confidence into my hand, holding the scythe tight, keeping him safe.

Nakaji, the he-man, taught me how to swing the scythe to prune shrubs at Shugakuin. Babe Ruth toured Japan in 1936. I calculated that Nakaji would have been around nine that year. His swing did look similar to a baseball player's. When he swung, the blade would slice a hundred leaves at once, smooth as butter. You could hear the wind resist his blade. When I did it, the air sat stagnant, or I'd accidentally dip too low, creating a huge crater on the shrub's surface. Or I'd swing so weakly that my blade could only scratch the leaves, tickling them. In essence, I was massaging the shrubs. Admittedly, in grade school, when the kids played baseball, I remember often being picked last for teams.

Nakaji demonstrated specific techniques for pruning hedges. If he was standing above a shrub and wanted to prune the top, he'd

----

swing the scythe as though he were hitting a ball with a bat, from right to left. If standing next to a tall shrub, some of them more than twelve feet tall and requiring a ladder, he'd swing the stick up and down. After an hour of practicing, I went over to look at the men's work. They had already sheared an area the size of three swimming pools! I trudged despondently back to my kiddie-sized pool. A few hours later, I was still making miserable progress. Sweat poured down my arms. I sighed. *Here I am, working alone again in a garden, with my boyfriend thousands of miles away.*

I felt tired and out of breath as I looked up and spotted a slender man of medium height, wearing an expensive, well-cut business suit, walking briskly toward me. There were no garden tours at that time of day, so I wondered what he was up to. Out of the corner of my eye, I watched him move closer, and hesitated in my swing as he came perilously close. Kei had wrapped an extra rubber band around the base of my scythe to secure my grasp, what he called "the beginner's scythe." But instinctively I held on to it with a death grip. The businessman stopped right in front of me and signaled for me to hand him the scythe. No introduction. I figured he could not have been one of Shugakuin's gardeners, given his attire. And no one from outside the company ever instructed us. In fact, it would be a downright insult for a stranger to step over Nakaji's authority. But I felt drawn to obey him. I handed him my scythe. I looked around and prayed my boss wouldn't come walking around the corner, or we'd both end up sliced butter on toast.

Putting both of his hands around the *uchigama*'s long wooden stick, he moved the left end of the scythe up while pulling the right down, as with a kayak paddle. He repeated the movement up and down, getting progressively faster to show me how quickly it could be swung this way. He sheared the side of a hedge in seconds. He spoke to me in fluent Japanese sentences during his demonstration, just like Nakaji did, and I nodded my head obediently, understanding none of his words but all of his meaning. He handed the scythe back. On my first try, the blade cut through the leaves beautifully. *Whoosh.* Surprised, I looked up at him with a smile. With a frown, he waved his hands for me to continue. He had no time for appreciation. Again I was able to slice the leaves with more power and control. I cleanly finished off a small area in a few seconds as the strange man stood watching. Then, as mysteriously as my knight in Armani had arrived, he strode off around a corner and disappeared.

At lunchtime I spied the same businessman walking around on the other side of the lake. I pointed toward him and asked Kei who he was. "He is the head gardener of Shugakuin." For once words eluded me. I went over the secret lesson I'd been given, and remembered the words of my American mentor, Dennis: "When I teach you something, Leslie, I am teaching you what I was taught by my teacher, and what that person was taught by his teacher, and on, and on. You now become a part of this lineage. We are all connected." Shugakuin garden's leader had taught me more than a clever trick; he'd handed me a tiny glimpse into the history of Shugakuin gardeners. By learning from him, I'd had a conversation with one of the first gardeners of Shugakuin, who'd pruned shrubs the same way almost three hundred and fifty years ago. This is why Japanese craftsmen pride themselves on doing as they are told by their teachers rather than jumping to electric hedge trimmers.

All day I tried to ignore the image of my scythe slipping out of my hand, flying into a group of unsuspecting tourists. The next morning I discovered that my hand had become so sore that I couldn't hold a pencil to write in my journal. But I still managed to grip the scythe. Only at lunch was I able to relax. The cool air hovered under the cryptomeria, forcing me to don a fleece hat by midafternoon, but the scene still felt enchanting. Mountains and woods surrounded me. Sunlight filtered its way through the leaves and sparkled softly on the dirt road. From several directions came the sound of trickling water. Birds, oblivious to the coming winter chill, chirped with lively spirit. They liked my spot. I sat, exhausted, against a fallen old tree trunk while the men retreated to the car for lunch, listening to noisy talk-radio shows. Their appetite for commercial intrusion in this green paradise annoyed me.

I thought about my boyfriend's visit the week before, replaying our scenes together, trying to determine whether things would have been easier for us if I had chosen an organic rather than a strictly traditional restaurant, a less tour-driven garden to visit. The songbirds called out to me from all directions in the little forest echo chamber. They distracted me from worries about Taylor. The wind blew hard, and branches swayed overhead. A pine needle whorl plopped onto my head. I looked up. Perhaps the ghosts of the garden wanted me to focus more on their trees. I listened awhile, resting against my mossy log, and looked up at golden maple leaves, dark green conifers, and bits of blue sky peeking in overhead. The high dome of branches held a certain elegance that reminded me of the magnificent War Memorial Opera House in San Francisco. From my season-ticket balcony-side seat, one could see the beautiful hand-carved ceiling of the opera house, with lights that look like embedded stars. Trees fill me with comfort and awe. They inspire me, as do the opera singers, who devote their lives to their craft.

I began to relax a little under the shadow of the pines at Shuga-kuin, and repositioned myself against the scratchy, stubby old fallen trunk, my pants damp from the moist ground. It was rather an unlikely spot to sit in an emperor's garden. Nevertheless, I felt my chest lighten, my worries about Taylor drop away. I breathed in deeply and breathed out the air flowing down the mountain, into my spirit. Looking around, savoring the sounds, sights, and textures of a beautiful garden, I finally relished a few minutes of peace. Nature held me close. I felt her singing her dramas to me inside the shimmering emerald opera house, known to others as Shugakuin Rikyu Imperial Villa.

Tanuki Discovers
Garden Spirits

It rained so hard while we worked at Shugakuin three days later, I took a break from the men and found a hot lunch on a street near the entrance to the garden. No one blinked an eye when I walked into an udon shop, a fair-skinned girl in a dirty gardener's uniform. I wrote in my journal as I sipped steaming broth, my damp sleeves smearing the words I'd just written. It was November, and I came home wet and tired. Cold air pushed through the cracks of my bedroom walls at night. I would wake up with throbbing pain in my arms from days of repetitive swinging. I silently wept, *How will I hold my tools tomorrow?* I coughed, my cold progressing, and then drifted back to sleep. The next morning, when Nakaji handed me my scythe, I stared hard at my hand, willing it. *You will hold!* Fear helped, for I needed to avoid killing Nakaji, who continued his habit of standing within a few feet of me as my blade whipped its wide circle at about the same level as his heart.

The maples around the emperor's lake began to turn color in patches as the week progressed. They looked as though they sported English tweed coats with a smattering of bright red, faded green, and dried brown leaves. The color spread up into the mountains. Still, I felt a little disappointed at my first real glimpse of

----

autumn in Japan. Only pinches of leaves turned color at a time. I'd yet to spot a shocking red velvet cloak of leaves that dazzle a garden, as I'd seen in many Japanese calendar photos. I felt tricked. Fooled by Kyoto's minimalist fall, perhaps by my whole experience with the craftsmen. Working as an apprentice in Japan had sounded thrilling. Yet the reality proved tiresome, mundane, and repetitive, and no matter what people had warned me, it was more difficult than I could have imagined.

The challenge of using the scythe became not just how to swing it quickly but how to swing it while standing on a bamboo pole that had been tied into the crotches of two spindly hedge branches, ten feet up in the air. The men regularly tied strong two-inch bamboo poles to tree branches, creating instant scaffolds inside a tree or between two trees where ladders wouldn't fit. Sometimes a pole would be placed so that a ladder could lean up against it in a spot where no branch existed. Certain shrubs at Shugakuin looked short from afar, but many rose twenty feet high, as tall as a two-story house. Nakaji showed me how to tie the pole close to the crotches of branches where the branch is strongest. But trunks and branches of thick hedges, where sun rarely penetrates, tend to be less strong than trees out in the open. So not only did our poles wobble a little when we balanced on them, but I was not entirely confident that the branches supporting them wouldn't snap. We'd have to place the pole high enough that our waists were above the canopy, where we could swing wide well above the hedge.

Regardless of the narrow pole beneath our feet, it was possible to keep from falling because the hedge was so thick. When pruning on a ladder or in a tree, I always make sure I have three points of my lower body supported, such as two feet and one hip, or a foot, hip, and thigh. With three points secure, I can move my upper body as much as I want. So with both feet on the bamboo pole, and dozens of branches below the waist to lean against, the men and I swung for hours. Still, my spindly perch wobbled with unpredictable support, and Masahiro and I sweated considerably, being the least experienced. The advanced craftsmen worked away flexibly, like birds cleaning their feathers at odd angles while balancing on electric wires.

Because of my cold, I had to take frequent breaks, hoping no one saw or heard me submit to coughing fits. Occasionally, my arm muscles would simply give out. Nevertheless, I managed to complete a few areas. There was just one problem. My sheared hedges weren't quite as smooth as the others. The guys' hedges looked formal and clean, all thick and flat on top. My areas looked as though they'd been gashed by a child. I'd tried. When swinging, I'd hit a coarse branch sticking up higher than others, and my scythe would dive in. Or I'd swing too high in midair, alarmingly fast. Thankfully, tour groups roamed far from me.

But when I watched Masahiro, I couldn't complain. He worked on the tallest and most dangerous jobs. The bamboo poles he balanced on were tied into branches fifteen feet off the ground. He worked on a long hedge stretching forty feet. He could barely keep from slipping off his pole as he wielded his sharp instrument, working as fast as he could. He walked around with a permanent anxious look, his clothes drenched with sweat. Yet he continued on, determined.

Inside the hedges, I found fascinating twisted conglomerations of plant species. Every hedge I've worked on in California is created from one plant, usually pittosporum or azalea. California hedges might be fifteen to thirty years old. Inside the ancient hedges at Shugakuin, I discovered dozens of plants making up one hedge: juniper, maple, dogwood, holly, boxwood, pieris, camellia, rhaphiolepsis, and bamboo. Who knows how old these plants were. Centuries? Standing over the hedges with a dangerous tool in hand felt less fascinating. I'd hang on to a leaf or two with one hand, fearful of falling into the dark, leafless pit below, and concentrate on shearing one small area at a time.

It eventually occurred to me that I had unlimited access to one of the most astounding gardens in the world. I felt I must stop conversing with my sitting log during every break and take some action. Without mentioning anything to Bossman, hoping he wouldn't be held responsible should I be reprimanded, at lunchtime I wandered the property with my camera, unable to resist the urge to capture all I saw. I began by circling the lake, walking right past imperial gardeners who pruned mountain trees from forty-foot extension ladders. They glanced over at me, then continued their work. Certainly this meant it was okay for me to keep going, right?

I eventually came upon a wooden sign that said in English DO NOT ENTER. It's probably okay to go in there, I reasoned; after all, we worked in that area yesterday. The wild maples in the forbidden area leaned heavily over the lake. I stood under them, inside the canopy looking up, and took photos of the light penetrating the frail cover. Standing inside the leaf tent, I felt safe. The maple held me inside a world of greens and browns, light and dark. I felt like an animal in the forest, undiscovered. I was fascinated by the vulnerability of the trees, about to lose their leaves and expose their bones, their inner realm.

I exited the hidden forest onto a wide-open path along the lake. But just before I stepped out from the trees, I spotted a tourist group approaching. I had grown shy of the Japanese tourists' curious reaction to me. With my back turned, I looked like a Japanese gardener boy, with my short stature, khaki outfit, white towel on my head, and traditional scythe in hand. When I turned around, visitors would spot either my pale skin or my feminine look, and they'd cry out, "*Gaijin!*" (Foreigner!) Everyone would run toward me at once and ask dozens of inquisitive, encouraging questions, none of which I could understood. I worried they might think, *Gee, this American doesn't understand any Japanese! She sure didn't do her homework! Why would this company ever let her work in our gardens?* even while they smiled politely. Western-looking tourists completely ignored me.

The Japanese women, on the other hand, were fascinated. Some who could speak English told me that they appreciated my study of Japanese cultural arts, admired my boldness in working in a man's field, and wished to one day run their own businesses, as I did in California. But one young Japanese woman told me she felt pressured by her peers to buy department store outfits, and that she spent too much money on clothes to afford going to architecture school in Italy, which was her dream. Another said executive positions in companies for women were rare. I found Japanese women in the winter of the year 2000 educated, smart, and ready to hold more positions of power in Japan, if only society would allow it.

I eyed the tour group walking around the lake in the far distance, and knew from past experience that it would reach me in about ten minutes. I made a split-second decision and slipped

----

behind a long, thick shrub that circled the outer perimeter of the lake before anybody could spot me. I waited. As the tour group approached, I became more still. The group passed right by me, their slender, stocking-covered legs and high heels at eye height, their shoes grating against the gritty white gravel path. *Ahhhh.* For once I felt a sense of peaceful distance from a tour group, like watching a movie in a dark theater. I could hear every word they spoke, their eyes gazing right over my location, never suspecting that I lurked behind the shrub. Completely camouflaged, with my khaki outfit and dirt-smudged cheeks, I relaxed. Just for the fun of it, I looked straight into a woman's eyes.

"Yiiieeee, tanuki!" she screamed, pointing toward me. Tanuki are little creatures that look a bit like raccoons, but they carry a certain mythical status. In folklore, they can shape-shift into many things, including human beings, and might account for mysterious singing or drumming coming from the forest. Little tanuki statues proliferate in Kyoto gardens, as ceramic gnomes do in other parts of the world, including California. The whole tour group rushed toward me. I had no choice but to stand up and reveal myself. Surrounded within seconds, I turned bright red while I hastily tried to remove the leaves from my hair. I looked down at the dirt on my uniform and attempted to step back a little so as not to sully the adorable purses and color-coordinated skirts worn by the gushing women. I was even better than a tanuki. "*Gaijin!*" they all said, and then upon closer inspection, "*Onna no hito!*" (A girl!) They swarmed me. I bowed sheepishly. Enthralled, they all spoke at once, asking me indecipherable questions. How I envied their gentle stroll in such lovely attire. We couldn't speak each other's language, but we had a meeting that likely none of us would forget.

I wasn't the only creature to be discovered at Shugakuin. The emperor's garden came alive the week I worked there as we crawled, climbed, and sliced through it. During the week, I spotted a salamander, a fox, and a tiny green frog. The little frog stared at me meditatively, as though he couldn't care less that I looked like a giant. His bright green skin glistened, even in the shade. Animals, including birds and insects, ran wild, disobeying path protocol. To notice the living nature of a garden, one must either work or sit among the trees quietly. This type of intimate interaction with a garden reminded me of getting to know someone. When icy dew permeated my thin cloth boots, the imperial garden challenged me by asking, "Do you care enough about me to continue?" As I came upon the old wooden boathouse, the garden recited a poem of age, decay, and beauty. And as I stared at the black, brown, and ochre leaves covering the moss, the garden nurtured me, diverting my troubled thoughts with a palette of visual treats. Mere photographs cannot capture the intimacy of a garden.

Nakaji bellowed his commands across the gardens of Shugakuin. Colors, like moods, altered daily with the coming season. His voice, or perhaps other seasonal influences, finally shocked the maple leaves into great swaths of bright red and orange en masse. The maples sighed one last, great, colorful breath before their syrupy sugars made their way down into the roots for winter. Nakaji reached my area and walked over to closely examine a tall hedge, which I thought I'd mauled, near the front entrance of the garden. I held my breath but continued to work at an increased pace when he came into view. He looked the hedge up and down, and, without a word, walked off. Wow, progress! Or complete failure.

- - - -

Nakaji asked me, after I had been coughing for several days, "Are you feeling sick?" I replied, "*Daijōbu*" (I'm fine). I refused to admit defeat to the men; it would be like letting down the entire female human race. Nakaji commanded me to switch from using the scythe to raking leaves. Suspicious that I was receiving special treatment, yet feeling weak, I obeyed. I raked a mass of fallen rust and gold leaves atop a damp, emerald moss carpet, feeling guilty about clearing away the beautiful scene, but grateful to take it easy.

Masahiro ran over and explained in broken English that when I'd gathered enough leaves, I was to come get him so he could carry my tarp to the truck, literally a five-minute jog away. Typically the men don't just carry debris to the truck. They fill the tarps with as many leaves as humanly possible, swing a load over either shoulder, and sprint to the truck. I realized at that moment that Bossman indeed had gone easy on me, so I resisted, "Oh, no, I'll carry it," I insisted. I didn't want the men feeling they had to work harder because of my sickness, "Yes, yes," he insisted. "No, no," I responded, planning to ignore him. Nevertheless, the very moment my large tarp was full, Masahiro would pop out of the trees, swipe my load, and run it to the truck. I glared at him and wanted to hug him the next moment.

One afternoon I brought a special snack for the men to thank them for their continued support of the American woman in their midst. I'd hidden in a paper bag a large bowl of homemade popcorn—without butter or salt, so the men wouldn't get their hands dirty. I wasn't quite sure how the hierarchical group would handle eating the popped snacks from one large bowl, but that was the only way I could think to serve it. At first they acted hesitant, just looking the bowl over as though the idea of popcorn mystified them. Then, after a few men reached for a kernel or two, they dove all at once, like animals. Someone threw a piece of popcorn into the lake to tempt an imperial koi. Nakaji yelled at him and made him try to retrieve it with a rake! But it floated further away while all the men teased the worker. One koi actually did swim nearby, but it glided right past the soggy white thing floating on its rooftop. I worried that a koi might choke on a kernel, but Nakaji and the men just laughed. It did not surprise me that the trees reflecting upside-down green snow cones across the lake put the men in a good mood, as the purpose of this whole landscape was to encourage serenity and light-heartedness for the emperor and his friends.

Out of the corner of my eye, I spotted an imperial guard approaching us with haste down the long path surrounding the huge lake. I'd never seen a guard without a tour group. Uh oh, I thought, my tranquility shattering. Who do you suppose will be blamed for a piece of popcorn spoiling the emperor's pristine lake? Sure enough, the guard headed straight toward us with a serious look on his face. As he neared, everyone huddled near Nakaji, trying to act innocent and well connected, avoiding eye contact with the guard. I wondered what Nakaji would do. Just as the guard reached us, he hesitated, and Nakaji stared at him with a blank look, in an aristocratic sort of way that only Nakaji, the he-man gardener of all gardeners, could carry off. The guard looked back, said "*Konnichiwa*" (Good afternoon), and continued on his way.

The next day, as I sharpened my tools beside a path, I thought I heard a female voice, so I looked up. Sure enough, walking by was a young woman wearing a traditional khaki gardening uniform with a white towel wrapped around her black hair. She was the second Japanese woman gardener I'd ever seen. She looked to be in her twenties and stood unusually tall. She had a slim but healthy build and beautiful broad cheekbones. She was chatting to my coworkers, with her back mostly turned to me. No one attempted to introduce us. I decided to play it cool and not go over to say hello, as I might have done in California. Maybe it would embarrass her. I went back to concentrating on sharpening my tool. I felt it more important to show the men that there were two serious women working in the imperial garden, and that we had more important things to do than chit-chat. I suspected that she worked more seriously than I could ever imagine. I looked up one more time to get a glimpse of her and then focused on sharpening my hard blade against the wet stone. We're working together, I reasoned; that's enough.

My last afternoon at Shugakuin, I worked way above the lake, behind an ancient stone building. As I focused on raking fast enough so that I could ignore my tired legs and arms, I heard an alarming cry. I whisked around, searching the dark brush for the source of the tortured moan. On a low wall ten feet away, watching me with inquisitive eyes, sat a foot-long mound of white fur. The cat stared at me confidently, displaying her refinement and beauty. Normally I can befriend even the most skittish of street cats. But for some reason not a single cat in Japan would let me get near it. Do American gardeners give off a strange smell?

I looked around, listening. No footsteps or bellowing of Nakaji could be heard. I debated my options and then put down my rake. I'd never seen anyone stop work or slow down outside of breaks. If Bossman discovered me petting a cat, all the remaining leaves at Shugakuin might drop at once with Nakaji's rage. The cat persisted with her tantalizing meows. Slowly, with anxious glances at the garden entry, I moved toward her as she stared back at me boldly. I stopped about five feet away and used my most clever cat-enticement method. I waited for her to come to me, calling her softly. She took a few steps forward. I tried to halt all but slight breathing. I relaxed my muscles. "Come here," I said softly. *As if she understands English,* my inner supervisor corrected. I risked moving in a bit closer. She moved again, and then I. Finally, I put out my hand and touched her soft, warm head. Silky fur pressed against my fingers.

When I first visited the imperial gardens two years earlier, to help me remember the garden's name I imagined a queen made of sugar standing on the water. I'd say to myself, "Sugar Queen, Shugakuin." I often associated Japanese words with visual images to help me memorize them. I looked down at the beautiful, pure white, fearless creature and thought, *Certainly, this must be the real Sugar Queen of Shugakuin.* After a bit more reckless petting, I resumed raking. Sugar Queen watched me with incredible concentration, like a spectator at a tennis match. When my rake moved left, her head followed left, and when it moved right, her head turned right. A friend joined her on the wall, and they watched together. Real fans!

I wondered again if there might be spirits in this three-century-old estate, and, if so, how they would appear. How would they feel about the noisy leaf blowers compared to the quiet garden rake? What would they think about this American woman working in their midst, struggling to match the fierce pace of Japanese craftsmen? Throughout the day, gray clouds grew and darkened. The temperature dropped, a sure sign of rain. But it never happened. For the first time in a week and a half, while I stood in the hidden garden with my new friends, the skies cleared and my head cold lightened. Just before we ended our final day in the emperor's garden, the craftsmen and I took a moment to watch a blazing gold sphere melt into a burnt tangerine horizon and descend into the rice fields.

Mother Makes
a Secret Offering

It was still dark when I saw Nakaji's car approach our predetermined anonymous street corner. I hopped in. The vehicle jerked back and forth as I struggled to wake up from my groggy state. We then picked up Nishizawa, who would join our team until the end of my apprenticeship, just before New Year. Nishizawa was a senior worker in the company who had been landscaping in Kyoto with the company's landscaping crew before he joined us. He looked like he could have been anywhere between his twenties and early forties. The gardeners in Japan I met looked so healthy, it was often hard to guess their age. Nishizawa's demeanor was easier to predict. He always gave me a big smile when I greeted him, and, while very skilled at pruning, he completely lacked any sign of arrogance. He would fit in very well with the California Japanese woodworkers I've met, who are laid-back and friendly but highly disciplined. It seemed as though the other men looked to him for advice.

We stopped to pick up Masahiro, and the four of us—minus Kei, who refused to work on his day off—drove across Kyoto until the truck pulled up to a middle-class house in a neat, compact neighborhood. I was curious about this home. In the front yard, a low fence revealed to passersby a garden that looked like a small forest. I observed that every tree and shrub had been attentively styled, including a detailed black pine silhouetted against a starlit dawn sky. Many of my California clients ignored their gardens in late fall, letting dead leaves pile up around half-used barbecues and old plastic chairs. This garden enthralled me. Nishizawa noticed my curiosity and said, "Nakaji-san home." Without a single flower, it felt captivating and atmospheric. It embodied winter's approach.

Distinct elements in a garden, such as the bare branches of deciduous trees, stylized evergreens, or a lack of flowers, can give the viewer the feeling of winter even without snow or freezing temperatures. To get ideas for winter gardens, I encourage my pruning students to take hikes in nature in the wintertime. In California's winter, the red twig dogwood, with its bright red bark, or the Douglas firs, with their small, handsome cones, would be fine plants to use in a California naturalized garden. In the little Kyoto garden, we stepped like cat burglars down a stone path in our silent dark blue *jikatabi* buttoned up to our calves, heading for the front door. The garden struck my laid-back Californian sensibilities as poetic in its sparseness yet almost too formal, with hardly a branch out of place.

I glanced down at a stone basin, filled with crystal-clear water that held not a spot of dirt at the bottom, and nervously thought to scrape some dirt off my jacket. The garden floor looked as clean and pure as a fresh layer of snow. With such a fine garden, I imagined I might be about to step into the home of an ancient Japanese warrior, and I straightened my posture. I soon discovered I wasn't too far off.

The front door slid open, revealing a woman wearing a modern dress covered by a housewife's apron. She smiled and beckoned

----

us in. We stepped into the most elegant *genkan*, entry room, I'd ever seen, the size of a small bedroom. The *genkan* normally sits at street level and the rest of the house is a step higher, so the boundary remains clear between the shoe-allowed *genkan* and the shoe-forbidden rest of the house. The main house rose up much higher, about three feet, accessible by a large step that also served cleverly as a wide bench. Square silk pillows had been placed on the bench, along with a tray containing a teapot, cups, and slices of chocolate swirl cake. The offering drew us forward. We had come to this house to gather work equipment, and we were about to spend our only day off working in the gardens of Nakaji's private client.

I knew from Kei that Nakaji worked on Sundays in order to run his own business, in addition to six days a week with Uetoh. According to rumor, some years ago, Nakaji had requested permission to leave Uetoh so that he could start his own private business. The head boss had so disapproved, he'd picked up Nakaji's heavy metal desk from the center of the room and dropped it in a corner. Nakaji apparently wouldn't quit without respectful approval from the company, so instead worked seven days a week. This story mystified me. Why didn't he just leave if he wanted to? My dad once said, "If something is deep in your heart, you have to do it." Dad obviously hadn't met a traditional Japanese craftsman.

Despite the tempting tea tray, we remained standing three feet away, stealing glances at the sliced cake rounds, the black and white swirled side by side, like us. No one knew exactly what to do until Nakaji barked loudly, *"Suwatte!"* (Sit!) We sat down at once. The bench, its grain looking as smooth as an undisturbed pond, held us all, with the tray in the middle. Nakaji looked closely at the teapot, lifting the lid, and then said something to the woman who had greeted us at the door. She laughed warmly, smiled toward us, picked the pot up off the tray, and left the room. She returned shortly with another pot. I assumed that the first pot hadn't looked sufficiently hot to Bossman. I also guessed that the woman was Nakaji's wife, but I couldn't be sure, as we were never introduced.

We timidly drank our tea and took polite, hesitant turns reaching down and grabbing pieces of cake. I shivered a little while looking around. The cold never bothered Nakaji in the garden, or apparently in his home. Along a deep wooden shelf on one side of the room were displayed precious items of the household: a forbidding antique vase, an elegant ornate plate, and a *maneki-neko*, a well-known Japanese cat statue seen at the entrance to shops in red, white, and black. Nishizawa pointed to the kitty and let out a chuckle. Only a senior in the company could get away with that. I surveyed the circumference of the room, finally noticing just inside the main floor of the house a giant tree trunk, cut just above the roots and below the canopy. This thick, gnarled trunk stood taller than Nakaji and was broader than his shoulders. The lacquered surface glistened with each twist. When he saw me staring at it, Nishizawa said, "A cypress tree, one thousand years old." My eyes widened. I wanted desperately to go up and touch it but stayed put. Nakaji invited us to step up into the living room while he gathered some things. As I passed the ancient cypress, I managed to graze the trunk with my left hand without anyone seeing.

As ordered, the three of us seated ourselves stiffly on the living room's black leather couch. I noticed some books on the coffee table and thought perhaps it would be okay if I looked through them; at any rate, I couldn't resist. I found a wide selection of Japanese garden photo books and flipped through them. I soon determined that each book featured a garden built and cared for by Uetoh Zoen. Insatiable curiosity comes in handy! Then I discovered a landscape architecture magazine article featuring a large public Japanese garden in Vancouver called the Nitobe Memorial Garden. Nitobe had been extensively renovated by Uetoh Zoen.

The year before I started my business, I'd done a solo trip up to Canada to bolster the courage I did not feel I had yet, and ended up in Vancouver one night, unable to find a place to stay. After an hour at a pay phone, calling places I'd looked up in a travel guide and feeling a bit frazzled, I succeeded in securing a night at a temporary summer dorm room on the University of British Columbia campus. I arrived at night, relieved that I didn't have to sleep in the back of my truck. The next morning I stepped outside the dorm to refreshing sunshine. To my surprise, right next door to the building I'd slept in was a distinguished Canadian Japanese garden called Nitobe. I loved wandering around the garden with its winding streams, mesmerizing overhead maple branches, and strikingly simple lake design, with white sand against blue-black water.

Sitting on Nakaji's black couch, I thought, *What a coincidence! The young man sitting next to me on this couch had once worked in the garden I'd found by chance four years earlier!* I looked over at Nishizawa, then again at the photos of Nitobe. In one photo, next to an enormous rock being moved with a tripod, stood Nishizawa. I wasn't sure which coincidence was more amazing: that my crew had worked at the garden I had visited, or that I had picked that particular book off the table. My whole time in Kyoto, in fact, felt just like that, like one big coincidence that almost didn't happen. A bit daunted, I looked down at the pile of books and magazines on the coffee table. I wasn't sure which book I should pick up next.

Instead I commented to Nishizawa, "Nakaji-san has worked on many gardens." Nishizawa could understand a little English if I spoke simply and slowly. "Do you know at what age he began his studies to become a gardener?" Nishizawa responded gently, in his proper way: "I believe Nakaji-san began pruning after he finished his training as a kamikaze pilot in World War II." He said this casually. *Jesus!* I thought. *He was a kamikaze pilot?* But I remained expressionless and just tilted my head a little, as though I was Spock reacting to one of Captain Kirk's dramas. I kept a tight rein on my emotions; I did not want to appear ignorant about our role in the war and our bombing of Japan. I also didn't want the men to think I would now fear Nakaji, even if he had brought me close to tears a couple of times. "Hmm," I said pensively. Had the men been holding out on me about Nakaji, worrying about my reaction?

The news penetrated my thoughts like a shovel cutting through hard soil. Nakaji, earlier in his life, would have considered me an enemy combatant. The shovel continued to dig. Later, he assumed the role of a thoughtful mentor for an American young woman. People since have told me that the realities and feelings of those chosen to become kamikaze fighters were complicated. Still, I marveled over Nakaji's life journey. True, he had never shown me any appreciation; but if he'd wanted to, he could have made my life miserable. Nakaji treated me with respect. He skillfully challenged me and thoughtfully encouraged me to believe in myself. He pushed me, wanting me to learn but not fail. Despite his gruffness, I admired the man who in his youth might have killed me if given the chance.

We drove to a private client of Nakaji's, and I spent hours raking autumn leaves. After a strong drop in temperature, the deciduous tree holdouts in Kyoto had finally turned color all at once and dropped leaves by the truckful. Maples, cherry, ginkgo, dogwood, and crepe myrtles strutted their fall outfits and dropped them on the floor like models changing quickly off a runway. In my effort to rake up as many piles as fast as I could, I mistakenly pulled up a good patch of moss with my rake. Nishizawa walked by and informed me, "It's better if you use a broom. An employee was fired once for not being careful enough with the moss," then walked off. I figured what I had done must have been pretty serious if Nishizawa thought he should break the craftsman's code of silence and speak to me, so I quickly began raking the torn moss to hide it under a big azalea *tamamono* shrub.

Yet danger approached. Bossman's bulky figure tromped briskly down the path, straight in my direction. Nakaji was far enough away that he could not decipher the contents of my pile but close enough to grow suspicious if I raked something under a plant instead of onto a tarp. *Please, make him walk another way*, I begged. My pile seemed to grow larger with each step he took. I tried to push it around with my rake and willed Nakaji to look at my hands or the rake handle but not the pile.

He's going to kill me, was my last thought before Nakaji came right before me. I stood frozen. He looked down directly at my pile of moss, looked back up at me, boomed for me to go to another area in the garden, and walked off. A miraculously easy send-off! Running to my new assignment, I whispered, "Thank you, God!" I felt he deserved a little credit too.

The cold affected me every morning. I crossed my arms a lot, trying to make my frame smaller, my clothes bigger. I added layers to my outfit despite the fact that I felt foolish doing so given that the men still dressed like it was summer. But these efforts remained fairly ineffectual because I was still running around in my thin *jikatabi*. As temperatures dropped, my toes and fingers would numb. I felt myself retract inward, my emotions becoming as exposed and sensitive as the bare maple branches. I thought about Taylor quite a bit. I replayed the same "Does he miss me?" tapes because I had no girlfriends with whom I could have gossip episodes.

That winter, I felt an affinity with one of my favorite plants, the laceleaf maple, known in horticultural circles as *Acer dissectum*. The laceleaf is more diminutive than other maples, often four feet tall maximum in Bay Area gardens, although it can grow up to fifteen feet tall in prime conditions. The laceleaf mounds into a domelike shape that cascades downward like a spherical waterfall.

Carefully thinning laceleafs after their first spurt of spring growth is no easy feat. Some pruners inadvertently shorten them into popsicle shapes. I like to open them ever so slightly so the puzzle-like inner branches can be glimpsed inside a see-through canopy. In winter the leaves die off and the shrub takes on a leafless, stark, and cool look—the complete opposite of its summer exuberance. By hand, I gently pull off shriveled brown leaves, revealing a beautiful inner world of twining branches.

Along the high mountaintops of Japan, where laceleafs naturally grow, as soon as temperatures drop, the leaves fall off. But in the Bay Area's mild climate, the leaves stick to the tree. The only way to get them off is by grasping and stroking the dead leaves gently downward, like combing a child's sensitive head. The pruner's skill is tested in winter. Any stubby, unnatural-looking cuts previously hidden under summer foliage become an exposition of shame all winter long.

Quality pruning helps the laceleaf show off as a refined winter sculpture—especially if a small light is placed underneath the tree, creating a living silhouette. The most photographed plant at the Portland Japanese Garden is an old laceleaf maple, whose twisting open structure allows for picturesque views into the garden. Before Japan, I always thought of laceleaf maples as a plant that expressed softness and femininity.

I still find them beautiful, but I also feel a certain sadness when I see them now. I'll look at the bare winter branches and think about how vulnerable they might feel, as I did during my winter in Kyoto. I wish them well in November as I gently pull off their leaves, knowing that by the winter's end, a few of the most shaded branches, deep inside the tree, will perish. I clean out these dead twigs when I repeat the spring thinning process. I'd never thin a laceleaf in a hot and sunny time of year such as late summer in Northern California, especially on the top. If the maple's bark is suddenly exposed to strong sunshine, it will burn.

This sadness does not make the laceleaf ugly to me—just the opposite. A while back, I discovered the Japanese word *mono-no-awaré* in a design book, *Japanese Garden Design*, by the Japanese garden landscaper and author Marc Peter Keane. He described *mono-no-awaré* as meaning "beauty, especially one of a subtle, ephemeral nature, or an emotional response to the inherent sadness of life itself." *Mono-no-awaré* perfectly describes the laceleaf in winter: lovely, weeping, full of sentiment.

Nakaji's private client, who looked about the same age as my mom, approached me in the morning. She asked where I was from, and we excitedly discovered that her daughter was going to school at Saint Mary's College, just over the hill from Berkeley. As we talked about her daughter, I felt a familiar tightening of my chest, my homesickness returning.

I went back to raking peacefully, trying to avoid pulling up any moss, when a garish loudspeaker blasted the ice cream–truck song through the garden. Sure enough, Nishizawa ran out to the street to flag down the truck. *Kyoto ice cream? It's cold, but I'm game!* But then I ran to look outside the front gate and saw a small truck with smoke coming out of its chimney. Nishizawa pulled out some cash and bought each of us a foil-covered bundle. I unwrapped my gift, which fit warmly in the palm of my hand, and discovered a steaming sweet potato inside. "Do you have such a thing in the United States?" the guys asked. "Only slightly like it," I replied, not wanting to delve too far into American children's sugary eating habits and love of orange Creamsicles.

After break, Nishizawa led me to the other side of the house, where a stone path led to a specific type of garden, with trees that remained mostly green year-round. A canopy of evergreen oak and cypress hovered overhead, held up by matchstick tree trunks. Narrow strands of light fell through slits in the canopy and flickered on and off the ground. Branches swayed overhead. This was the tea garden leading to a wooden teahouse that the client had probably built at great expense. Like a mother hugging her child who has come home from school, the tea garden is an intimate, enclosed space. Planting trees closely together creates a dense forest feel, which can help relax the visitors exiting their busy work lives, moving toward the tea house, preparing to enter the reflective inner world of the tea ceremony.

The landscaper of this particular teahouse garden, or *roji*, used plants native to Japan, perhaps from the surrounding forests of

Kyoto. By using native plants familiar to visitors, the landscaper hoped to encourage an easy, familiar setting rather than a fascinating, unfamiliar one.

While it is true that I enjoy summery rose gardens—I am dazzled by butter yellow Julia Child cultivated roses—the understated traditional *roji* takes me back in time, and in spirit, to the little forest behind my childhood home, where my friends and I explored plants, insects, birds, and our private thoughts.

Nishizawa patiently explained to me that the main stone placed in front of the entryway of the teahouse was called *tobi-ishi*. To help myself remember this new Japanese word, I visualized my toe stepping on the rock, *to*, and thought of the middle of Nishizawa's name, *ishi*; putting these two together I got *to-ishi*, leading me to *tobi-ishi*. Nishizawa holds my ranking as the number-one humble Uetoh Zoen craftsman. He worked skillfully yet with such good nature. He had an irresistibly friendly personality. I never saw him get angry, and when he laughed it was for a sincere reason. I got the feeling that he looked out for the other workers. After that day, every time I saw a *tobi-ishi* stone, I thought of Nishizawa.

Despite Nishizawa's kindness, I waited for break impatiently. I'd worked on a Sunday, after all, and hoped there might be some sweetness to the day. Finally, the tray was delivered silently by Nakaji's client, the mom. Everyone said together, "*Arigatō gozaimasu!*" (Thank you very much!) as she stole away. On the tea tray lay the most expensive snacks I'd ever seen. Inch-thick medallions sat in a shiny pile, each artfully wrapped in silver foil. I leaned against a plastered teahouse wall. I later learned this was forbidden because of the live nature of the walls, which pick up oils and show stains if one leans against or touches them. Exhausted, I slowly unwrapped my treat to savor it, drinking my much-appreciated green tea. At the same time, I felt a bit resentful about my Sunday gardening duties. I asked myself, *Why do I let gardening take up my whole life? Here I am working thirteen days in a row! What about play? I do so much for the gardens; do they have to take every bit of my life?* I bit into the delicate, crisp dessert and tasted a buttery puff pastry filled with a sweet puree.

I asked Nishizawa, "What's in this?" He responded, "Kabocha squash." That sounded weird. A squash pastry? I thought about the kabocha and remembered it was sometimes referred to as the Japanese pumpkin. Hmm, Japanese pumpkin in a puff pastry, in November. My family had celebrated Thanksgiving three days earlier. Now I understood.

I pictured the daughter talking to her mom about her American Thanksgiving dinner. I realized I may have just been delivered a secret gift, the closest version of pumpkin pie a Japanese mom could come up with on short notice. I looked again at the delicious kabocha pie in the palm of my hand, and emotion welled up inside me. I reflected on this mysterious offering from a nurturing mom who would understand a girl's homesickness on a holiday far from home. I thought about how the client made no mention of the dessert, no special eye contact when she dropped off the tray. The men wouldn't understand the connection, so I stayed silent.

I spent a bit more time looking over my pie, and then polished it off. I felt like an idiot for all the time I'd spent thinking *I'm so tired, I'm so cold, I'm so lonely,* while everyone else might have been running around, strategizing on how they could do something thoughtful for the American. Sometimes the connections we make in gardens aren't just with the plants but with the

- - - -

people. In *Japanese Garden Design*, Mr. Keane says that in historical context the Japanese word for garden, *niwa*, included "humans in nature as an inherent and indivisible part of it." The garden in Kyoto brought us together—client, garden, gardener. Bite by bite, I savored my kabocha pie and wiped the excess water from my eyes. *It's just plant allergies*, I tried to mentally communicate to the men. I got back to work.

The amount of time the craftsmen spent immaculately cleaning the garden struck me as surreal. First we shook the trees hard by grabbing onto their trunks and mimicking a hurricane. Then we ran around raking fallen leaves like frantic young ducklings paddling after their mom, only we went *scrape, scrape, scrape* instead of *quack, quack, quack*. One of the guys used a loud blower to push the remaining leaves into piles. He then reversed the airflow to suck up the tiny fragments of broken leaf.

Last, we picked up the few remaining leaves by hand and washed down the curbside gutters, starting three houses above our client's property, so no leaves would later be pushed down by wind or water to sully our masterpiece. Nakaji watered down the garden walkways and the path leading to the front door as we backed toward the truck. I turned off the spigot for him. Then he had to water down the front path once again because I'd accidentally left muddy footprints when I walked down the path to return to the truck instead of walking on the moss. Everyone waited and watched while we did this. We did group bows to the mom-client as we stepped backward toward the car.

The sun had just begun to set by the time Nakaji dropped me off on my windy street corner. I headed quickly toward home, wearing two fleece sweaters, a winter jacket, and the thickest hat

I'd brought with me to Kyoto. Not nearly warm enough! I worried inwardly about colder days ahead.

The scene made me think of another Sunday I'd spent just outside Kyoto a few weeks earlier. My Kyoto landlord, David, owned a tiny shack in a rural area, which he used to visit to get away from the crowded city. He took me with him one day. When we arrived he struck up a conversation with an elderly farming woman at work in the fields. The farmer, tending her row of vegetables, looked to be older than seventy. Her body stooped as she walked down the field, making her silhouette look like an upside-down L against a gray, overcast sky. I'd worn a thick coat but still hugged it tightly, wishing I'd brought a thicker hat. Upon our introduction, the woman said, smiling, with David translating, "I can't wait for winter." Her sentences swayed up and down, making her comments sound dramatic and tortured. "This weather makes me so hot!" She wore a thin cotton shirt with sleeves rolled up. I admired and envied the farming woman.

Wind whipped around me and the Kyoto concrete as I made my way home. I pulled down my fleece hat to cover the lowest tips of my earlobes, envisioning sleeping under several layers of covers that evening, which would probably make me sweat a little. I couldn't wait.

Room with a
View of Nature

I finally had a precious Sunday off after thirteen days of gardening with the men. So what did I do? I went to a bonsai show, spent an hour staring at a tree, and then cooked dinner with my coworker, Kei. Hovering at the back of my mind was the fact that the crew and I would leave before dawn the next morning to work at a private client's home out of town. I'd become immersed in the demanding schedule of the Kyoto craftsmen. Small surprises and tiny intrigues became my rewards.

After months of working with the men, I'd do just about anything to spend time with a woman. So when an American friend who lived in Kyoto, Shannon, asked if I would like to look at stylized plants at an annual Kyoto bonsai exhibit on my day off, I responded, "Look at plants? Yes!" Walking through the show, we chatted nonstop about plants, my boyfriend, her husband, her design and textile business, and our opinion on just about everyone and anything within sight. I adored spending time with her—a woman at last. Shannon personified everything the men weren't. She was emotionally expressive and chatty. She wore a snug skirt that showed off her lovely, delicate, feminine figure. She allowed her long blonde hair to tumble in loose waves about her shoulders.

As Shannon and I covered every topic possible, I barely had time to look at the huge bonsai passing our vision.

I explained to Shannon, "*Bonsai* simply means 'plant in a pot.' You can impress your friends if you pronounce the word *bonsai* properly by making the first 'o' long and saying the second part quickly, 'bone-sayee.'" The trees in the exhibit sat spaced apart on long tables like paintings in a museum. These masterpieces grew as we spoke. The exquisite plants we walked past had been watered, fed, root-pruned, and styled for decades, even centuries. In their prime, they'd be brought inside the home or to a bonsai show for display, then taken back outside to a garden if the home-owner liked caring for them, or to a bonsai nursery if a professional looked after them. Many of my clients do not realize that almost all bonsai need to live outdoors. "If you buy a plant," I advised Shannon, "you'll need to water it regularly, perhaps every day in the summer. My little nephew kept track of the constant watering schedule by watering his bonsai with the leftover dog's water, each day that he freshened up the water bowl. Eventually we can teach you how to trim it. It's sort of like a pet."

The bonsai techniques I learned near the beginning of my pruning studies still guide me two decades later. Faced with a difficult plant to style, I go straight to bonsai principles. I explained to Shannon, "Bonsai are not meant to look cool or manipulated—quite the opposite. Look at these plants and imagine real trees enlarged in the landscape, just like when you look at a landscape painting and imagine real scenes. Paintings are made simply of canvas and paint, whereas a bonsai is actually a living plant. So using one's imagination with the plant shouldn't be so hard. The bonsai artist studies nature carefully, takes into account horticultural science,

----

and hopefully allows the spirit of the plant to have some say. A skilled bonsai artist would never dominate or manipulate her plant."

I've noticed that, in any bonsai show, even the most unsavvy bonsai enthusiast can separate the bonsai that looks overmanipulated from the one that looks natural and filled with drama. It's okay with me that not all bonsai are masterpieces. I'll hang any painting created by someone I know. But most of us have managed to see a few masterpiece landscape paintings in our lives. These are the paintings that enchant us into believing that we are almost in the painting, feeling the scene. The same goes for bonsai. Many bonsai artists just have fun and try their best; only a few can style a two-foot bonsai crabapple tree in such a way that when we look at it, we imagine being a child again, sitting under the shade of its drooping branches, ready to pluck a secret treat.

Shannon and I walked and chatted so intently that I hardly noticed even the most spectacular bonsai. Her bright spirit outshone them. As she was telling me a story about her husband, I spotted an old man sitting on a bench facing a rather smaller bonsai than the rest. The plant caught my eye too, even though it had been placed at the end of the table rather than in the center. It looked to be only a foot or so high, whereas the others stood well over three feet. Tiny red fruits hung from this crooked tree—I recognized the bonsai as a dwarf pomegranate. There must have been fifteen spectacular larger plants within view. But this small plant was the only one to pull my attention away from my golden girlfriend.

I asked Shannon if she wouldn't mind going ahead, that I'd catch up with her. She strode off toward the plant bazaar. I waited at an inconspicuous corner of the room until the old man vacated his spot. I didn't want to rush him. After about fifteen minutes, he left, and I walked quickly to his warm seat, trying to act nonchalant. I wasn't sure why he was looking so intently at the pomegranate, but I felt drawn to sit where he had sat.

Delicate bright green leaves covered the small plant, which was dotted with red fruit. A skinny, twisting, sinuous trunk led down to a wide root base lifted so high off the soil I could see a hole through it. This hollow spot reminded me of a favorite tree at UC Berkeley— a buckeye with a rotting lower trunk, rumored to perhaps be the oldest tree on the 150-year-old campus.

The pomegranate leaned to the right, its branches spread out like bird wings, with leaves for feathers. Less than an inch wide, miniature pomegranates dangled enticingly. I assumed the bonsai artist who guided this plant had purposefully left these fruits. Perhaps there had been more and he had removed them. Or maybe less fruit had shown up in previous years, and he waited till the right year in order to display this plant. In my imagination, the pomegranate sat in an abandoned orchard, hence its untended, asymmetrical look. Upon more careful inspection, I noticed that a few of the pomegranates had popped open, bruised and slashed, as though a crow had just been pecking at them. I pictured the pomegranates ripening in late summer, about to drop and rot into the earth.

I marveled at how every detail of the small plant presented a thoughtful collaboration between the plant's will to grow and the patience of the bonsai artist's hand. A slit in one of the fruits exposed its fertile seeds. I laughed, remembering how the other day I'd tried to explain to Kei the difference between the words *fertilizer* and *fertile*, as in "a fertile woman." That conversation had ended quickly.

I couldn't help but stare at the pomegranate searchingly. I had turned thirty-five that year. I felt strong but also a little ripe myself, or at least heading that way. My heart felt pecked at. Wind, cold, trees, and men had pushed me quite a lot of late. The little bonsai also looked lonely among the bonsai giants, many of which had thick trunks and vibrant needles.

Then something occurred to me. The plant before me wasn't just an old plant to be pitied. No. Its bruised fruit captivated me, just as it had the old man. The pomegranate had been placed at the end of the table not because it was to be ignored, but so that it could be admired. It drew me over to take a closer look. In its story I found emotional resonance and beauty. I rested there awhile longer until I began to feel guilty about taking up the seat. So I got up to find Shannon.

My shoulders ached by the time we left the exhibit, because I carried all the work clothes I'd need for a three-day work trip to Hishima. I planned to meet Kei at his house for dinner prep and sleep over there so we could bike together to work in the morning. No buses ran that early. Kei had kindly, but with some hesitation, offered to play host. *What would we talk about for so many hours?* I wondered. I looked forward to our dinner—homemade pizza.

Kei took the duffle bag and groceries from my hands as soon as he opened his door. We fell into an easy rapport. I told him about the bonsai show—a geeky pruner subject. I mentioned that one of the prize plants in the show had been done by a student of my American mentor. Kei did a subtle double take when I mentioned this tidbit, as had Nakaji when I'd told him. I enjoyed trying to get an emotional reaction out of the men.

After I gave Kei a pizza-making lesson, we sat satiated on the tatami floor, still talking about this or that. Since Taylor's departure, I couldn't help but continue to admire to Kei. He could prune like an Olympian and nurse tiny plants on the same day. He had become a symbol of human connection in Kyoto, where sights, sounds, smells, and taste were all foreign.

Could there be something between us? I dared wonder. *Something more than just being friends? Is this why he grew so silent before my boyfriend's visit? Or was he simply becoming a quiet friend? Or worse, was he angry at me?* I fretted. I felt a growing desire to know the answer so I could cancel out the what-ifs and move on. Loneliness caused me to feel even more reckless. So I considered exploring the Do Not Enter garden of my friendship with Kei. Unlike almost everyone I've ever met from Japan, Oklahomans are direct and to the point. So I knew I should just end the conversation right there before my impetuous ideas took hold. But then I thought, *Oh, why not ask? I need to find out what's going on.* "Kei," I ventured forward softly. "So," I meandered as my pulse rose. I thought fleetingly of the image of Taylor saying "I love you" through the taxi window, and then how he'd made no effort to contact me since. "What do you think, Kei, about—" I stuttered down a sharply curved Japanese garden path, its destination hidden. "Kei, what do you think about us being more than friends?"

Lately gardening had become a muddled meditation. I'd focus on pruning the plants one moment, and then quickly other thoughts would enter my head. I'd try to return my focus to the plants, but over the past few weeks my main thoughts had been as repetitive as sheared azaleas in Kyoto: *Plants, tired, plants, boyfriend. Plants, tired, plants, hmmm, my friend Kei.* Back and forth

I went. I looked to Kei; he remained silent. He lay on his back, looking upward thoughtfully. Not a single movement or expression allowed me entry into his thoughts. *What an idiot I am!* I fretted, hoping for something positive to arise out of the mess I'd just created.

With the calm voice of someone used to reining in his emotions, Kei finally responded, "I like Leslie as a pruner." He hesitated before continuing, "I like Leslie as a friend." He seemed to be composing a haiku. "That is how I like Leslie." Then he smiled all friendly up at the ceiling, signaling an ending to his poem. *Brilliant!* I thought, rejected without the use of a single negative word.

After a second or two of prolonged silence, I popped out, "Okay!" and we picked up our conversation about whatever we'd been talking about before my inquiry. Eventually we went to sleep, he in his tiny bedroom, me on the tatami near the toaster oven. I slept restlessly, destined to feel lonely in Kyoto forever. But I still had to smile at Kei's cleverness with the expressive Californian. To my surprise, I'd also felt an immediate sense of relief that Kei and I would remain just friends. That feeling lasted, so I knew it was the right one. I appreciated Kei for his translation abilities and for his diplomacy with a sometimes emotional American gardener.

By the time we reached Hishima the next morning, the birds hardly peeped; their dawn outburst had ceased several hours before. As Masahiro and I sheared like the dickens, running from shrub to shrub, I had time to study all the varying landscape styles on the large estate. Each garden had a different atmosphere. Beds leading to the front door felt like walking through a modern art museum with all the tightly sheared shrubs and symmetrical marble sculptures. The landscape facing the back bedrooms looked like forests of fall color, with maples and evergreen live oaks. Near the side kitchen, I discovered farm-to-kitchen vegetable beds. I even peeked around a tall fence enclosing a tiny garden off a bathroom window. This scene, with the right imagination, might turn a brief shower into a mountain waterfall plunge.

On the outside, the gardens felt disjointed. But because the Japanese mostly view their gardens from inside the house, one room at a time, the variety of the gardens was just fine. At new California jobs, I ask my clients if I can enter their home to look at the gardens from inside. American homeowners walk, play, and relax in their yards much more than Japanese do. But busy Americans forget that most weekday nights and many cold winter days, they also view their gardens primarily from inside.

I have a client with a large backyard apple tree outside her dining room. It offers shade to an outdoor picnic table and provides her fruit. She leaves most of her apples for birds because the tree produces so many and the fruits are mushy. I call her fruit Snow White apples because of their black-red color. Each year I cook with them, labeling my jars "Snow White Apple Sauce." I asked my client if I could sit in her dining room chair the first time I worked on the tree, as she told me that most days of the week she liked doing office work in that spot. I'd found the primary viewing point for the apple. From there I could see where to prune the Snow White tree, high enough so a view to an uphill neighbor could remain screened, and low enough so more sunlight could enter the room.

Masahiro and I raked up enormous piles of leaves. On my way back from one particular dump run, I took a shortcut around a rather huge sheared shrub and found myself in the company of some new, and friendly, colleagues. Snow White and the seven dwarfs, painted statues each about a foot tall, marched in formation beneath a wide azalea shrub, which I hoped might bloom in spring Technicolor. I wondered if these statues emphasized the garden's deep forest theme or just held our Japanese client's imagination in the light way the fable held mine. This was indeed my most interesting question of the day.

When we arrived at the Japanese inn where our client had paid for us to stay for several evenings, a receptionist whisked me away to my private room. The men would sleep in a shared dorm room somewhere else in the hotel. She opened the door onto a luxurious space with a central futon covered with a cloth of such delicate floral print, the woman might just as well have strewn fresh petals on top. *Perhaps she's taken me to the wrong room!* I thought anxiously. A glossy lacquer tray with a tea set sat nearby on a short bedside table. An elegant wooden screen hid my private bathroom. With smudges all over my face and my clothes covered in dirt, I felt like I'd entered the magical attic room of one of my favorite childhood books, *The Little Princess*, only set in Japan.

The inn's thick futon bed looked inviting after a long day. The receptionist mistakenly thought I was staring at the lacquer tray, so she walked over to show me how to use the teapot, cups, and strainer. She opened the tea tin and tilted it for my inspection. Inside I saw shriveled green tea made from the leaves of *Camellia sinensis*, the shrub that Nakaji had me smell. As soon as the receptionist left, I tipped my weary body onto the bed and remained motionless, looking up at the ceiling, corpse-style, for a while.

For once, I thought, *being the only garden girl at Uetoh Zoen has paid off*. According to Kei, the men had to share one big tatami room. I wondered if they were jealous.

Glancing around, I noticed a small rectangular alcove built into the wall, about the size of a wine crate. Inside rested a vase of holly branches with a painted scroll of a snow-covered forest scene hanging behind. The alcove reminded me of a *tokonoma*, a much larger display shelf commonly found in Japanese teahouses.

A typical *tokonoma* alcove—about six feet high, five feet wide— might display flowers with a calligraphy scroll behind them. Regardless of the physical size of the *tokonoma*, the scene is meant to represent a much bigger, or even limitless, scene in nature. Just as a poem is the essence of a story, the *tokonoma* represents the essence of nature, hinting at a certain scene, atmosphere, or message. I looked at the little alcove in my room and imagined a winter holly shrub inside a snow-covered grove of pines. Although my inn bedroom had no windows, which normally might have felt claustrophobic, the little alcove acted as a make-believe peephole into imaginary nature.

I also found that my room had a real *tokonoma*, a large, tall alcove raised slightly off the floor. In it sat a television, computer, and telephone, with a factory-made landscape scroll hanging on the wall behind. Did this display represent a landscape of technology coming to the Japanese countryside?

The idea of my own room sounded fun, but as I looked at the blank computer screen, I sensed loneliness creeping up. I pictured

----

the men spread out in their huge tatami room, joking around, snoring in unison. Back home in Kyoto, I'd gotten used to the company of traffic horns and the morning monastery drums.

Silly Leslie, I told myself, trying to cheer myself up, *you know the men envy you getting a private room!* Right before I'd separated from the men in the lobby, Kei informed me, "We'll eat in the main dining area at seven. Normally we wear pajamas." Before I could ask what that meant, the men walked off. I showered and waited on the futon, which was so much more luxurious than my flattened futon back in Kyoto, contemplating pajama options.

My relaxation ended when the phone jarringly rang at six-thirty. Masahiro, who could hardly speak English, said in a shaky voice, "Dinner is now," and hung up. I had decided that I definitely wasn't going downstairs in my preferred bedtime attire, a thin cotton shirt and undies, so I stepped out in a fleece sweater and sweatpants.

I found the men in the dining room sitting quietly, legs crossed, on flat pillows. I thought at first that they were meditating. But it's just that I was late, and they'd been waiting for me. They hardly spoke during most meals. The guys wore T-shirts and pajama bottoms. I'd guessed correctly this time on the Western ladies' proper inn attire, although a pink negligee might have livened up the serious group a bit. I tried not to stare at Nakaji's outfit, a stiff, perfectly ironed kimono with a bold abstract print. I found out later that Japanese men and women often wore *yukata*, kimono robes worn after the bath, at traditional Japanese inns. Masahiro's hands shook during the whole meal. He came from a rural island in Japan, and the guys told me that this was his first experience eating freshwater fish, perhaps eating in such a fancy restaurant. I felt a bit jittery myself, sitting across from my boss while he was wearing a bathrobe, even if it was hand-stitched and manly looking.

Our table had a lovely view of an outdoor stream and landscape through a wide glass window. Just like a *tokonoma*, the inn courtyard garden was small, but it felt much bigger in my imagination. As the meal progressed I wanted to ask questions I normally didn't have time to ask at work. Nevertheless I held my silence, not wanting to bother Kei for translating. I had a whole reservoir of questions saved up. I'd learned that in Kyoto if I waited before asking a question, the answer would usually appear on its own. I thought up what seemed like millions of questions each day. Yet I had to pick and choose the most important ones to avoid overwhelming the men.

That day, I asked Kei just two questions: "When do we bike to Uetoh?" and "What time is dinner?" Some of the questions I wanted to ask him were: "Where else does Uetoh go on work trips?" And "How much did this cost our out-of-town client?" (At the end of the trip I estimated nearly three thousand dollars for one fall pruning.) And "Do any of the men have hobbies like ikebana (the Japanese art of flower arranging), bonsai, or poetry outside of pruning?" A month later Nishizawa told me that he did ikebana, "as an amateur only, for fifteen years." And "What was Nakaji's favorite garden?" Nakaji happened to answer this question during a tea break, saying his favorite garden was Katsura Imperial Villa, "for the pines." I held myself back from asking what I needed to know that night: "Does my inn room have a heater?" I never found one; I just used lots of blankets and two hats.

The moonlight struck the little pine in the courtyard garden, rendering its needles a mass of green spider legs. I nibbled quietly on my fish and pickled vegetables, gripping my chopsticks tightly for fear they'd tumble out of my hands and onto the tatami, disturbing the peaceful meal. The men finally relaxed and began to chat, in Japanese. So I pretended I traveled alone on vacation, enjoying a delicious meal in an inn on my own with a fine view of a forest and stream, which anyone would enjoy in solitude, wouldn't they? Keeping me company during my dinner was the feminine maple that leaned over a rock, gurgling water flowing among boulders, a prickly pine pruned by someone else, and the reflected moonlight, which captivated my attention the most with its fleeting spirit.

Feminine Strength
in the Maple Grove

One morning the following week, I showed up at the office looking like the incredible garden-girl hulk. I'd overslept through two
alarms, thrown my work clothes right over my pajamas, and run
to my bus stop with my hair crammed into a bright blue fleece
hat. Wearing two layers of clothing, and with my hair a mess, I
had a difficult time walking and felt even more self-conscious
than normal traveling through town. Later that day, I met some
women whose uniforms were different, and much more beautiful, than mine. I sat in the back of the bus and tried to comb my
hair with my fingers. But no one gave me a second glance. I had
a chance to "slim down" in the women's bathroom, undressing
to take off my pajamas. Ironically, I made it to work on time, and
by chance the men showed up late, so I got to act as number-one
worker for half an hour.

Loading the truck under Bossman's loud instructions made
me physically jittery, but mentally I was unfazed. I understood
at this point that when it came to yelling commands, Nakaji was
an equal-opportunity boss. Once the men arrived, we zigzagged
through the streets of Kyoto. We passed commercial shops blanketed in neon signs and street-side altar gardens brimming with

plants. The city was modernizing at an unstoppable rate, but tradition and nature were still held closely.

I became distracted by memories of Berkeley's November lemon and orange trees ripening in the sun. I looked out onto the cold Kyoto street and noticed we'd entered a completely different neighborhood. The buildings had turned from busy glass-fronted shops to simple wooden structures of traditional design, with almost no signs. The neighborhood looked old and handcrafted. Pedestrians, who filled the Kyoto main streets during rush hour, had all but disappeared. It felt as though we'd driven onto an empty movie set of *The Twilight Zone*. The only movement was that of bamboo blinds swinging back and forth in an invisible morning breeze.

I turned to Kei and tilted my head. Still my closest friend in Kyoto, he understood my question. "We are in Gion, Leslie, a historic neighborhood where geisha live," he explained. "Today we are working at an *okiya*, a traditional lodging where women live when they are training to be geisha. *Okiya* are almost like family." "It's so quiet," I couldn't help but mention. "The geisha are still asleep. They worked very late last night at the bars." He spoke the last sentence as though he had personal knowledge of this fact. This made me feel a bit annoyed, and amused.

The men's voices rose an octave. They're interested too, it occurred to me. I felt terribly curious myself about the possibility of seeing these highly trained and beautiful women of Japan, but for a different reason than the men. I recited a silent prayer: *Please surround me with more than just testosterone today.*

We arrived outside a front gate leading to the *okiya*, which was a large white modern building. We waited in the truck while Nakaji gained permission to enter. The property was enclosed by a naturally plastered wall, which from the inside had been lined with wide strips of tree bark. Towering maples grew over the wall, and a huge, dense forest hovered inside. Young women, practically girls, in bright kimonos fluttered past our truck, laughing softly and whispering to one another. The men watched their approach attentively through the rearview mirrors, trying to act as though they weren't. I turned my head to follow their path, wanting to see every detail of their exquisitely designed kimonos. I did slink down a bit in my seat, hoping the women wouldn't notice my masculine attire. I felt shy being so close to these soft-skinned women.

When walking into cafés in Berkeley at the end of gardening days, seeing office girls in stylish skirts standing next to me, I feel awkward and invisible to men. I love working with the trees, the soil covering my skin, little spiders finding their way up my sleeves. But pruning requires sacrifice for a social young woman. On my days off, when I wear slim jeans tucked into black suede boots, I notice myself being noticed.

A car pulled up very close to our work truck, and a tall woman got out, wearing a kimono with a formal, subdued print. She walked toward the front door with a certain power and elegance that drew everyone's attention. *How does she do that?* I wondered, watching her stride, trying to deduce her method. Exiting the truck myself, I instinctually made sure my door did not touch hers, even in the slightest. Kei watched me. "Be careful, Leslie. That car belongs to the headmistress."

Stepping inside the garden wall, I was enveloped by a mass of scarlet foliage overhead and brilliant moss underfoot. The ground sloped downward from the outer garden wall toward the building, embracing its occupants. I observed multiple floors, each with a

----

view out onto the upper portion of the forest through one huge window per apartment. Each room had its own living landscape painting through a window, a portrait of an ever-transforming geisha garden.

This painting would alter over the course of a year, from a tender springtime portrait to a lush foliage-filled summer painting. As fall approached, new colors would appear, slowly at first, the artist painting them one by one, and then all at once, as though an invisible hand pricked the canvas with a pin, spilling blood across the canvas. In winter the tableau would become cool, with bare maple branches silhouetted against blue skies. Kei mentioned that *maiko*, apprentice geisha, entertained clients from their rooms, so the beauty and care of the garden held great significance for them. "They entertain from their rooms only during the day," he clarified, sensing where my thoughts had strayed.

He explained that the *maiko* learned traditional songs, dances, musical instruments, and dress. *Maiko* even studied the art of pleasant conversation, about current politics, for example—a lost art form in America's Southern states, where my dad's Republican and Democrat friends used to tease one another mercilessly, in friendship, every afternoon over lunch at their favorite diner, the Lunch Box.

I watched Japanese films obsessively throughout college, including one about a modern geisha. I felt intrigued by filmmakers who saw their world through an aesthetic lens tinted with nature. One of these films, *When a Woman Ascends the Stairs*, told the story of a cocktail lounge hostess in a small Japanese seaside town in the fifties. Similar to a geisha, this hostess entertained male customers at night for money, climbing stairs to an upper-story bar. The men accepted her as simply a conversational companion, even if they sometimes propositioned her. I identified with her as a sensible woman, determined to earn her own living, sometimes allowing herself to fall in love, at times with the wrong man. Occasionally, when I arrive home from work to my two-story home, exhausted and loaded down with workbags, I think of this woman as I climb the stairs to my front door. I asked Kei if he thought contemporary geisha were in any way intimate with their patrons. He responded firmly, "Leslie, Japanese men look to geisha as entertaining conversation companions, and that's it." *Friends only*, I repeated to myself to be sure I remembered his point.

The early morning cold in the geisha garden dominated most of my ruminations. Despite the handmade cardboard insoles I'd cut for my thin-soled *jikatabi*, my chilled feet pinpricked with pain as I walked over the lumpy, icy moss during the first three hours of work. In the early hours of a Kyoto November garden, the ground released the cold it had gathered overnight, pushing frosty air into my soles. I pruned ferns from thick clumps down to three or five fronds per plant. Therefore, not only was I standing on a sheet of ice, I was hardly moving. I glanced over at the men. They didn't wear sweaters yet, much less hats. I tried to push my discomfort as far inside as possible. I hoped my feet and hands might go numb rather than become painful. *It's just a feeling*, I told myself, trying to accept my situation; *you won't die*.

Nakaji walked over to where I crouched, next to a fern that almost looked like the native California sword fern, and pointed to my well-worn leather gloves. He spoke disapprovingly. I understood his message. I'd heard it before. Bossman obsessed over clean gloves, donning brand-new white cotton ones every day. I had never thought twice about my gloves' age or cleanliness. And daily glove donning was contrary to my environmentalist and frugal nature. One worker told me employees snagged Nakaji's day-old gloves out of the trash can every night to use the next day. I felt tempted, but the trash can was claimed.

My Uetoh coworkers showed up to work every morning in clean, pressed uniforms. These uniforms seemed to demand respect, in a way that made me think the torn jeans of the California garden outfit encouraged the reverse. Almost every person I met in Kyoto talked about the craftsmen in a deeply respectful way. I'd tell them I worked in the gardens, and they'd ooh and aah as though I were working on a doctorate. In California, if I mention my occupation, people often respond, "How relaxing to work outside!" as though I've figured out a clever way to hang out at the beach all day.

On top of respect, Japanese society paid the most experienced gardeners and company owners well, and the Japanese government assured garden craftsmen a lifetime of free health care and affordable housing. And in return, the Japanese craftsmen, like doctors and geisha, trained in their craft for years, if not decades, before starting their own businesses. I sometimes wondered, though, what inspired my crew, many of whom were still very much in training and earning low pay. They worked so incredibly hard, every freezing winter day, six days a week, nine to ten hours a day. Why did they push themselves beyond what might be expected of a good worker?

Nakaji had already hinted to me weeks ago about getting new gloves. I'd tried to compromise by simply washing my gloves each evening. Apparently they still looked too dirty. So I washed my gloves under the freezing outdoor faucet, right where the men could see me during first break, and wore them wet for the rest of the day, acting the martyr. When Nakaji saw me washing them, he pointed and loudly said to the men, *"Bimbo!"* They all laughed in unison while my complexion turned a color matching the fall leaves overhead.

How could he know this obscure English word, I thought, furious, *and announce it in a women's garden?* Traditionally, the geisha business consists exclusively of women: students, teachers, and even owners of the places where apprentice geisha live and work. I watched the proprietress of the *okiya* we worked at through a large window on the first floor. Over the course of several days, I saw this elderly lady sitting on a cushion in front of a low table piled with papers, working away for hours on end. And she could see us. After the B-word was spoken, I ran extra quickly, carrying several ladders at once as the men often did, mentally daring Nakaji to use that word again.

When I got home that evening, I told my American landlord about Bossman's sexist insult. He doubled over laughing. He explained that Nakaji had actually said *binbo,* which means poor person in Japanese slang. I laughed too, realizing I'd never survive if I actually understood what Nakaji said half the time. The next morning, I stopped off at a local 7-Eleven to buy a twelve-pack of gardener's fuzzy white cotton gloves to last exactly twelve days.

It took me a while to realize that Nakaji's obsession over white gloves did not necessarily mean he was looking for people's respect, even if he got it. He didn't strike me as the type who waited for other people's approval. White gloves pointed to one of the more difficult to understand ethics I discovered working alongside the craftsmen.

The men ran between jobs and pruned furiously, almost competitively, as they searched for ways to do a little more than what was expected of them. Their pride did not necessarily come from high achievement, or from high pay, fancy titles, and retirements, although I'm sure they appreciated such things. I noticed that the Uetoh craftsmen's main source of job satisfaction instead seemed to be effort and sacrifice.

When I returned to California, a pruning colleague asked me, "What did you learn in Japan?" My impulse was to answer, "Life is hard." Years later I reformulated that answer after I'd gained some perspective: "Gardening is very hard work, but at the end of the day, like raising a family, it is deeply satisfying." The men taught me to put a little extra time into my work than what was expected, and to increase my speed over time. They taught me that if I do a little more than is asked of me every day, if I work with heart, I will feel a sense of pride before anyone tells me "you are so skilled."

Particularly because I am a woman working in a traditionally male field, I have to feel good about my work from the inside. It makes me sad to see other dedicated, brilliant American gardeners suffering from low self-esteem. By asking me to wear new white gloves every day, I think Nakaji was trying to teach me that if I act like a premier craftsperson, I might feel like one.

By afternoon the glorious sun warmed up the geisha garden. Nakaji and the other workers enjoyed watching me try to feebly shake dead leaves out of the maples. I didn't want to hurt the poor trees! I pulled the trunk back and forward carefully, causing a few leaves to tumble down. I shook the tree a little harder, and a bunch of leaves fell on my head. Not bad! I smiled at Bossman, congratulating myself. Wrong. Nakaji let out a distressed sigh. He motioned me aside. He grabbed ahold of the trunk and jerked it so hard I thought it would snap. Leaves fell as though a tornado had hit. Looking up afterward, I understood why he had used this violent method. Every single shriveled, brown leaf had fallen out of the tree, and all that remained was an exquisite, blood orange canopy silhouetted against the sky. This was the image that had inspired me for decades in Japanese garden photos. In reality, the leaves of maple trees go into fall color in spurts, leaving lots of brownish leaves mixed in with the colorful ones. Only with a gardener's intervention was I able to view this stunning maple scene. The geisha at the *okiya* appreciated this scene so much that they hired us to do the same job two weeks later.

High up in the maples, I had a chance to study branch patterns. "Coarse to fine," I noted. Like all trees, the maples began with tiny roots under the earth, melding into a wide base, called the root crown, above the earth. This grows into a trunk, breaking off into thick branches, then smaller ones, then hundreds of tiny branchlets, the outer canopy of the tree. With this gradual upward structure, fine roots to coarse trunk to fine branches, the tree held quite stable, without rigidity.

An excellent example of a tree's combined strength and flexibility can be found at the Oklahoma City National Memorial, dedicated to those who died or survived the domestic terrorist bombing in 1995. A few years ago, my best friend from third grade, Karen, and I walked around the memorial reflecting on the uselessness of all that death. One of the women who died belonged to the hippie Catholic church I grew up in, a church that focused

----

on social equality and justice. To kill someone trying to help poor people, who encouraged understanding between diverse human beings, seemed the ultimate stupidity.

I felt a bit numb at the memorial, so I walked over to investigate a large tree on the site. The reverberations from the bomb blast caused the windows at my father's law office, five blocks away, to shatter. An elm tree directly across from the blast became webbed with shards of glass all over its trunk and had all of its leaves shredded off. People said for months that the tree looked like it might die. But it still lives today because of its coarse-to-fine structure. People call it the Survivor Tree. Its huge root structure, with thousands of fine roots clinging to the soil, and its massive trunk held the tree firm, but the upper branches flexed so the tree didn't snap. Sometimes I tell my clients who reluctantly neglect their gardens while they are busy with careers or family, "Don't worry; plants are forgiving."

The geisha garden's maple canopy also looked fine and clean. In pruning classes, I ask people to look at trees in the distance, at the fine canopies. Our subconscious knows that a tree's outer perimeter is soft and even, even if our conscious mind would not be able to put this into words. This is why a poorly pruned tree, a "butchered tree," with coarse stubs on the ends and long reactionary sprouts sticking out of its canopy, looks wrong even to a non-pruner. The craftsmen were quite careful to prune the maple branches properly, at intersections, so that no stub cuts could be seen.

Wrestling another maple on foot, I climbed into the tree and shook every branch within reach. Then I used a hook on a long pole to shake even higher branches. We seemed to prune and shake every square inch of the forest. Then about thirty feet up one tree, I spotted a particularly messy-looking area that just wouldn't shake clean. I climbed up to it feeling frustrated and stubborn; it was quite high. Peering over the mess, I discovered a small nest, skillfully woven out of moss and twigs. I marveled at how it had survived the garden craftsman storm. The tiny home looked so tender against the bright sky. I stared at it wistfully, wishing I could climb inside the soft bed and take a brief nap. My heart, beating erratically from all the shaking and climbing, slowed to gentle thumps. I sighed deeply, and went somewhere else where I could shake the tree again before Nakaji found me idle.

We used noisy leaf blowers in the geisha garden, we raked around every trunk, we picked up fallen leaves by hand, and we swept crumbs off the rocks with our *tebōki*, hand brooms. I tried to enjoy the moment. After all, we were inside a private garden, in one of Kyoto's oldest neighborhoods. But climbing forty-five feet into a spindly maple, I just didn't feel like it. Instead I felt remorse because I'd accidentally raked up a fairly sizable chunk of the moss carpet off a rock. *You'll never learn*, I reprimanded myself. I tried to transfer some new moss onto the spot, patting it into place like fixing a hole in a piecrust. But none stuck. So I left the hole bare and hoped no one would notice.

Nakaji did his half-time yell to signal lunch. *Rumble, rumble.* The doors of a room on the ground floor slid open. For a moment, I thought I had fantasized that an elaborate picnic for a princess had appeared. I blinked. Sure enough, resting on the edge of the tatami sat black lacquered trays holding oranges, sweets, cakes, and a tea service. The geisha, experts in entertaining, hadn't forgotten the dirt-smeared gardeners. As we enjoyed our meal, the rock with a mile-wide bald spot sat smack in the middle of our

----

view, a few feet away. No one said a word. They knew it would be worse for me that way.

Ring, ring! A young man rode into the garden on a bike. *What's that?* I wondered. He opened a wooden box on the back of his bike and lifted out five steaming bowls of udon, covered tightly in plastic wrap. Scallions floated ever so delicately on top of the steaming broth, as though they had fallen from the maples. I felt a moment of peace, and I silently thanked the proprietress for allowing us to relax and enjoy the fall colors with a nourishing meal. Not only did she help train female geisha apprentices, but that day she helped a female gardener apprentice. The men remained silent and contemplative as they ate. Their fierce work ethic, intertwined with their ability to appreciate refined beauty, was what allowed them to build premier naturalized gardens. I ran around and took photos, and in one adjusted a bucket of an old well to frame the shot. When I returned to the car, where the men had retreated to listen to talk radio, Nakaji said, "Don't touch the well around the other side of the building. It is over a hundred years old."

On my way home, I instinctively headed for warmth in my local *sentō*. On any given evening, I'd find all sorts of neighborhood women there—from older wrinkled ladies to skinny girls to considerably plump middle-aged women. I'd even seen a little girl jump into the icy cold plunge and swim like a baby koi. I'd never had the opportunity to see so many types of female bodies on a weekly basis. One late night I saw a woman at the bathhouse about my age, naked, with bruises all over her body. Every woman was welcome at the bathhouse. We cleansed and warmed ourselves together.

The evening after working in the geisha garden, I stood in a steaming tub up to my stomach and noticed a big red bump on

- - - -

my hand. Did I have a disease? I looked more closely this time. It finally occurred to me that I had a blister. I looked at it fondly. It had been such a long time since I'd gotten a blister, almost twenty years. I'd trained in ballet as a child and teenager, dancing four hours a day, five days a week. I loved my sweaty lessons. My teacher, Louise, was both a ballet teacher who could spin six turns on one toe *and* had a black belt in karate. She was tough. I had plenty of well-earned blisters back then. But not one blister since high school until now. I saw myself as a young girl running to class, so excited to work out. I eventually found myself too short in height and on talent to dance professionally. I'd also felt a desire to explore the world more than the demanding ballerina schedule would allow. Quitting ballet in college, I began searching for something I felt equally passionate about. I stared at the palm of my hand. *It's right here, Leslie, in the hand that holds your shears.*

Guardian Angel
Tells a White Lie

December finally arrived. One morning, I stood at my Kyoto bus stop, hugging myself for warmth, when down from the sky floated a perfect snowflake. It landed right on my workbag, where it promptly melted. As more fell, I tried to guess where they might land. They blew in every direction. I pulled my hat down over my ears and sensed a feeling coming on that I'd experienced little of lately—exuberance. Real snow! I hadn't felt snow since I was a child in Oklahoma, where we'd sledded down the soft slopes near our forested street. I looked around and saw that my bus stop companions remained expressionless, their reactions kept hidden.

I'd often see a middle-aged woman at this bus stop, a transfer point on my way to work, wearing colorful silk hair scarves tied under her chin. She talked to me in rapid Japanese that I could never understand, much to my chagrin. My mind was hardly functioning at six-thirty in the morning, yet despite my inability to respond in any coherent way, she never gave up on her attempts to teach me new Japanese phrases. When I'd see her, I'd say to myself, *Oh, no, here comes the friendly woman.*

That morning I felt worn out from week after week of fast-paced physical labor with the craftsmen, six days a week, sometimes seven. I was nearing the end of my apprenticeship, and as Christmas approached, so did my homesickness. I stood daydreaming about Christmas trees when the friendly woman silently snuck up next to me and burst into a high-pitched, unintelligible monologue. "*Ohayō gozaimasu!*" (Good morning!) On and on she went, speaking—as though I understood her! I turned and stared at her in disbelief, and in doing so, happened to spot the bus I needed to catch driving toward our stop—a full ten minutes earlier than expected. It normally took fifteen minutes for my transfer bus to arrive, and I'd been at the stop only a few minutes. I barely had a chance to wave it down. Once I'd sat down, frazzled, I looked at my watch and realized the bus had actually arrived at its normal time. How could this be? Where had the time gone? I tried to think back, willing my brain to wake up. The answer found its way, like morning light piercing a dark canopy. I must have fallen asleep at the bus stop while standing up! The friendly woman had spoken to wake me up. She'd saved me from missing my bus and showing up late for work, a dreaded prospect. But she'd done so in such a subtle way, without embarrassing me or calling attention to her favor. Forever afterward I'd see her and react instinctively, *Oh, no!* but then I'd feel warmth inside and think, *Here comes my guardian angel.*

I admired the way my angel and my coworkers communicated ideas and messages indirectly. I'd had little practice in this art form. Oklahoma pioneer culture tends to be pretty direct: "A man is as good as his word," and "walk your talk." American culture in general also tends to reward direct communication. For example, one Halloween evening in Berkeley, a tiny soft-spoken ninja showed up at my door. The three-foot-high figure barely managed to whisper "trick-or-treat" so that she could grab one of the small chocolate candies I held out to her. Her mom gently but firmly reprimanded her, "Look at the woman when you speak!" I myself was taught early on to politely say thank you, shake hands firmly, and to look people right in the eye out of respect.

Every Monday morning, the Uetoh workers gathered to listen to the boss's speech. They stood silently with their heads bowed and eyes politely averted. During the meetings, I stood with my hands together in front of me and my head bowed like a traditional Japanese craftsman. But I'd still glance up with my eyes, looking directly at the company leader, partly out of rebellion, partly out of childhood habit. It felt odd not to look at someone who was speaking to me, especially someone higher than me in the Japanese hierarchy— elder, teacher, and leader.

One of the few times I experienced indirect communication in America came from my friendship with Mas, my Japanese American bonsai instructor. Mas was born in America, moved to Japan when he was three months old, and returned when he was thirteen. He eventually served as a U.S. soldier in World War II. Afterward he became a well-known landscaper, bonsai artist, and teacher. I met Mas while he was instructing me and several others on how to move thousand-pound rocks, using his eight-foot-tall wooden tripod with a pulley system. I'd volunteered, under Mas's direction, to help build the landscape to surround the prestigious Bonsai Garden at Lake Merritt in Oakland, California. Some of us women volunteers secretly planted my *Xena: Warrior Princess* doll in the soil right near the entrance gate to promote female power in the garden. Sure enough, an American female bonsai artist, Kathy Shaner, trained and awarded in Japan, became acting director of the garden.

After completing the volunteer project, I began chauffeuring eighty-something-year-old Mas to my community college once a month so he could teach pruning at our Merritt College Bonsai Club, the only bonsai club in the state run by volunteers, without dues or fees. In exchange he'd take me out to sushi dinner before each class. Over these meals Mas hardly spoke, but what few words he said, I remember. One such evening, as I picked up the last piece of nigiri sushi between my fingers (Mas told me it was acceptable not to use chopsticks), I asked him a question that had been in the back of my mind for a while. It was a month before I was to leave for Kyoto in search of my apprenticeship. "Mas," I spoke hesitantly, "to be honest, I'm not sure I'm good enough to work in Japan. What if I'm a burden to any company I end up working with?" This was hard for me to ask, but I trusted Mas. "Don't worry," is all he said. I figured that maybe his focus was on his *chirashi*, a small bowl of rice with raw fish and traditional Japanese vegetables on top. It usually took him about an hour to finish, while I chatted away and drew sketches of him or anything else in my vision.

The following week, Mas called to ask if I wanted to come over to his house to prune the tallest pine in his backyard Japanese garden, where he cared for and displayed his bonsai, including the juniper featured on the cover of the 1994 edition of the book *Sunset Bonsai*. I was thrilled. The pine that needed work stood more than fifteen feet high, taller than any conifer I'd ever pruned. Mas had styled it for more than thirty years. It leaned over his big koi pond, where "Mama," a fat two-foot-long orange koi, would come to Mas and eat fish food right out of his hand when he stomped on the pond's edge. Mas's bonsai plants poetically dotted the perimeter of the pond. He'd tell me, "My trees are old, you know, just like me."

Despite my eagerness to prune a tree in a famous garden, I dreaded my new assignment. Dennis warned us, "If any of you are asked to prune in Mas's garden, you'd better know what you are doing. If you botch the job, people will find out, and your reputation will be ruined."

Dripping with sweat, I worked several days on the multi-branched pine. Mas worked from a nearby chair, delicately snipping one of his bonsai, perhaps the first bonsai he ever collected fifty-seven years earlier, a Sierra juniper, one of the three that he later donated to the prestigious Pacific Bonsai Museum in Washington. I had to regularly move a fifteen-foot ladder around the pond, maneuvering it around his potted bonsai plants. "Do you want help?" he'd ask, yelling out from the other side of the pond. "No, no, I got it!" I'd stubbornly insist. How could I ask an eighty-year-old to help me carry a ladder? I tried my best to be careful while I navigated the twisting paths. But sometimes I'd come perilously close to his priceless black pine bonsai from the 1915 San Francisco Panama-Pacific International Exposition, estimated to be more than four hundred years old, or to the large potted pine said to have been smuggled out of the Golden Gate Park Japanese Tea Garden the night before rioters attacked the garden during World War II.

At such moments, I'd feel the tail of my ladder being steadied, and I'd look behind me to discover Mas guiding me to just the right spot, where I could reach the next branch I needed to work on. Just as silently as he'd appear, he'd go back to his bonsai and recommence his patient, tedious styling. I worried every minute about my competence. At the end of three long days, we looked together, and even I had to admit that the hundreds of zig-zagging branches that Mas had touched for years, and that I now touched, looked beautiful silhouetted against the azure sky. Mas said, "That's good work, Leslie." Before he'd even said it, I felt deep down that I was ready for Japan.

The day my guardian angel saved me at the bus stop, the crew and I worked in a formal garden, the Kyoto Prefectural Reception Hall, under vibrant green pines and red-flowering camellias covered with a light dusting of snow. Uetoh Zoen had previously built the garden in one of many future collaborations with international Japanese landscape designer Shunmyo Masuno.

As I raked thousands of fallen leaves and red petals, I watched curiously as Masahiro placed several floating bamboo poles in a pond, forming a half-circle. I eventually deduced that if leaves fell into the pond while we pruned the maples above, the poles would create a sort of drifting fence, holding the leaves in a small area so they could be easily dredged out later with rakes. Told to shake dead leaves out of trees above another pond, I searched for some bamboo poles. I learned new tricks each day, silently observing the men while working on other tasks. A Japanese landscaper I met called this type of learning "stealing knowledge."

Not only did the craftsmen teach me indirectly, but the gardens did too. For example, if I saw a black rope wrapped around a rock in the landscape, I'd slow down. Most Japanese visitors know that a black rope signifies "Do not step past here" or "This is a sacred place" without needing a sign to spell it out. Likewise, a visitor might walk down a path and come upon an extra-large flat stepping stone. Subconsciously, she might slow to a stop, the wide stone allowing her to stand comfortably with both feet. The visitor might then look around, noticing a particularly striking view. The use of a large stepping stone is a common landscaper's trick to invite visitors to slow down and feel as though they've discovered a vista all on their own. Japanese landscapes guide the visitor, her pace and path, gently.

A fascinating high-tech design featured in the Reception Garden was so subtle that most nighttime visitors experienced it without knowing about it. I later found an article written by Shunmyo Masuno about the Reception Hall garden in the journal *Process Architecture* in 1995 discussing how a computerized lighting system was installed in place of nighttime spotlights. Lights came on and off in different areas of the garden throughout the night, in a preprogrammed pattern that could be altered into different arrangements. Each time a visitor looked out from the main building, a different waterfall, rock, or plant would appear under the light's focus, entertaining the mind both consciously and unconsciously.

Toemon Sano, Uetoh Zoen's leader, also wrote in this special issue of the journal. He said that although the gardens of Masuno, when first built, might look "somewhat demure in character," the quality of his gardens "becomes apparent with the passage of time." He said that Masuno was not so concerned with "making" a garden as with the "raising of a garden." Like a child, a garden needed to be guided and raised with care to develop into a mature beauty. Hence, a Japanese garden combines the designer's plan with the gardeners' care, the pruners' encouragement, and nature's influence over time. Mr. Sano's final words stuck with me.

The mixture of traditional plants and modern lighting at the Reception Hall struck me as impressive, but to be honest I couldn't have cared less about its enchanting beauty or sophisticated design. All I focused on was what Kei had told me earlier in the day: "Leslie, we're traveling to another out-of-town job next weekend." I already had plans for that weekend. My American friends and I intended to put on a festive Sunday dinner. If I worked out of town with my crew, I'd miss Christmas in Kyoto.

Christmas in Kyoto almost always fell on a weekday, so most Americans I'd met just skipped it. One expat mentioned that he'd felt so depressed after years of not being able to find a Christmas tree in Kyoto that he decided to drop Christmas altogether. Hearing that made me so sad. This year Christmas Eve fell on a Sunday, so my most warmhearted American friend, Maya, and I had dreamt up finding some kind of branch to take the place of the Christmas tree, as well as having a celebratory feast. Ever since Kei told me about the work trip, I imagined my friends gathering in Kyoto while I endured inn isolation—the men all in one room at the hotel, me by myself in the other. My disappointment grew throughout the day, and my actions became equally weathered.

No matter how many floating bamboo fences I constructed, thousands of dead leaves clogged the water. Despite the fact that the ponds, connected by streams, had a clear flow downhill, the men decided to clean the leaves out of the lower ponds first, moving up to the highest ones last. This meant that as we cleaned leaves in one area, more streamed down from upper ponds, clogging it back up. In these kinds of circumstances, I'd learned to scratch my head and do as I was told; there was always a good reason for doing what looked odd. But this day, I proclaimed the

----

process stupid in my thoughts. I walked to an upper pond and began raking by myself. *If I have to go on the Christmas work trip, then at least I'll do things my way today*, I reasoned spitefully, with a certain emotional immaturity that sometimes besets me when I'm overwhelmed by loneliness.

After a while, Masahiro hiked up to where I was busily cleaning and motioned for me to work downstream with the others. I simply pretended I couldn't understand him. I looked at him with a sweet smile and proceeded to carry out my duties. I felt I had a slight grasp of the indirect communication thing and devised using this newfound power to my benefit. *They'll know I'm right*, I insisted. Finally, Kei came over and explained, in English, "Leslie, you must work in the lower area." I acted surprised and innocent, "Oh, that's what Masahiro was trying to tell me. Sorry!" I knew I was being childish, and passive-aggressive to boot, but I couldn't help myself. I'd join the men and be good for a while, then fall back into plotting new ways to annoy them the next. My silent rebellion persisted most of the day.

At the end of the day, back at the office, Kei approached me with his second announcement of the day. He said, "The office found out that, due to housing problems, you cannot join them for the out-of-town work trip." I almost hugged him. I actually allowed myself a slanted grin a brief second, before responding, "Okay." Later I wondered about my sudden ejection from the work trip. Toward the end of my stay with Uetoh, Kei told me, "Next time you come to Japan, you should do some reading on culture and traditions." I defended myself, "But I read three Japanese culture books and interviewed countless people," adding, "You have no idea how many times I kept silent when I wanted to speak out!"

- - - -

Kei, nonplussed, added, "Oh, we knew how you felt." "But I never said anything!" I exclaimed with big eyes. "We watch your emotions," he finished with a sly grin. Oh. I'd never considered covering up my facial expressions. Damn. The men knew how to steal knowledge from the American girl.

My mom would pick huge, enchantingly perfumed snow white flowers from the southern magnolia tree outside my parents' bedroom. She'd float a single blossom in a large bowl of water, and warned me when my tiny fingers reached too close, "Don't touch the magnolia flower or it will die." I passed this information on to many friends as an adult. Not until twenty years had passed did I realize that touching magnolia flowers did not kill them. They wouldn't even bruise! My mom's story was what I call a white lie, an innocent fib told for the greater good, a noble attempt to keep a flower-enraptured girl from crushing a delicate petal. I could never be sure why Uetoh higher-ups canceled my participation in the Christmas work trip. Could they have noticed my agitation and made up a white lie about lack of housing to help sooth my burgeoning homesickness?

I had encouraged my dad to plant a rare species, little gem magnolia, behind his house in Oklahoma to complement the white swans that circled his lake. Little gems are a dwarf version of the huge traditional southern magnolia. Years later in San Francisco I had the opportunity to prune a whole grove of little gems on the terrace of a contemporary San Francisco sculpture garden owned by one of my clients. Remembering how my father, just a few years before his death, had loved watching his little gem magnolia grow, I tried my heartfelt best to preserve as many of these San Francisco blossoms as possible each time I pruned them.

- - - -

One evening, an extraordinary man would walk under these very little gems on his way to a special fundraiser dinner held at my client's house. I felt so proud that President Barack Obama had strolled under the trees I'd had the opportunity to prune. My dad would have been thrilled to vote for Obama, but he died two years before he had the chance. Yet he did campaign for Obama, in his own indirect way. He participated in many antisegregation protests and restaurant sit-ins in Oklahoma before I was born, so that all Americans could have opportunities. Gardens morph and seasons change. Clients give birth to children who play under the trees I prune. Clients grow old watching these trees; some clients die. Trees grow old, and I recommend to my customers that they plant new ones for future families to enjoy. I'll style a tree over many years, helping it find its beauty, its place in the world. The delicate scent of the magnolia still entrances me.

Finding Heart
in the Landscape

Forgoing a beautifully mowed front lawn, Kyoto private homeowners often build a tall fence completely enclosing atmospheric
three-dimensional gardens. Five days before Christmas, I opened a
sliding wooden door to one such garden, stepped off the sidewalk,
and entered a rich landscape that reminded me of the wooded
area around my first childhood home. Outside the garden wall on
the street, cars with honking horns sped by, kids rode bikes while
talking on their cell phones, and old ladies tottered by carrying
crinkly plastic bags. Inside, nature thrived, looking like a compact
forest. Houses on either side sandwiched my client's property,
but they were so cleverly hidden you'd never notice them. The
perimeter trees and shrubs of the inner landscape were kept just
high enough to distract from surrounding buildings, allowing the
viewer to feel enveloped by a forest.

Just as a curious passenger in a boat cannot see where the winding river leads, the visitor entering this garden could not see the
whole path at once. The path meandered softly for a while, then
turned sharply behind a short bamboo fence at the last minute,
blocking a view to the front door. I felt pulled forward along the
stone walkway to resolve the mystery. The path did not zigzag like a

drunken sailor from one side to the other, nor did the stones greatly vary in shape or color in an exaggerated attempt to look interesting. Instead, I walked along good-sized flat stones, easily navigating the bends in the path, glancing around while I headed toward the front door on my brief but satisfying walk through nature.

Many features of a naturalized garden suggest direction. A pine tree slanting right guides the visitor right. The see-through essence of a pruned laceleaf maple entices curiosity. Bushy shrubs screen the air-conditioning unit, discourage closer inspection, and encourage moving along. Plants, interspersed with large stones, allow for a sense of depth that may not exist in a short front-yard garden. A simple trick such as planting a wide-leafed rhododendron near the beginning of the path, and then a small-leafed azalea toward the end, gives strollers the feeling of being drawn into a scene, as though they were walking with a huge magnifying glass. Just as a painter uses tricks to turn a plain canvas into an imaginative world with depth and perspective, the Japanese gardener uses plants, and long-term styling, to turn bare soil into a journey surrounding the visitor.

But a garden craftsman must use more than tricks to create a powerful garden, just as a technically skilled painter does not always make a great artist. I once renovated a small path for an American client who was over ninety years old. She told me she often walked a specific direction through her garden, from her beat-up garbage cans down a path to reach a favorite natural streambed. From the garbage cans, the stream wasn't visible. Because of budgetary constraints, she'd asked me to use only items from the property to do a little renovation. I found a small concrete statue of a bunny behind one of her bushes. It looked as

----

though it had been part of her garden for a while but had been forgotten. I placed the bunny on a flat stone right next to a step midway down the path. I led my client to the beginning of her path,
the garbage cans, and she looked toward the step suspiciously for
a while because her eyesight wasn't very good. Then she gasped,
"My sweet bunny! I thought I'd lost it years ago!" and she walked
without further prompting down the path toward the stream. My
attempt to draw her forward had worked. But also this object had
touched her heart. Now, on her way to her streambed, she had an
old friend to greet her, to guide her to her little oasis. A special
rock, plant, or color can draw a viewer into a naturalized garden
scene just as well as, and much more subtly than, a concrete bunny.

Reused material can add a feeling of age to a garden, if it's not
too distracting. I've seen old concrete or terra-cotta roof tiles used
in the gardens of Kyoto. Age in a garden adds temporal depth and
can bring out a story. In a samurai's garden in Kanazawa, Japan,
I once came across a short tree with a four-foot-wide trunk. At
the top of the tree, braces of wood and rope held in place rotting stubs. The garden caretakers had taken care of the dead part
of the tree as much as the living. I tried to guess its species but
couldn't, and finally searched in the garden's brochure. It said,
"Central to the garden stands a crepe myrtle, over five hundred
years old." I'd never seen a crepe myrtle with more than a one-
foot-wide trunk; no wonder I hadn't recognized it! I wanted to
wrap my arms around the myrtle's marbled bark and climb up to
wrap a few safety lines around the stubs myself.

Many of my American clients move into new homes, cut down
old, seemingly useless trees, and plant their contemporary favorites.
They celebrate flowering cherries in spring and harvest organic

apples in summer. But they miss out on the thought-provoking stories told by trees such as the samurai's crepe myrtle. Who saw that
tree over the past five hundred years? Which kids had climbed it?
Who had fallen in love under it? Or dueled to the death? Perhaps
the samurai had looked at the tree every morning as he'd exited
his home, or shot it with arrows to practice his archery. People had
some four hundred years to cut it down, but no one had. I'm not
against cutting down all trees, but certain ones have so much heart
because of their age.

Old pines, podocarpus, and camellias lined the secret Kyoto
garden path. Over the years craftsmen had pruned these trees so
they did not shade the rest of the little garden too much. But the
pruners allowed each plant to grow tall enough to look natural to
the untrained eye. Even though the landscaper and pruners used
tricks to manipulate visitors, the scene looked untouched. Japanese gardens reflect nature, particularly natural scenes that touch
the heart, the special scene that you just can't forget, like the huge,
weeping tree offering shade after a long hike, or the meadow at the
foot of a mountain, with tiny wildflowers pushed by gentle wind.

In the private Kyoto garden hidden by a fence, the homeowner
would view the garden on the way home. In theory, one could
bring a chair outside in the sun and rest one's bare feet on the
soft moss under the shady podocarpus tree, although this is more
likely how a Californian would behave. Enclosed, the garden felt
intimate, embracing, and maternal. Tree branches hung over the
path, creating a womblike ceiling of green canopy.

The men led me around the side of the house. The landscape
altered dramatically, with a backyard that appeared to be under
renovation. Paths had been taken apart, and stones mounded to

----

the side. The men dug a new path with shovels and tied certain trees with red plastic ties. "Leslie, cut down the trees with the red tape," Kei instructed me. *No pruning today*, I sulked. I had only a few weeks left with the company before my return home. Part of me wanted to learn more, while another just wanted to retreat from the cold. Each morning that week, as soon as I figured out how to keep myself warm with new socks or a different hat, the temperature would drop further.

The garden behind the house was like a disaster scene, with trees overgrown and strangling each other. Someone had planted the garden carefully, but it hadn't been pruned or styled for many years. Yet, similar to a stray dog, gardens that required a gardener's help often look this way at first. With a little design work, thoughtful pruning, and tending of the plants, it could eventually look as lovely and comforting as the beautifully enclosed front garden. Even the smelliest, most flea-ridden old dog becomes fluffy and perks up with some food, a bath, and a little love. Quite often, when I first approach a stray-dog tree, neglected and unappealing, I say to myself, *Why me? Why can't I get better plant material to work on?* I'm not a natural lover of stray dogs. Yet I know deep down that every tree or garden has its own beauty that can be revealed with pruning and nurturing. Even if it has only a smidgen of beauty, it's there.

I looked over at a rather weedy spot and saw something that stilled my ruminations. I had been searching for it for weeks. In a shady corner of the garden stood a rather messy fir tree, about nine feet tall, shaded out by a larger tree overhead. The fir had a shiny plastic red tie around its neck. I'd found it, the perfect Christmas tree. I'd been on the lookout for a tree or branch I

----

could cut down and use as a Christmas tree. None were sold in Kyoto. But of all the jobs we'd visited over the past two months, not a single one of them had a tree, or even a branch, that I could use for a planned celebration. I touched the fir needles to make sure it was real. *Stay calm*, I told myself.

Maya and I had been hard at work over the phone for weeks, strategizing holiday plans. We both thrived on social gatherings. In college, my politicized Berkeley friends and I complained that the Christmas spirit had been corrupted by commercial interests. So I'd tried various ways to downplay the holiday's significance, such as refusing to purchase Christmas trees. Instead, I'd use cut branches from my gardens or find a tossed conifer from the dump, my favorite environmental alternative, and make it into a tree. Most of them ended up quite lopsided. I maintain this habit even today. A leafless winter branch of the red-stemmed Sango-kaku maple makes an outstanding Christmas tree. Wrapped with white lights, it looks like a winter deciduous tree in a snowy, star-lit forest.

Despite my reluctance to revel in all that is Christmas in America, I yearned for a Christmas in Japan. I searched for my Christmas branch in every garden we visited. But the Kyoto gardens were just too perfect. All branches had been painstakingly developed for fifty to one hundred years. I had almost given up hope, until I saw the little abandoned fir tree in the back of the secret garden. It was the perfect orphan we could love. Back in California, I reserve the most beautiful cut branches for an ikebana teacher I know, dropping them off at his house late at night on my way home. In an arrangement for a museum or memorial, a beautiful dying branch has one last chance to shine.

But how to get the Kyoto fir tree over to Maya's house? I knew it would look odd for an apprentice to ask any question, much less request a favor. The men always appeared hardworking, never greedy. I decided to let them throw it in the truck without knowing I wanted it, then just remove it from the debris pile once we returned to the office. About half an hour later, as I was focused on setting stepping stones, I turned around and saw Kei and Nishizawa cutting branches off the little fir so they could lay it flat on the debris pile! Shocked, I ran over thinking, *Get your hands off my tree, for God's sake!* I barely resisted tackling them or throwing myself over the debris pile to save it. Instead, as I neared, I got their attention by just looking intently at them for a few seconds. This worked. I asked softly, "Oh, can I keep that?" I could have just finished a yawn. "Yes," they responded, their faces blank, not wasting time by asking me why. They threw the tree aside, a bit too roughly for my comfort, and continued working.

Later, back at the office, I sifted through a huge debris pile to find my treasure crushed between a one-armed *Podocarpus gracilior* and an overzealous *Fatsia japonica*. I dragged it off like a thief, as it was quite dark by then, and left it behind a toolshed, figuring I'd deal with it the following day. I had no idea how I'd get it home, and prayed all evening that no one would find it in a cleaning fit and chop it into little pieces before morning. I just couldn't figure out how to tell everyone in the office, including the head of one of Kyoto's top landscaping companies, "Leave the dead tree alone; it represents a deeply held American symbol of Jesus and presents."

That evening, Maya told me over the phone, "No one has a car—how can we get it back to my house?" Most of her professional Kyoto friends used bikes and the efficient Kyoto bus service. During the midnight anxiety session, an idea came to me, and I contrived a plan. I concealed my contraband smuggling equipment in my workbag the next morning. I could barely wait for the end of the day. As soon as I stepped outside the office door, dusk settling in, I ran behind the shed. There lay my misshapen tree, with all its glistening branches shooting out from its slender trunk. I breathed a sigh of relief. It takes at least three months after a conifer dies in the ground for its needles to turn brown. The conifer's insistence on life makes me admire it all the more.

I pulled an old white sheet and some rope out of my bag and cringed, but I knew what I had to do. With my lips pressed together, I sawed four feet off the bottom of the fir. A small tree was better than no tree. I slowly pressed the side branches as tightly against the trunk as I dared, remembering what Mas taught us in bonsai class: if you move branches very slowly, they will bend without snapping. I wrapped the rope around the pressed branches and rolled the whole package up in a sheet, tying it up until it looked like a fat five-foot-long joint. I figured I'd just carry it on the bus. What would anyone say? The word *no* hardly exists in Japanese.

Stepping on the first bus, barely able to breathe, I handed the bus driver my coupon and hung tightly onto my mummy. Perhaps the people on the bus would simply think, *The crazy American is at it again!* The driver remained expressionless as I passed him. I dragged the tree to an open seat and acted as though it was normal to block the aisle with what looked like a dead body. When I repeated the whole transaction on the second bus and sat down with my cargo, I got an appreciative glance from a young man in the row next to me. I danced jubilantly inside my head but tried to look normal till I exited.

- - - -

As I unwrapped my package at Maya's, three Americans and one Japanese stood speechless. Kei had joined us, as he was best friends with Maya and had a curiosity for all things American. My friend who hadn't seen a Christmas tree in eight years was there. Kei helped by cutting the base of the pine flat with his Japanese saw. He worked with craftsman speed and sacrifice in Maya's freezing enclosed courtyard, building a stand according to Maya's steady flow of directions, while we watched through the windows, inside the warmth. No one had ornaments stored in their attics. But within two hours, the tree was covered from head to toe with strung popcorn, newspaper streamers, and meticulously folded origami cranes. The paper birds spun energetically each time someone opened the front door on the windy evening street. Their colors lit up a tree that needed no Christmas lights to brighten it.

Sunday's Christmas Eve dinner finally arrived. We all were swept up in the moment, playing charades around Maya's short *kotatsu* table with a view of the magical tree, savoring *clafoutis*, French custard made with extraordinary Japanese organic milk and butter. Japanese cows live the opposite life of the craftsmen, resting in meadows and munching on grass, instead of running in landscapes and pruning most plants in sight. The Christmas tree had been placed in Maya's *tokonoma*, where it represented more than what I had previously seen as the inevitable commercialism of Christmas. I saw that occasionally a dream could come true, thanks to a bit of whimsical creativity. I realized the Christmas tree represented depth in time, like an older tree in a garden. The fir tree connected me to my family and friends past, present, and future. I could almost touch the tree that my

----

now-deceased grandmother had touched, and all the ones my future family, friends, and I would adore. It didn't need to be the biggest, brightest, or newest tree to be cherished. We all sat together on the straw tatami mat looking at the tree, which leaned a bit to the left. The little fir brought us together.

I woke up the next morning with a Christmas Day chalky mouth, feeling exhausted. I wasn't used to getting to bed past nine, much less eleven. It had been a while since I'd felt warmly surrounded by friends, so I could barely get myself to exit my warm cocoon for a Monday workday. By noon on Christmas Day, the crew and I had already felled four eighty-foot conifers off a steep mountainside. Rest never lasted long with the men. The company owned land on the western edge of Kyoto Hills, where they harvested timber for profit.

We met Toemon Sano, the elderly father of Shinichi Sano, the active leader of the company, on the mountain. At eighty-three, he'd lived forty-eight years beyond my age that winter, so I bowed to him deeply, wondering when he might retire full time. He walked over to a large tractor with a backhoe, jumped in the driver's seat, and took off up a steep mountainside, out of sight. My regular crew had left Saturday for their out-of-town work trip, so I worked with a completely different crew made up of Toemon; a senior employee, Saito, whom I hadn't seen since my first month at Uetoh; and a few new faces.

A short, dense man with a chain saw approached us. He looked to be about eighty-five, with cropped gray hair and wrinkles like the cracks of baked earth—a Japanese Santa Claus. I rarely saw elders working in the States, much less in the physically demanding profession of an arborist. Then I was introduced to his wife, who looked to be about eighty-eight and sported her own chain saw. I gazed at her with keen interest, and she stared back, sizing me up. She muttered something in Japanese. I understood. She'd said under her breath, "*Onna no ko*," a young girl. I felt a touch of pride and fascination. I imagined what it would be like to work fifty more years. Everyone ran off in different directions, beginning work. I looked over at the wiry white-haired woman and told myself, *Well, Leslie, I have no idea what you're supposed to do here, but you'd better move five times faster than she does.*

Saito eventually motioned for me to follow him up the mountain carrying ladders, cables, and rope. He and the man who looked like Santa Claus signaled for me to fetch cables while they set up a complicated maze of ties to direct the trees as they were chainsawed. Running, as we always did, I scrambled and stumbled through the dense underbrush on the steep hillsides, bruising and nicking my face and wrists. Despite the freezing temperatures, I was exhilarated. The heavy scents of the conifer trees refreshed me, and for once it didn't seem so cold. I love wild nature and feeling the pines playfully scratching my cheek. I felt at home in the forest on this Christmas Day.

I suspected that the new men in my crew had decided to treat me cautiously, or rather, like a girl. They gave me light branches to carry and ordered me not to climb ladders. Of course that made me run even faster. One time I had a cable in my hand and ran straight toward the arborist's handmade worn wooden ladder. Someone needed to climb it to attach the cable to the tree. Saito yelled out from a distance, "*Dame, dame, abunai!* No, no, be careful!" But I pretended I didn't hear him and darted up the ladder, its rungs rounded from years of use, as fast as I could, before they could reach me. No one could stop me from climbing a possibly hundred-year-old ladder. Besides, how hard is it to climb a ladder? The arborist said something to Saito, mentioning my name. Then I heard Saito tell the old man I was twenty-eight years old. For once, I had no problem remaining silent, being thirty-five years old at that point.

The arborist sliced a sixty-foot tree down at its base so that it fell in an exact, predetermined spot. Toemon Sano drove the tractor up a steep winding slope and dragged the tree, attached to a chain, down the mountain. A hundred-foot crane then lifted it off the road to an open site. The husband cut branches off while we women separated the piles. The smallest kindling was thrown into a small fire. I couldn't believe how strongly my older female companion worked, using her chain saw to deftly cut large branches into smaller ones for our piles. Smells of sap, fern, and ash mingled and penetrated our musty clothing. By late afternoon, we ended the job by huddling around the fire to drink tea, with embers and sparks swirling around us.

Back at the office, under fading light and dropping temperatures, I was introduced to Toshi, my boss for the remainder of my time at Uetoh. I didn't know it yet, but my crew would be on the out-of-town work trip for much longer than I'd anticipated. Toshi was a tall, wiry man near forty or fifty who often seemed to be in a sour mood. He immediately began ordering me around. I realized we needed to take advantage of the few hours of light remaining. He told me to move dozens of fifty-pound bags of soil off trucks to another location. I could barely lift the bags by the end of that day, although other men working alongside me could manage two at once. We'd stack a number of bags on the truck, then drive them to other parts of the property and take them off. Sometimes Toshi would change his mind and tell us to put the bags back on the truck and move them to a third location. *Why couldn't he have strategized better from the start? What a waste of time*, I'd think, with little patience at the end of the day.

He pointed for me to carry about fifteen bags, one at a time, by hand, down the road to a certain spot. I thought I had misheard him, given that the bags sat in the back of the truck and the spot was located sixty feet away. Why couldn't we drive them to the spot rather than carry them? I hesitated, *"Asoko?"* (Over there?) I asked in what my grandmother would call uppity, sarcastic speech. Toshi went red in the face and stared me down hard. He grabbed two bags from my hands, walked them forcefully over to the spot, and threw them down to show clearly what he'd meant. Nakaji had never really been angry with me, so I felt a bit shaken. But I got the point. I picked up the bags—I couldn't sling them over my shoulder—and half ran and half dragged them as nonchalantly as I could, cursing under my breath. The project seemed ridiculous and cruel. I felt frustrated and singled out. Then I felt frustrated with my reaction. After months of seeing every level of worker publicly reprimanded, I still reacted emotionally.

We continued our inefficient game of sack checkers for hours, until darkness and the temperature fell. My hands and feet began their crawl toward numbness and pain, which had never happened in the evening, only the morning. We worked for about half an hour more in the dark. My hair was plastered to my skull after hours of sweating. I limped a little on my way back to the icy cold concrete bus stop. "Christmas evening," I muttered. The

----

glorious first half of the day with loving nature made the last part of the day with the grumpy boss all the more difficult to take. I bought a can of warm green tea from a vending machine near the stop and held the can under my jacket to warm my belly.

I stopped off at a quiet bar on my way home where I usually ate dinner alone before the regular customers, the midnight crowd, took over. Just as well, given how dirty and disheveled I was each evening. I generally felt embarrassed to be seen in public in my work clothes. As he'd done every night for several months, without a word exchanged, the cook from his open kitchen prepared me a warm meal I'd randomly chosen. I couldn't read the menu, so I'd just point. If the chef didn't like what I had picked, he'd shake his head, making negative noises until I pointed out a dish he approved of. The chef gave me an unusually large serving that night after I said, "Merry Christmas!" In turn, I gave him a wrapped box filled with chocolates. I knew I'd soon be leaving Kyoto and had earlier planned to give a Christmas present to the man who cooked my dinner and did my dishes every night. He helped me make it through the evening that night as he had many others. He gave me just a bit of nurturing, a little rub under the scruffy puppy's neck, and allowed my difficult and magical garden journey to happen.

My intention had always been to finish my apprenticeship to the end, but that night I wasn't sure. Pulling the covers over my head for maximum warmth, I tried to reason out my emotions. *Well,* I thought, *given that everyone works as a team, maybe Toshi was frustrated too.* But my thoughts kept circling back to what I perceived as a particular meanness emanating from his actions. I thought and thought, until drifting off, I began to see embers, sandbags, and French custards circling a fir tree lit up with stars. Family and friends I loved sat around the tree, the light playing on their faces with dancing shadows. I watched them nearby from a dark corner. They kept calling to me, asking me to join them. But I shook my head. No. Not yet.

Black Coffee Warms
the White Garden

I debated later that night whether it felt as cold inside my bedroom as out. I might as well slide my shuttered windows open, I reasoned, so I can see the sky while lying in bed. On nights when I couldn't sleep, I'd look out at the stars. My worries lessened compared to the universe's enormous and sparkling black-and-silver garden. So I scampered out of bed, slid the two wooden frames open, and ran back, the ancient floorboards singing their lullaby under my feet. After a few minutes of star wonder, my worries at last calmed. Then a cool breeze entered the room. So I got back up and closed the shutters with a click. The room grew slightly warmer, or did I only imagine it? Like much of my journey with the craftsmen, I wasn't sure if what I experienced was fascinating or simply disagreeable.

The following morning, I tried to squeeze toothpaste onto my brush, but the tube wouldn't budge; it had frozen solid overnight. Then I got milk out of the fridge for my breakfast muesli and noticed that it felt warmer inside the refrigerator than in my kitchen, a strange sensation. I packed backup clothing in my workbag: silk underclothes, fleece sweaters, plastic rain gear, and my warmest Machu Picchu wool hat. I even crammed ski pants into my bag, just in case. I loved the way my thin *jikatabi* shoes felt like wearing socks in the garden—in summer, that is. I had only a few weeks left with the traditional craftsmen at Uetoh, so buying new winter *jikatabi* boots was out of the question. I assumed I'd never wear my Creature from the Black Lagoon *jikatabi* back home in California. Years later, separated-toe shoes became all the rage.

At night I slept with covers so heavy, I imagined my fifteen-pound cat, Fat Boy, sleeping on top of me. He'd never want to work till he sweat, to run around for hours in gardens, although the idea of hiding behind a sweet-smelling camellia, ready to pounce on an unsuspecting mouse, might have piqued his interest. I briskly readied for work in my aesthetically pleasing, freezer-worthy wooden Kyoto home. Back home, perhaps at that very moment, my cat may have been sleeping warmly near my mom's feet, on her queen-size bed in her well-insulated, conventional California stucco home.

Although daylight grows longer after December twenty-first, it felt as though it continued fading as New Year's approached, only a little more than a week away. Still, the sun shone almost every afternoon, causing *Camellia sasanqua* to burst open, pink and rosy as my cheeks. I felt a little silly with my bulky workbag full of clothes sufficient for a trek to the North Pole, especially on warm, sunshiny days. On a sunny Tuesday morning, it looked as though the three of us would be crammed into the front seat of a truck, so I stuffed just a few items into my bag tightly, hoping the men wouldn't notice, and left the remaining layers in my locker.

My regular crew was still out of town on their work trip. I sat in the front seat of the truck with a senior worker and my new boss next to me on a bench seat. Staring out the window, I fell slowly

----

into hibernation mode. We drove through Kyoto, past city boundaries, and out into the countryside. I'd close my eyes, and then open them for seconds at a time, peeking groggily out the window. I saw farmhouses with long bamboo drying racks out front, hung with hundreds of long white slender daikon radishes, a farmer's winter's harvest. Fields, buildings, and trees passed, looking like low-resolution black-and-white prints covered in frost. On the distant mountainside dark green conifers and orange trees rippled across the hills, mingling with strips of bare earth stabbing upward from the fertile valley below. I could hardly budge my eyes open, but the beauty still touched me.

A chill penetrated my wool hat, so I doubled it near the bottom and fell into a soft slumber. The truck firmly braked, and I awoke to find we'd arrived in the large parking lot of a rectangular building, a nursing home, with institutional, symmetrically sheared plants. Really? I thought, laughing a bit. Yet another boring job my last week in the company, I said to myself. With my regular crew absent, we'd really hit the dregs. *What did you expect, another imperial garden? The company has to work where it is needed, not where you want to work*, my businesswoman side retorted.

With Masahiro gone, I tried to fulfill my role as number-one *kōhai*, the lowest-ranking worker in the company. I jumped on the truck to get ladders off before anyone else, hauled multiple loads of debris at once, and, at ten o'clock on the dot, ran to find the tea tray. The men ignored me, in speech and gaze, and I just had to guess what to do next. I brought a book with me about an American studying at a Japanese monastery as a short-term apprentice like me, but at a temple instead of a garden company. Training in a Japanese monastery looked surprisingly similar to doing an apprenticeship at Uetoh. The lead priest in the temple askcd each monk, regardless of rank, to treat the American apprentice as an equal. Sometimes the American would be told to do advanced duties with senior monks and then to work on basic projects when working with novice monks. I had always been treated in this manner at Uetoh Zoen. But with Masahiro gone, the switch between duties grew, confusing me more than usual.

One minute I'd pull weeds, the next I'd style a pine. In retrospect, I realized the variety helped me see the breadth of company duties. But I'd grown weary during my last week. I'd become more like Fat Boy, dreaming simply of sleep. Yet the craftsmen had no intention of letting up.

I finally hit my frustration limit at the nursing home garden, which I'd dubbed "the icicle courtyard." The air in this garden, where we stood still and pruned pines for hours, held such a cold humidity that my feet and hands throbbed with pain for three hours. It felt like someone was smashing them repeatedly. I almost began crying several times, with my boss working right next to me. But I willed myself to hold out until I could find a private place at first break. When I felt really bad, I'd visualize things that brought me comfort, like tea with milk and sugar, or babies with brown eyes and dark curly hair. At breaktime I went to the women's restroom, where I let myself cry, risking puffy, bloodshot eyes. Before returning I rinsed my face with cold water to lessen the evidence.

I realized that the double socks I'd put inside my *jikatabi* were a mistake. The booties hugged so tightly that the wool socks couldn't insulate—like a down sleeping bag pressed too flat. So I removed a pair, which helped, but the thickening clouds overhead did not. Sipping hot green tea, I tried reassuring myself. I thought back to how I'd confided in Kei the week before. "Do you feel the cold?" I asked. He responded, "My hands do not get cold, and typically I do not wear hats in the winter." Of course I took the hat comment personally and could hardly swallow my tea, choking back tears while thinking of his words. *Fine*, my mind yelled at Kei, *no one understands*! Quickly, I resumed my visualizations: yellow flowers, funny friends, grilled cheese sandwiches on buttery Wonder Bread.

Pruning that day, I wore thin gloves instead of thick ones in order to do detailed work. But trembling fingers don't function well either, so I brought out my thick ones again and decided to keep them on, no matter what, even if they got ruined from sap. Just before my cry break, I was taken off pine pruning and told to pull some weeds with thousands of barbed seeds on their tips. Not only did they drench my gloves with dewy frost, but they blanketed my cheap cotton gloves with hundreds of seeds, making my hands feel like human pincushions. I felt the new boss had gone overboard to make me miserable.

Accustomed as I was to Nakaji's fairly predictable command style, my new boss's behavior took me by surprise. While Nakaji worked long and hard and expected us to do the same, the new boss seemed to relish giving me the worst possible jobs. Our clients revered Nakaji, and I felt loyal to him. Nakaji never gave me a single compliment, but with each command, I'd feel as though he yelled on a bullhorn, "You can do it, Leslie, dammit, you will!" In comparison, I suspected the strange boss of giving me jobs that guaranteed failure.

And for most of the day, for the life of me, I couldn't remember my new boss's name from our brief introduction the day before. I feared it would be insulting to ask. I didn't trust my new *senpai* enough to confide in him, so I spent the day contriving ways to address my boss without using his name. I worked anxiously, afraid he'd guess. I spent most of first break trying to pull seeds out of my gloves. They'd hooked deep into the knitted material. The appalling thought of spreading the seeds throughout the garden, and my religiously tidy nature, forced me to pick them off, one by one, wasting my precious time off. Seconds before we ended the first break, the boss handed me a new pair of clean gloves.

An hour before noon, snow began to fall in elegant, feathery clumps, turning the nursing home garden into a strikingly beautiful scene, worthy of a Japanese garden calendar. I felt grateful for the extra fleece sweater I'd kept by chance. My fingers began to ache again. I prayed for lunch, when we could jump into the truck and at least find some comfort in the moderate warmth of heat from three people in a small enclosed truck. One minute past noon, I stood next to the truck and waited patiently for the men to climb inside the truck first. After they'd settled, the boss opened the car door for me from inside, motioned with his hand to say something about it being too crowded, handed me my bag lunch, and closed the door on me with a resounding click. I sighed, standing there while snowflakes noiselessly encircled me.

A small sliver of a feeling that the new boss didn't like me had found its way into my thoughts, like a forgotten splinter. Now I felt like someone had whacked me hard, pushing the splinter deep. Could the boss have figured out that I didn't remember his name? I had been so careful. Was he an unhappy person? Was I threatening as a woman? Or was I treated like any other apprentice in Japan? I asked myself all these questions. I could never be sure of his intentions. Yet in the midst of these swirling thoughts came the understanding that the cold and sleepless nights were making me think in crazy ways.

He may have desired to toughen me up, just like any other Japanese craftsman, just as I'd wanted. But I could no longer think straight. I sat down on the parking lot curb, as close to the truck as I could manage, to try to protect myself against the wind. Fine, I thought spitefully, I can adapt to this situation, like all the other workers would. I ate my lunch with my back turned to the men, my silent protest.

Then a woman wearing a lovely tailored skirt came running out of the nursing home toward me, slightly shielding herself from the wind and snow. By that third month, I still could hardly understand any Japanese outside of obscure garden terms. But she communicated with hand gestures and miming, speaking to me in rapid Japanese, as my guardian angel at the bus stop had done many times before. She asked if I wanted to come inside and eat lunch. "Come inside and get warm," she said. Not hard to understand that. I responded with a slight smile, "*Iiee, iiee, arigatō gozaimashita*" (No, no, thank you so much), while inside I told myself resolutely, *None of the other apprentices would go inside to eat lunch, no way*. She hesitated. She held her skirt down with her delicate bare hands, just inches from my face. "*Arigatō gozaimashita*," I said again politely. Stubborn pride surpassed discomfort. The woman retreated inside. I hunkered down.

Then she came out again. As she got closer, I saw she was carrying something steaming, a hot cup of black liquid, coffee. She drew closer and held out the coffee until I took it from her hands. Her motherly compassion reached out to me at the same time, across a veil of falling snow between us, a warm arrow seemed to fly right into my chilled heart. I grasped the warm cup and instinctively held it near my chest.

I tried to keep my emotions in check. I felt determined not to cry in front of the men, especially this boss. But her gesture conveyed such kindness. As soon as she turned her back on me, tears began to run down my cheeks. I couldn't wipe them away. The men might be watching me from the side mirrors, I told myself despairingly. My back was still turned to them. If I don't touch my face, they'll never know. I tried to sip my coffee and pantomime normal activity as tears rolled down my cheeks, collected on my chin, free fell, and splashed into my cup. They melted into the hot liquid, like snowflakes.

My thoughts swirled. I wasn't sure I could take the stress anymore. Even trees have limits. Teaching pruning classes, I remind students of a key difference between aesthetic pruning and most pruning taught in books: aesthetic pruners know when to stop. Books mention all sorts of reasons to style trees: to prune out crossing branches, to remove the dead or diseased, to cut branches going straight up or down, or to angle into the canopy rather than out. But rarely do the books explain when to stop pruning.

Before even beginning, an aesthetic pruner first considers how much of the tree to prune. An easy rule for a novice pruner is to remove no more than a third of a healthy plant. If the tree has numerous problems, a few can be addressed each year. Nudge the plant. If a plant looks old, weak, or just planted, then prune no more than a tenth. Never prune a diseased plant. I too needed some time to recuperate between thinning cuts. But Japanese craftsmen simply do not slow down.

As I sipped my cooling cup of coffee, with lovely, icy snow falling around me, the woman came out again to retrieve the cup. I looked at the ground so she couldn't see my tears. But she kept saying something to me over and over. I finally looked up. I must have looked a sight. I watched her expression turn from polite friendliness to horror then to tenderness in the space of a second. She understood. She took the cup without a further word and quickly walked back inside, her heels clicking on the icy pavement. I struggled not to feel ashamed. Surely she must have understood my determination to act strong, like a dedicated craftsperson. But deep down, I felt exposed and overly sensitive. What I believed was our female pact, to suffer in silence, made me cry even more.

The wind and the snow swirled around me, and gradually I sensed nature encircling me too. Nature in her most sincere form helped calm me down, and my tears subsided. A few minutes later, Toshi opened the car door, stepped out, and signaled for me to hop into the car. I climbed in the middle of the bench, between the two men, without uttering a word. I pulled out my Agatha Christie book, so that wise, elderly Miss Marple could help me to defend against these men and redirect my thoughts away from bursting into more tears.

On the drive back I kept my eyes open, but the rest of me had pulled inward. I stared at the passing vista. The mountains had darkened to charcoal green and burnt red-orange streaks. Smoke rose from burning trash piles on open farmlands. Whitewashed traditional wooden homes sat motionless under an amber waxing moon, more than half full. I like that, I thought, seeing things more than half full. I tried to hold on to the idea. Then I closed my eyes and allowed myself to hide in the darkness. When we reached the office, I fled in silence to the bus stop.

I stopped at Kentucky Fried Chicken on my way home—my reward for having endured a particularly hard day—and sat on my futon bed, trying to comfort myself with extra-crispy chicken pieces, usually a very effective weapon against strong emotions. But each time I bit into a crunchy piece, I'd think of the soft snow falling on the truck. And with my soft biscuit in hand, I pictured an icy gray concrete curb. Once the tears returned, I could not stop them. I decided I needed to talk to someone. I could think of only one person who could understand how I felt without thinking that all Kyoto craftsmen must be crazy.

Rather than calling Taylor, I decided to phone a good friend from Berkeley, Ichiro. As has happened with many Americans I've met who have done much longer garden apprenticeships, the Japanese work ethic strains a Western relationship. Most Americans aren't used to people working six days a week, sometime seven, for decades, running between jobs with a ten- to twelve-hour-a-day schedule. My relationship with Taylor had grown distant. He couldn't understand why I worked so hard for a garden company. I felt a particular friend might understand my situation better without jumping to harsh conclusions regarding a traditional Japanese company. Ichiro excelled as CEO of an American Japanese corporation. He lived on and off throughout his life in the Bronx, New York, and Japan. His top karaoke act on business trips was singing "New York, New York" with an exaggerated Japanese accent. "Japanese businessmen love it!" he exclaimed. Ichiro was wise and full of good humor when it came to cultural interactions.

I couldn't figure out the time difference, but took a chance and called him. He picked up his phone, sounding alert, telling me it was 5:00 a.m. and he had just woken up to get ready for work. For several minutes he just let me cry. Close to many women in his life, Ichiro knew how to handle emotions. I told him my story leading up to the snow day in almost incoherent emotional sentences, ending my tale vehemently with, "I'll never go back! I only have about a week left before the end of my apprenticeship. I'll quit. I'll cause trouble for the new boss. He hates me! Do you think he hates me, Ichiro?" I asked, beseeching him to both agree and contradict me. "Do you think he hates Americans?"

I had nothing left to say. We both sat in silence before Ichiro began to speak. "Of course," he reasoned with me in a soothing voice, "your three months of work in the company has been very trying. The hours have been long, with little time off compared to what you are used to." He hesitated between sentences. "Loneliness, Leslie, has taken its toll. It's cold." He said this matter-of-factly, without indulging me too much. "You've been keeping all your emotions inside, while your subconscious knew the end of your apprenticeship was near. The Japanese push hardest right at the end, whereas here in America the last few days at a job can be the easiest. This was the extra push," he said. "It just took you by surprise."

I hadn't realized Japanese push hardest in the end. In all my interviews with ex-apprentices and all my Japanese culture books, no one mentioned this fact. And Ichiro's explanation sounded reasonable, I had to admit. At the end of an eight-year UC Berkeley job, I'd cruised through the last week and relaxed my last day at a going-away work picnic. "The dam holding all your emotions back wanted to burst," Ichiro continued. "It simply cracked a few days early." He spoke clearly and gently—half pep talk, half lullaby. "Most likely the boss doesn't hate you. He was just pushing you very hard at the end of your apprenticeship inside the company. The ethics you leave with demonstrate to others the ethics of the company. They want to make sure you represent the dedication and sacrifice of Uetoh Zoen craftsmen."

"So you think I should go back tomorrow?" I asked him feebly, taking a few gulps of breath, still hardly able to talk. I felt defeated by his logic. I didn't want to return, but as long as he thought the boss didn't hate me, I could possibly consider it.

Eventually I hung up. I crawled deep into my covers and pulled the blanket up just below the base of my chin so I could still breathe the fresh air of my dark room. A question from my mentor popped into my thoughts: "Do you understand the word *gaman*?" Dennis had almost dared us to understand this concept. "*Gaman* means to bear the unbearable." It sounded romantic, courageous, even passionate at the time. My pruning classmates and I were sitting in a warm room when he gave us this speech. Was this what he meant? The struggles of others looked worse. Should I return tomorrow or impose my revenge on the new boss? I breathed in deeply, resigned. I knew I'd return the next day.

If I returned to work, I strategized cautiously, I'd bring multiple layers of warm clothes. If the boss asked me to do something difficult, I'd expect duties to become more difficult the next command. I would not let my guard down again. Trying to bolster my courage, I told myself, *Whether you succeed or fail is not the point. Just do your best.* The house sat still and silent.

Craftswoman Turns
the Kaleidoscope

Wham! I transferred icy sections of neon green moss from plastic nursery flats onto the soil on the last day of my apprenticeship with Uetoh Zoen, New Year's Eve, 1999. I lifted the shovel over my head and slammed it down hard on the moss, connecting the moss to the earth as instructed. It felt satisfying to pound Kyoto's ancient ground cover, transferring the discomfort in my hands back into the ground. I'd been upset a good part of the morning. My regular crew would not be returning from their work trip in time for us to say good-bye, and tomorrow would be the first day of their vacation. We'd all be carried into the new millennium—separately. I could hardly believe I'd never see them again. *If only Kei had told me they'd be working out of town more than just a few days*, I grumbled to myself. He should have known.

"Uhhn!" I groaned like I might not be able to continue, allowing the craftsmen to feel extra macho. I told myself that I didn't care anymore whether the men thought I was strong. I'd done my best. Even though I did care. *Slam*! The shovel smashed a thick slice of brilliant moss to a fourth its size, startling the songbirds into brief silence. The moss bounced back to its original two-inch-thick form, and the birds began again chirping away. *Tweet, tweeeet, tweet*. The transferred moss felt right at home in its new walk-in freezer home, with icy water leaking through its earth-blackened walls. I was the only one who still felt foreign in the beautiful Kyoto gardens.

We worked in a private residential garden with a little bit of everything during my last day. I walked under a wooden gate that had been shaved by carpenters to such smoothness I wanted to rest my cheek against it. I raked around a framed-in bench area that no one could sit in, as we had to keep moving. We picked up old bits of leaves along a curving streambed fed from a softly gurgling waterfall. One of the craftsmen shook dead needles from stylized pines, foot by foot. The conifers surrounded the scene with playful twisting branches.

What in the past would have looked like one of the more artfully rendered landscapes I'd ever witnessed now appeared commonplace. Only by looking back through photos of my work with Uetoh Zoen years later did I see how spectacularly designed were the gardens I worked in day after day, and how rich my journey was, all the way to the end.

I cleaned and raked the garden with worn, stubborn effort and wondered if my new coworkers had heard about me breaking down in the snow several days earlier. My Japanese friend who taught ikebana explained to me a few years later that the craftsmen might not feel pity for the homesick Western girl but instead would admire my struggle. "No matter how fast I tried to prune, even timing myself to try to speed up, the men would always prune faster!" I told Shuji. "Of course the Japanese craftsmen pruned faster; they weren't going to be beaten by a girl!" he responded, sending us both into a laughing fit. Shuji understood

the play between the craftsmen's reserve and my American open-
ness because he was born in Japan and his husband was from
Oklahoma.

Entering the garden that cold morning, I glanced around, and
everything looked, well, already done. To my standards, the garden
appeared perfect. The pine's silhouette cut into the sky with perfect edges, the paths had already been swept clean, and the moss
beds grew thick without a single weed. What else could we do?

Like all excellent Japanese craftsmen, we cleaned the garden
more. Traditional New Year's garden cleaning in Japan required
cleaning in corners, under pebbles, and around rocks. Every part
of the garden had to be tended to. The men shook the conifers,
searching for dead needles. They used reverse blowers to suck up
dust particles from the garden's moss and pebble carpet. They
emptied water basins, scrubbed them clean, and refilled them
with clear, icy water. Japanese homeowners also cleaned inside
their dwellings intensively before New Year's Day. I loved the idea
of a delicious cleaning, inside and out, once a year.

Sogyu, whose company I worked with at the beginning of my
stay, invited me to an end-of-the-year party, which he said was "a
symbolic time for all his workers to celebrate the previous year's
accomplishments and to leave last year's resentments behind so
everyone could start the New Year afresh." I wished I could feel the
same way toward my crew. In my weariness, I eyed my new boss and
the others with suspicion. I felt I'd lost Kei's friendship. Consuming
my thoughts, the question grew, *Who's on my side and who's not?*

Toyoka, whom I hadn't seen since my first month in the company, rejoined the crew. I trusted him enough to ask him the name
of my new boss. Perhaps I worried too much my last week. But

just in case anyone was within hearing, I silently pointed to the boss whom I suspected hated Americans, and asked Toyoka softly, *"Onamae wa nandesu ka?"* (What is his name?) I sensed that my gentle coworker understood my vulnerability. I heard years later that Toyoka left the Uetoh Zoen company to become a farmer. He responded quietly, close to my ear, "Toshi-san."

It began to occur to me that certain workers indeed had heard about the snow day. They seemed to be protecting me from Toshi. For example, in the morning, I listened as the boss did a good morning reprimand of each coworker, and then listened more carefully as footsteps headed in my direction. I increased my raking pace. A craftsman whose name I didn't even know showed up for no apparent reason, walking past Toshi's line of sight. Distracted, the boss yelled something at him brusquely, then walked away and left me in peace. These may have been coincidences, but things like this happened repeatedly throughout the day.

Another time, I leaned a broom against a finely plastered garden wall as I raked sodden leaves into my tarp. Toyoka caught my attention by waving at me. No craftsman had ever warned me of an impending infraction during silent work time. He pointed to my broom and shook his head, "No, no." I looked over at my broom, trying to discern the problem. I still didn't understand the long-term delicacy of plaster walls. Not only was the garden's plaster wall alive that December morning, planning to show its patina spots over time, but the wooden gate would also age and change color over the years in a manner Japanese woodworkers considered living. Carpenters avoid sealing up wood with stains for this reason, so the wood breathes naturally. No antiwrinkle cream for the wooden gates of Japan.

In the dead of winter inside the private Kyoto garden, the plants, plaster, wood, clients, and gardeners all pulsed with life. I moved my broom away from the wall and placed it on the ground. Toyoka returned to stroking his rake on the pebbles with calming, repetitive strokes. *Scratch, scratch, scratch.* The crew surrounded me that day. Whether I succeeded or failed, they'd succeed or fail with me.

I had a hard time focusing on my work that morning because of more than just concerns about my new boss. The previous day I'd finally received a note from my boyfriend. Just as I'd entered the house after my normal Sunday morning excursion to buy fresh fried tofu for breakfast, which was like eating bacon when I slathered it in sweet miso, my landlord handed me an envelope with Taylor's scrawling handwriting. *Finally*, I thought, both anxious and excited that I held something in my hand that Taylor had held in his. At the beginning of our relationship, he'd written me long letters the old-fashioned way, even though we lived in the same town. I ran upstairs to my bedroom for some privacy and sliced the envelope carefully with my pruning shear blade. I loved reading letters.

I reached into the envelope and pulled out a single photograph. I instantly recognized the plant in the photo, a California huckleberry, my favorite native California plant. *Vaccinium ovatum* is known for its delicate leaves and tiny bluish fruit. It grows very slowly, some say only an inch a year. I've seen it on parched, windy slopes of Point Reyes, hugging the rocks for warmth and moisture.

Taylor had taken this photo on one of our hikes through Huckleberry Botanic Regional Preserve in the hills above Berkeley and Oakland. I remembered the shot because, without Taylor's knowing it when he took the photo, a small bird had been hovering under the huckleberry in the shadows, probably scared to death of the two giants passing by. Taylor said the huckleberry plant made him think of me, sweet and tart, slow and sure in pursuing my goals. I teased Taylor that the little bird in the photo reminded me of him and his desire to hide from the world behind his camera with his natural reserve.

I turned the photo over and squinted at the writing. "Shall we meet in the preserve when you return? T." Sort of a hopeful message. But a bit disappointing nevertheless. I searched for other meanings but found none.

I walked over to my window, and rested my head on the ledge. I stared out at the big cherry tree with all its bare, shiny branches, pulsing with life. Despite its aliveness, the tree just stared back, leafless and gray to my eyes.

"What do you think?" I asked the tree. A response came back quickly, right into my thoughts: *Don't worry, Leslie.* I don't know really where these responses come from. The tree continued, *Have patience.*

The conversation ended there, in brief, typical fashion. Years before I went to Kyoto, a garden craftsman from Japan, who led a pine pruning workshop in California, suggested this practice to me. During the workshop, a question popped in my head. I waited for all the other participants to talk with him first while I debated asking my question. I hesitated, and then still kept quiet during a period of silence at the end of the workshop. The question just wouldn't go away. So with a shaky voice, I raised my hand and asked, with a translator helping, "When the weather is freezing cold or uncomfortably hot, when the pine is as prickly as sharp sewing needles puncturing your skin, why do you keep going? What is your inspiration?" He thought about this question a bit. After much quiet thoughtfulness, he responded, in a way I'd never expect from a skilled Japanese craftsman. He said, "Sometimes I tell the tree about my day, or about troubles at home. Sometimes I tell the tree, 'I'm going to make you as pretty as my wife.'"

At first I didn't know what he meant. Over time, I sensed that he was wiser than I'd assumed. I tried talking to trees a few times on blind faith. It occurred to me that perhaps he understood that I felt lonely in the gardens. And by talking a little to the trees here and there, I began to realize that I wasn't alone, that in fact the trees were living beings. I'd never really given this much thought while I pruned.

Strange that it never occurred to me, after all the years I spent feeling lonely in the gardens I worked in, that friends were right there, that trees and plants surrounded me. Plants, like me, live, grow, die, and break down into the soil. I don't say much to them. I mostly think about pruning theory. But, now and then, when a branch slaps my face, I might reassure the tree, "Don't worry, I know what I'm doing!" Or I ask them little questions, "Do you think this or that person is being mean to me?" and the strangest, and wisest, answers appear. I didn't understand what it all meant; I still don't. But many of my other pruning friends tell me, "It is the tree's spirit, Leslie." I don't know if I believe them. So I decided to leave the tree's message as it was.

I met another person who was willing to talk to trees. I met her at Tassajara Zen Mountain Center near Carmel Valley in California. Some people go to Tassajara to study Zen Buddhism, and others visit to relax with lovingly cooked vegetarian meals, hot springs, and nature. I like to volunteer at Tassajara, both to support the community there, who work hard to contribute to world peace, and to take a break in nature, with no computers, radios, or electricity, only a little solar lighting.

I was busily pruning a California native shade garden at Tassajara, designed by a local landscaper-ecologist, when a beautiful older woman with cropped hair walked out of her cabin nearby. I recognized her immediately. My mom listened to her records in the late sixties. I still listen to Joan Baez's enchanting album *Diamonds & Rust* on my turntable. I'd seen Joan off and on for days at Tassajara, singing with visitors, dancing with members of local native American tribes, graciously saying hello to anyone who approached her.

I tried to act normal as she approached, even though I could barely breathe. When she saw me, she asked kindly, "Hello, what are you doing?" I answered, "Pruning the shrubs around your cabin." I was at work on some plants at the entrance to her cabin. A gurgling stream ran along the back for both of us to hear as we talked.

"What's wrong with this one?" she pointed to a half-dead medium-sized tree that when healthy would bloom in spring with hundreds of tiny blue flowers. "It's commonly known as a California lilac," I said in a robotic way, because I'd worked with this plant for years and also because I could hardly speak with someone I admired so much in front of me. "Scientifically it's known as *Ceanothus thyrsiflorus*. Ceanothus is not long lived, and this one looks fairly old. I think it's dying simply from old age."

I kept going. "I'm considering two options for it. I could either cut it down, as not much will be left after I remove this

----

dead branch. Or I could just remove the dead wood and give the remaining small living section just a little more time." Baez listened quietly. This encouraged me to go on. "Seeing as you are staying in this cabin," I offered, gathering what remained of my breath, "why don't you decide?"

She looked at the shrub awhile, touching it, peering into its canopy like a proper aesthetic pruner might do. She then turned back to me. She said, "The shrub is telling me it wants to stay for now." I didn't realize anyone else got specific information from the trees, so I felt a little taken aback. *Should I believe her?* my talking-to-trees skeptic wondered. How can any of us know what a plant wants? Do these responses come from our own minds, or somewhere else? But I thought, *If Joan Baez says the tree wants to hang out awhile longer, then I'm going to let it be!* She then asked me graciously if I could teach her to prune, so I gave her a simple lesson on how to cut at the intersections of the branches to get the most natural look. I wasn't sure who was teaching whom. Finally she walked on, and I got back to work on the shade garden.

The day at Tassajara had been dry and hot, even in the shade. But my last day in Japan, in the little Kyoto garden, chilled me thoroughly. I whined inwardly, *Will this day ever be over? Will I ever be cared for by anyone else than the gardens?* My thoughts jumped around because I'd run breathlessly most of the morning, a tarp in each hand. At break I closed my eyes unsociably, ignoring the men. For lunch I planned on reading my English mystery. I'd already dropped studying Japanese or writing in my journal at breaks. Oddly, I found over the past week I'd begun to lose my ability to speak Japanese, except for the simplest sentences. Phrases I'd used for months escaped me, as though my mind was in a state of rebellion, preparing to leave Japan.

I worked myself up into an "I'm not going to cry" sweat, filling my tarp with brown needles and muddy pebbles until my wrists broke out into an itchy red rash from the prickly pine needles. Toshi gave me the undesirable task of cleaning out the dead leaves from a stringy, wet iris clump. It seemed a simple enough task on first inspection. I carefully pulled leaves out from their base. But I soon realized that the plant was located on the north side of the house, a permanently shady spot in winter, where it was particularly cold and damp. I had to remove my gloves to get a good hold. The icy leaves clung to the dormant clump. I'd imagined meditatively raking sand in Japan. I hadn't predicted that I'd be working on a decayed, freezing iris clump the last day of December. I told myself, *I'll show Toshi-san just how clean I can get these irises!* I pruned dead leaves as close to the ground as possible. My fingers became swollen and numb. *Your hands still work,* I reminded myself with my old tough-love attitude. I snipped and tugged carefully around the rotting patch, full of resentment and resolve.

Then I began to notice what had been covered: fragile, budding tips of next year's iris plants appeared, previously hidden under last year's brown leaves. They popped up just above the earth's surface, like moist violet and green jewels. The more I cleared away the decomposed leaves, the more the circle of purple, pink, and green buds emerged. The end result looked mesmerizing, a delicate kaleidoscope sitting amid a still winter's garden.

To experience the true beauty of a kaleidoscope, one must hold it up to the light and turn it playfully, allowing its magic to unfold. Interacting with a garden allows for a different experience than simply looking at it. I would never have discovered the gem of the rotting iris if I'd quickly glanced at the garden. I had to work in the garden, with my bare hands, for hours in the cold. The circle startled me out of my dark thoughts. The budding irises reminded me that even in darkness, life returns, even stronger.

In California I turn the kaleidoscope in many ways. Sometimes I hike or bike in the rain. Few people understand how much fun this is. In the wet season, I have nature all to myself. Once I danced in a rain shower at night with other revelers at People's Park, a community green space where the homeless are fed and students play volleyball. We all danced together. Sometimes I sit in a chair in my garden, drinking tea, with leaves falling on my lap, ants marching toward my slice of cake, weeds calling out. I must sit quietly to notice the ants and leaves. When I am much older, perhaps just struggling to sit upright in bed near a window, I will turn the kaleidoscope by opening the window and feeling the breeze.

I did a particularly fine job transforming the iris patch in the little Kyoto garden, then I stood back, trying to look nonchalant, waiting to see if anyone would notice. Toshi walked by and glanced down at the patch. He hesitated, and looked up to say in a surprised tone, "*Ii desu yo!*" (Very good!) Even he couldn't help noticing the luminescent spot. He had given me my first verbal compliment in Uetoh Zoen. Before I'd worked in Kyoto, this sort of first-ever compliment might have been a big deal to me. Instead, I found it a little humorous. I no longer needed the outside appreciation. For months, Nakaji had complimented me by giving me successively more difficult projects every day. I failed so often because, as soon as I figured one thing out, he'd give me something more difficult to learn. He had faith in my ability to learn, and I'd become more interested in finding new challenges than achieving success. The person I had grown accustomed to relying on for approval was myself.

Four of us cleaned the already clean private garden till late afternoon, then we made our silent bows to the client, my last in Kyoto, and sped back to the office before dark. Stepping inside, I saw many other workers—some I knew and many I didn't. It appeared that everyone had come back one last time before the New Year's holiday! I spotted my three garden musketeers, Kei, Nishizawa, and Toyoka, huddled around a humming space heater, warming their hands. My heart lightened. Nakaji stood near Masahiro in a nearby corner. I sighed. I regarded them all from across the room, feeling sentimental, even though my strongest desire was to return home. I looked over at my crew, while they traded stories in a language I still couldn't understand. Walking over to join them, I noticed that, without saying a word, they'd moved aside to let me stand closest to the heater.

It seemed as though dusk descended in a blink, and everyone gathered in the main room as we had done the first morning when I arrived at Uetoh Zoen, all buzzing with anticipation. Then the room dropped into silence and everyone faced the company leaders. Shinichi Sano handed each worker an envelope, except me. I assumed they'd been given a year-end bonus. Quite unexpectedly, as happened on my first day in the company, I was motioned to stand in front of the group and say a few words. I should have known this would happen, but I hadn't thought out the situation well enough. I could remember almost no Japanese at that point, so I fumbled through a brief "*Dōmo arigatō gozaimashita*" (Thank you very much), my cheeks turning red, with a bow. Maybe they'd think it was the heater. I recovered enough to remember the thank-you

----

gifts I had prepared for weeks, which I'd intended to hand out to each person in the company with whom I'd had contact. I grabbed my bag and began pulling them out, everyone watching me. I'd spent quite a bit of time choosing which gift went to whom, and in what order to hand them out, given company hierarchy.

Each gift held special meaning. For instance, I'd observed that Toemon Sano, the elder at Uetoh Zoen, did not drink green tea in the mornings but instead sipped coffee prepared with an automatic drip coffee maker. So I handed to him a full pound of Peet's coffee that I'd brought with me from Berkeley, wrapped and tied with an authentic ribbon. Plastic ribbons do not compare to real fabric ribbons, just as bright plastic flowers cannot compare to even the most common daisy. I'd never give a plastic flower to a Japanese craftsman. Next, I handed Shinichi Sano, the active leader of the company, a wrapped bottle of California wine made by California traditional craftsmen, farmers, and vintners. This present seemed appropriate for the man who seemed most involved in running the company, as it took the most physical sacrifice for me to carry it from California.

For Nakaji, I'd wrapped with particular attention a big tin of fine English black tea. If given the choice at breaktime, he'd always choose black tea over green. His present seemed lacking in pizzazz, but what else do you give a man who has a thousand-year-old tree trunk in his entryway? I handed out to each of my *senpai* wrapped gifts of chocolate, nuts, and postcards of Berkeley in the best hierarchical order I could negotiate. Normally we communicated only through nature, so I hoped these choice gifts would signal to them how much I appreciated their efforts to train a temporary stranger in their midst. One of the secretaries painted botanical watercolors of cherry flowers for the company, a tradition that went back for decades. She gave me a watercolor of a delicate cherry branch with fading, transparent pink blossoms. It reflected how I felt that day—tired, released from the intensity of working with a highly skilled, all-male crew.

I felt I didn't have to give anything to Toshi. He'd only acted as my boss for a week or so. Honestly, all week I'd imagine the scene of not giving him anything. *Forget it!* I'd say to myself each fading day, *no way*, and imagine him not caring.

Two days before, a strange thing occurred. While sweeping pine needles off the moss under a stylized pine, I had plenty of time to think when I should have been paying attention to the moss. I again went over why Toshi did or did not deserve a gift. *He may be trying to toughen me up, but instinctively I just know he's spiteful*, was a common thread. Then a new, and different, voice piped up: *If anyone deserves a kind gesture, perhaps it's the one who appears most bitter.* I looked over at a craggy old pine next to me, eyeing it suspiciously. Its healthy, sharp needles had poked me right through my glove just a few seconds earlier while I swept. I didn't know where that voice came from. But it stuck.

I'd handed out everyone's gifts and glanced surreptitiously over at Toshi. He looked as though he was trying not to care that he'd been left out, looking up and around, at his hands, behind his back, anywhere except toward me. Or did I imagine this? *If anyone deserves a kind gesture, perhaps it's the one who appears most bitter.* The thought persisted.

Even on the freezing cold days, I never gave up on the gardens, just as the waitresses at the Japanese restaurant in Oklahoma never turned away from the silly, giggling girls. They smiled at us, moving their fans back and forth. The waitresses, and the crafts-men, inspired me to see beauty and to create beauty. A plant can't grow without water.

So I prepared one last special gift earlier that morning. I pulled it out of my workbag and handed it to Toshi. His eyes widened in a slightly astonished look. He took his gift, a box of chocolate and nuts, wrapped with a special bow for a boss. He flashed a big smile. I'd rarely seen a craftsman express emotion. I felt a little surprised myself. I realized in a brief second that, just barely, I had done the right thing. I'd turned the kaleidoscope. Almost everyone said their good-byes and departed, but Toshi disappeared into another room and came back just as I was about to leave, with his hands cupped, holding out to me a pile of small, individually wrapped rectangular black bean candy, *yōkan*—soft, sweet, dark. He tried to hand them to me all at once, but some spilled on the floor. My small hands could only hold so many. I stooped down to pick up the few that had dropped. I love *yōkan*. The black candy perfectly reflected my adventures in Japan, a journey as dark as night on the outside, yet sweet and close to my heart throughout. I smiled up at the craftsman and headed home.

Acknowledgments

I am most grateful to three exceptional editors: Jay Schaefer, whose advice helped me develop a sixty-chapter journal into a living story; Mimi Kusch, who made my words shine much like the Japanese craftsmen prune trees; and Sheila Ashdown, who drew out key themes. Thank you Timber Press for bringing focus to gardens and gardeners.

Uetoh Zoen, I am forever indebted to you for allowing an American woman a glimpse into the traditional arts of Japan. I hope this book will teach others like my special crew taught me.

As the youngest of four sisters, I am comfortable listening to expert criticism. Thank you to my skillful editors: Barbara Haya, Rosana Franciscato, Patrick McMahon, and Eve Goodman. Appreciation to readers who carried this memoir all over world, offering advice in everything from gardening to Japanese traditions. Cappy Coates and Veronica Selver, earthen plasterer Emily Reynolds, Rafael Olivas, Jocelyn Cohen, David Song, Pete Churgell, and Yuki Nara. Many published authors took the time to offer advice. Thank you Ed Brown, Kendall Brown, Liza Dalby, Pico Iyer, Rosalind James, Marc P. Keane, Zachary Mason, Shirley Streshinsky, and Andrew Trouhy. David Chadwick, your book kept me company in Kyoto. Thank you to my client Everal Mitchel for allowing me to do a photo shoot, twice, in your beautiful Shigiru Namba–designed Japanese garden.

Without devoted mentors, who would I aspire to be? This Kyoto journey could not have happened without the following teachers: my most important mentor, Dennis Makishima, who takes trips on weekends to check up on his students; Stew Winchester, who taught me to love California native ecosystems by shaking my tent so I could sketch a sage at sunrise; Louise Ingber, who taught me ballet and how to be a poetic athlete; David Slawson, who reminded me that "Sometimes what we need to say is bigger than us"; and to Elaine Sedlack of the UC Botanical Garden Asian Section for continuing to bike up that hill!

Many inspired, encouraged, and listened to make this book happen. Thank you Sogyu Fukumura of Planet Sangha and crew for your faith in me. Thank you North American Japanese Garden Association for organizing Japanese garden gatherings for everyone, Merritt College Pruning Club teachers and volunteers, Sadafumi Uchiyama and dedicated gardeners at Portland Japanese Garden, Doug Roth of Sukiya Living magazine, my initial Canadian referral Gerald Rainville and Corky Facciuto who have both worked for Uetoh Zoen, Carol, Alison, Monica, Maya Blum, Asher Brown, Debra Lande, Julie Pinkerton, Sukey Parmelee, Ron Sullivan, Arlene Lueck, Sayuri and Hugh of Suzuki-Ya Tools, Lillian and Joe, Maryann Lewis, Diane Renshaw, Malcolm Scotchler, Marcello Goo, Suji Ikeda and Kent Jones, David McCormick, Shai Lavie, Mrs. Ishizaki, Maggie Kane, Pat and Patrick Mapps, Janet and Jeff Rulifson, Karen and Bruce Joffe, Maureen Perata, Richard Seibert, Karen Braley, Blake at Cole Coffee, David DeGroot, Mike Jones, Dale Oxley, Hakusha-Sonso Shrine volunteer garden company, Takanobu Mizumoto, Masuume Okiya; Carolyn, Jimmy, and

Acknowledgments

Rose of Meal Ticket; East Bay Bike Party, and sailors at Cal Sailing Club who remind me of Japanese craftsmen.

I could not have written this memoir at home, and so I thank my writing spots: Far Leaves Tea (Keko and Brad), Crixa Cakes, Masse's Pastries, Cafe Bartarelle, Tassajara, Green Gulch, Krotona Library, Ojai Valley Inn, Elizabeth's home, Pablo's garden, and Clive and Marion's outdoor bed where I found inspiration watching quails and listening to coyotes under the pepper tree.

I think of you, all those who reached out to help a woman realize her dream.